Political Transformations and Public Finances

How did today's rich states first establish modern fiscal systems? To answer this question, this book examines the evolution of political regimes and public finances in Europe over the long term. The book argues that the emergence of efficient fiscal institutions was the result of two fundamental political transformations that resolved long-standing problems of fiscal fragmentation and absolutism. States gained tax force through fiscal centralization and restricted the power of rulers through parliamentary limits, which enabled them to gather large tax revenues and channel funds toward public services with positive economic benefits. Using a novel combination of descriptive, case-study, and statistical methods, the book pursues this argument through a systematic investigation of a new panel database that spans eleven countries and four centuries. The book's findings are significant for our understanding of economic history and have important consequences for current policy debates.

Mark Dincecco is Assistant Professor in the Research Area of Economics and Institutional Change at IMT Institute for Advanced Studies in Lucca, Tuscany. His research focuses on economic history, political economy, and public economics. He holds a Ph.D. in economics from the University of California, Los Angeles, and has published in several academic journals.

POLITICAL ECONOMY OF INSTITUTIONS AND DECISIONS

Series Editors

Stephen Ansolabehere, Harvard University
Jeffry Frieden, Harvard University

Founding Editors

James E. Alt, Harvard University
Douglass C. North, Washington University of St. Louis

Other Books in the Series

Alberto Alesina and Howard Rosenthal, *Partisan Politics, Divided Government and the Economy*

Lee J. Alston, Thrainn Eggertsson and Douglass C. North, eds., *Empirical Studies in Institutional Change*

Lee J. Alston and Joseph P. Ferrie, *Southern Paternalism and the Rise of the American Welfare State: Economics, Politics, and Institutions, 1865–1965*

James E. Alt and Kenneth Shepsle, eds., *Perspectives on Positive Political Economy*

Josephine T. Andrews, *When Majorities Fail: The Russian Parliament, 1990–1993*

Jeffrey S. Banks and Eric A. Hanushek, eds., *Modern Political Economy: Old Topics, New Directions*

Yoram Barzel, *Economic Analysis of Property Rights*, 2nd edition

Yoram Barzel, *A Theory of the State: Economic Rights, Legal Rights, and the Scope of the State*

Robert Bates, *Beyond the Miracle of the Market: The Political Economy of Agrarian Development in Kenya*, 2nd edition

Jenna Bednar, *The Robust Federation: Principles of Design*

Charles M. Cameron, *Veto Bargaining: Presidents and the Politics of Negative Power*

Kelly H. Chang, *Appointing Central Bankers: The Politics of Monetary Policy in the United States and the European Monetary Union*

Tom S. Clark, *The Limits of Judicial Independence*

Peter Cowhey and Mathew McCubbins, eds., *Structure and Policy in Japan and the United States: An Institutionalist Approach*

Gary W. Cox, *The Efficient Secret: The Cabinet and the Development of Political Parties in Victorian England*

Gary W. Cox, *Making Votes Count: Strategic Coordination in the World's Electoral System*

Gary W. Cox and Jonathan N. Katz, *Elbridge Gerry's Salamander: The Electoral Consequences of the Reapportionment Revolution*

Continued following Index

Political Transformations and Public Finances

Europe, 1650–1913

MARK DINCECCO

IMT Lucca Institute for Advanced Studies

CAMBRIDGE
UNIVERSITY PRESS

CAMBRIDGE
UNIVERSITY PRESS

32 Avenue of the Americas, New York NY 10013-2473, USA

Cambridge University Press is part of the University of Cambridge.

It furthers the University's mission by disseminating knowledge in the pursuit of education, learning and research at the highest international levels of excellence.

www.cambridge.org
Information on this title: www.cambridge.org/9780521192330

First published 2011

A catalogue record for this publication is available from the British Library

Library of Congress Cataloguing in Publication data
Dincecco, Mark, 1977–
Political transformations and public finances : Europe,
1650–1913 / Mark Dincecco.
p. cm.
Includes bibliographical references and index.
ISBN 978-0-521-19233-0 (hardback)
1. Finance, Public – Europe – History. 2. Tax administration and
procedure – Europe – History. 3. Decentralization in
government – Europe – History. I. Title.
HJ1000.D56 2011
336.409´03–dc22 2011006135

ISBN 978-0-521-19233-0 Hardback
ISBN 978-1-107-61775-9 Paperback

Contents

Contents

Figures and Tables

Figures

Acknowledgments

This book is the result of work that I began as a graduate student at UCLA. First and foremost, I thank my dissertation adviser, Jean-Laurent Rosenthal, for his dedication, guidance, and insights. Jean-Laurent generously read the entire manuscript and gave many valuable suggestions. I also extend special thanks to Naomi Lamoreaux for her kind and patient commitment to this project and to Philip Hoffman for well-timed words of encouragement.

Many scholars have graciously provided comments and data over the past several years. I thank Carlos Álvarez Nogal, Daniel Bogart, Richard Bonney, Peter Brecke, Albert Carreras, Mauricio Drelichman, Rui Esteves, Giovanni Federico, Alexander Field, Wantje Fritschy, Oscar Gelderblom, Knick Harley, Geoffrey Hodgson, David Jacks, Hans Christian Johansen, Joost Jonker, Heleen Kole, W. L. Korthals Altes, Peter Lindert, Robert Margo, Maria Eugenia Mata, Christopher Meissner, Kris Mitchener, Patrick O'Brien, Michael Pammer, Leandro Prados de la Escosura, Jaime Reis, Albrecht Ritschl, the late Kenneth Sokoloff, Mark Spoerer, Enrico Spolaore, William Summerhill, Marjolein t'Hart, Nuno Valério, Wietse Veenstra, François Velde, Marc Weidenmier, Jan Luiten van Zanden, and several anonymous journal referees. I also thank participants in presentations at the All-UC Group in Economic History Workshop in San Francisco; Bocconi University in Milan; UCLA; the Canadian Network for Economic History Conference in Montreal; Carlos III University in Madrid; the Cliometrics Conference in Tucson; the Collegio Carlo Alberto in Turin; the Economic History Association Conferences in Pittsburgh and Toronto; the Economic History Society Conferences in Exeter and Warwick; the European Association of Evolutionary Political Economy

Conference in Athens; the European Science Foundation Summer School in Paris; the European University Institute in Florence; the Finance, Institutions, and History Summer School in Venice; the Frontier Research in Economics and Social History Meeting in Florence; IMT Lucca Institute for Advanced Studies; the Institutional and Social Dynamics of Growth and Distribution Conference in Lucca; the International Society for New Institutional Economics Conference in Berkeley; the NSF/NBER/ CEPR Workshop on the Evolution of the Global Economy in Cambridge, Massachusetts; the University of Oxford; the Paris School of Economics; the University of Pisa; Santa Clara University; the World Congress of Cliometrics in Edinburgh; and the World Economic History Congress in Utrecht. Likewise, I thank Eric Crahan, editor of history and politics at Cambridge University Press, for proposing this book and directing the publication process from start to finish, and two anonymous readers for useful suggestions.

Upon finishing graduate school in 2006, I became an assistant professor at IMT Institute for Advanced Studies in Lucca. I thank the director, Fabio Pammolli, for his enduring support; past and current colleagues Leonardo Baccini, Lucia Bonfreschi, Maria Elena Cavallaro, Jing-Yuan Chiou, Stefano Gattei, Andrea Giannaccari, Giammario Impullitti, Gabriel Katz, Morgan Llewellyn, Antonio Masala, James Melton, Luca Polese Remaggi, Mauricio Prado, Francesco Sobbrio, Mauro Sylos Labini, and Andrea Vindigni for lively conversations; and the IMT staff for their cheerful assistance. I cannot resist also thanking Danne Cosmopolita Food, Opera Caffè, Pasticceria Piccola Soave, and other bars, enoteche, osterie, pizzerie, and ristoranti for making life in Italy so very delicious.

Finally, I thank my wife, Kimberly Crawford, for her love, musical taste, and sense of humor. Our son, Julien Lee, was born in January 2010. I dedicate this book to them.

Weak and Strong States in Historical Perspective

Powerful fiscal states underlie today's advanced economies in the West and beyond. Wealthy governments typically gather large tax revenues as shares of GDP and spend great sums on the military, infrastructure, and social programs. How rich European countries first established modern systems of public finance is a fundamental question in economic history. It is the key question that this book tackles.

The answer, which involves centuries of political reforms, wars, revolutions, defaults, technological change, and economic growth, has profound implications for current political debates. The financial meltdowns of the late 1990s in East and Southeast Asia and Latin America illustrate the vital links between fiscal policy and development. Beyond financial crisis, emerging economies also face fiscal problems resulting from the lack of tax resources available to provide basic public goods like transportation infrastructure. Yet fiscal troubles do not affect developing countries alone. One of the most pressing issues that advanced nations must confront over the coming decades is how to keep entitlement programs solvent. No country is immune to fiscal imperatives.

To meet fiscal challenges, political regimes will have to evolve. The process of institutional transformation finds crucial antecedents in history. Links between politics, taxation, and public spending and debt are long-standing. Today's world certainly differs from that of the past. However, it is clear that a solid understanding of the establishment of modern systems of public finance will enrich current debates about how to best design and implement efficient fiscal institutions, for both emerging and developed nations.

1.1. Fiscal Fundamentals

A large literature in economics emphasizes the negative effect of executive predation on economic growth.[1] This view suggests that institutional constraints such as parliamentary control over government finances protect property rights and encourage investment by limiting the ability of rulers to expropriate. Figure 1.1 plots the average score of constraints on the executive from 1995 to 2004 from the Polity IV Database of Marshall and Jaggers (2008) against average log real GDP per capita over the same years from the Penn World Tables of Heston, Summers, and Aten (2006) for nearly 100 countries. Consistent with arguments that link predatory states with poor economic performance, there is a clear increasing relationship between ruler limits and income.

Though illustrative, Figure 1.1 masks the role of history. Many of today's rich states were not established with parliamentary institutions intact. Rather, executive constraints are the culmination of a long and arduous historical process. The political transformation from absolutist to parliamentary regimes and its fiscal effects are among the main themes of this book.

The literature's focus on executive predation, moreover, discounts the positive economic roles that robust governments may play. Political scientists argue that traditional local elites such as bosses, chiefs, clan leaders, landlords, and rich peasants in parts of sub-Saharan Africa oppose fiscal control by national governments, leading weak states to underinvest in public services that increase productivity. The successful development experiences of Asian Tiger nations, by contrast, took place under powerful fiscal states.[2] Figure 1.2 plots the average share of total taxes collected by central governments as a percentage of GDP from 1995 to 2004 from the Government Financial Statistics Database of the IMF against average log real per capita GDP for the same set of countries as before. There is a strong positive correlation between

---

[1] For theory, see North and Thomas (1973), Brennan and Buchanan (1980), North (1981), Levi (1988), McGuire and Olson (1996), and North, Wallis, and Weingast (2009). For empirics, see De Long and Shleifer (1993), Knack and Keefer (1995), and Acemoglu, Johnson, and Robinson (2001, 2002, 2005).

[2] For Africa, see Migdal (1988), Herbst (2000), and Bates (2001). For East Asia, see Wade (1990) and Kang (2002). There is also a recent related literature in economics. See Acemoglu, Robinson, and Verdier (2004), Glaeser et al. (2004), Acemoglu (2005), Besley and Persson (2008, 2009, 2010), Acemoglu, Ticchi, and Vindigni (2011), and Dincecco and Prado (2011). Finally, Lindert (2004, 2009) argues that social spending on public services like mass formal education is a major determinant of long-run economic growth.

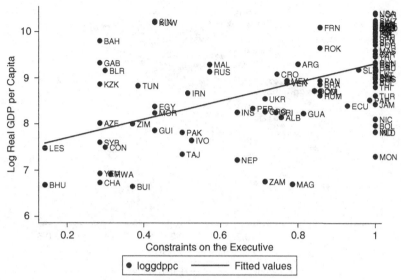

FIGURE I.I. Constraints on the executive and income, 1995–2004. Constraints on the executive are the average constraints on the executive index normalized from 0 to 1 between 1995 and 2004 from the Polity IV Database. Log real GDP per capita is the average log GDP per capita over the same years in constant U.S. dollars expressed in international prices, base year 2000, from the Penn World Tables, Version 6.2. The set of 96 sample countries is from Dincecco and Prado (2011).
Sources: Penn World Tables, Version 6.2, of Heston et al. (2006), Polity IV Database of Marshall and Jaggers (2008).

tax revenues and income, which is consistent with claims relating fiscal strength to better economic outcomes.[3]

However instructive, Figure 1.2 also neglects history. Fiscal prowess did not always characterize wealthy states. Instead, fiscal strength is the result of a deep process of political transformation. The establishment of robust tax systems and their effects on public finances is another of this book's core themes.

Overall, today's advanced economies strike a balance between weak and strong fiscal elements. Rich states typically possess a set of political institutions that link powerful centralized tax structures with parliaments that limit executive control over public finances. They are thus able to gather large tax revenues and can channel funds toward public services with positive economic benefits.[4]

---

[3] Excluding the outlier countries Bahrain (BAH), Croatia (CRO), Kuwait (KUW), Lesotho (LES), and Madagascar (MAG) only strengthens this correlation.

[4] Acemoglu (2005) refers to this type of outcome as a "consensually strong state."

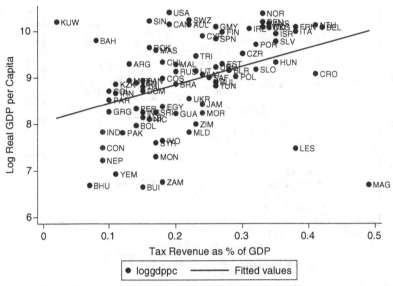

FIGURE I.2. Tax revenue and income, 1995–2004. Tax revenue collected by central governments as a percentage of GDP is the average between 1995 and 2004 from the Government Financial Statistics Database. Log real GDP per capita is the average log GDP per capita over the same years in constant U.S.dollars expressed in international prices, base year 2000, from the Penn World Tables, Version 6.2. The set of 96 sample countries is from Dincecco and Prado (2011). *Sources*: Government Financial Statistics Database of the IMF (2010), Penn World Tables, Version 6.2, of Heston et al. (2006).

But how did wealthy countries achieve regimes that are both fiscally centralized and politically limited? Many of today's advanced economies were not "born" with efficient fiscal and political institutions. To answer, this book examines the evolution of political regimes and public finances in Europe over the long term, from the height of the Old Regime in 1650 to the eve of World War I in 1913. Sovereign governments in Old Regime Europe generally faced two key political problems: fiscal fragmentation and absolutism. Though rulers exercised weak authority over taxation, they wielded strong control over spending. Under this equilibrium, executives were typically starved for revenues and often spent available funds on foreign military adventures rather than public services like roads that would most benefit society. To improve fiscal outcomes, states had to gain force by implementing uniform tax systems at the national level. They also had to restrict power by establishing parliaments that could monitor government expenditures at regular intervals. This book argues that the emergence of modern systems of public finance is the result of the resolution of these two fundamental political problems.[5]

By adopting a long-run perspective, this book enhances both historical and current debates over weak and strong states. The study of the development of public finance systems over the long term is valuable in its own right. Knowledge of the long-run process of fiscal change also has major implications beyond economic history. A proper understanding of the European experience translates into useful lessons for today's emerging and advanced countries, not the least because governments around the world have implemented European forms of fiscal governance.[6] Fiscal challenges from development policy to entitlement reform are with us to stay. To guide the course of future debates in useful ways, we must understand the past.

1.2. The Approach

Two seminal works form the core of this investigation. The first is North and Weingast (1989).[7] They claim that institutional reforms in England with the Glorious Revolution of 1688 enabled the king to make a credible commitment to responsible fiscal policies. Since the new constitution granted the national parliament the regular right to audit government finances, the ruler could keep promises to execute fiscal plans in time-consistent ways. By tying its hands, the executive was able to borrow much larger sums. The second seminal work is Epstein (2000).[8] He argues that institutional fragmentation within European polities, and not fiscal abuse by rulers, was the key source of fiscal troubles prior to the nineteenth century. Since provincial elites had strong incentives to oppose fiscal reforms that threatened

---

[5] The term "state," which is used interchangeably with "polity" throughout the text, has no normative connation.

[6] See La Porta et al. (1997, 1998, 1999), La Porta, Lopez-de-Silanes, and Shleifer (2008), and Nunn (2009).

[7] Also see Dickson (1967), Jones (1972), Stone (1979), Hill (1980), Brewer (1989), and Schultz and Weingast (1998). Scholars disagree over the fiscal impact of the Glorious Revolution. Clark (1996) argues that there were secure property rights in England from 1600 onward. O'Brien (2001) claims that England made key constitutional and administrative reforms in the 1640s. Stasavage (2003) highlights the development of cohesive English political parties in the 1690s. Sussman and Yafeh (2006) argue that the parliamentary innovations of 1688 did not lower British capital costs over the next century. Finally, Drelichman and Voth (2008) claim that fiscal repression rather than political change enabled England to sustain large debts.

[8] Also see Henshall (1992), Hoffman and Norberg (1994b), Hoffman and Rosenthal (1997, 2000), Rosenthal (1998), and O'Brien (2001).

traditional tax rights, there was a classic public goods problem whereby each locale wished to free-ride on the tax contributions of others. By establishing national tax systems with (high) equalized rates across provinces, states could gather much greater revenues. England – whose fiscal revolution epitomizes North and Weingast's argument – had centralized fiscal and political institutions from medieval times, making it exceptional.

The book claims that the political transformations that North and Weingast and Epstein identify are complementary components, and not competing or contradictory ones, of sound public finances. The book's long periodization makes it possible to fuse the arguments for fiscal centralization and parliamentary reforms into an integrated analysis of institutional change. Many studies of European fiscal history (including that of Epstein) finish with the fall of the Old Regime at the end of the 1700s.[9] These works often focus on weak-state problems of jurisdiction fragmentation. Other studies concentrate exclusively on the institutional shifts that took place during French revolutionary and Napoleonic times from 1789 to 1815.[10] Finally, studies of the nineteenth century after 1815 tend to emphasize the growing role of parliament.[11] The total result is to downplay or miss the key links between these diverse eras.

By contrast, the period under analysis in this book (1650–1913) spans fundamental transformations in political systems, as European states moved from fiscally fragmented and absolutist regimes to fiscally centralized and politically limited ones. The book thus examines the fiscal effects of both institutional changes, and not just one or the other. The findings support the argument that fiscal centralization and limited government alike led to major improvements in public finances. The results also indicate that the establishment of modern fiscal systems provided a solid institutional basis on which national governments could play positive economic roles, both during the Industrial Revolution over the late nineteenth century and during the rise of the welfare state over the twentieth century.

The book uses systematic methods of analysis to test for the impacts of political transformations both within and across European countries over time. Since North and Weingast focus on seventeenth-century England, and Epstein draws heavily from medieval Italy, one may worry that characteristics particular to those polities and eras drive their findings. The investigation in this book, by contrast, is general and applies the same set

---

[9] Also see Hoffman and Norberg (1994a) and Bonney (1995, 1999).
[10] See Godechot, Hyslop, and Dowd (1971), Woolf (1991), and Grab (2003).
[11] See Carstairs (1980), Flora (1983), and Cardoso and Lains (2010a).

of analytic tools to nearly a dozen sample countries. There is an intrinsic trade-off between historical breadth and depth. The broad scope of this book's inquiry compensates for any (necessary) loss of specific details. In this regard, the investigation complements works that rely upon chapter-by-chapter case studies.[12]

Most long-run comparative analyses of European fiscal history are qualitatively oriented.[13] This book constructs a new yearly database for three key fiscal indicators: free-market yields on long-term sovereign bonds, per capita revenues collected by national governments, and ratios of budget deficits to revenues. It also assembles new datasets for external and internal conflicts, economic growth, fiscal and monetary policies, and other elements. These data are used in a variety of ways. The book first characterizes fiscal time trends with respect to political transformations and other economic and political factors by country. It then subjects the data to a standard battery of rigorous tests. The book employs two distinct statistical procedures: structural breaks tests and regressions that exploit the panel nature of the data. The breaks tests assume no a priori knowledge of major turning points in the different fiscal series but let the data speak for themselves. The panel regressions incorporate a wide-ranging set of control variables to evaluate the fiscal effects of political transformations. In total, the empirical inquiry indicates that the resolution of weak- and strong-state problems – that is, the establishment of political regimes that were both fiscally centralized and politically limited – had significant positive fiscal effects.

Finally, the book moves beyond the analysis of sovereign credit risk alone. The fiscal history literature typically focuses on the links between

---

[12] See Hoffman and Norberg (1994a), Bonney (1999), Bordo and Cortés-Conde (2001), and Cardoso and Lains (2010a). This book also analyzes case histories.

[13] See Tilly (1990), Bonney (1995), O'Brien (2001), and Karaman and Pamuk (2010). Two econometric exceptions for the period before 1800 are Stasavage (2005, 2011). There is also an econometric literature on sovereign debt for the classic gold standard era from 1870 to 1913. See Bordo and Rockoff (1996), Obstfeld and Taylor (2003), Flandreau and Zumer (2004), Ferguson (2006), Ferguson and Shularick (2006), and Accominotti et al. (2010). Similarly, Lindert (1994) performs an econometric investigation of the rise of social spending in industrial nations from 1880 to 1913, while Aidt, Dutta, and Loukoianova (2006) and Aidt and Jensen (2009) examine the fiscal consequences of democratization from the 1800s to 1938. Other works that employ historical data series to test for the fiscal impacts of economic and political variables include Neal (1990), Willard, Guinnane, and Rosen (1996), Brown and Burdekin (2000), Frey and Kucher (2000), Sussman and Yafeh (2000), Mauro, Sussman, and Yafeh (2002), Reinhart, Rogoff, and Savastano (2003), Mitchener and Weidenmier (2005), Brown, Burdekin, and Weidenmier (2006), Tomz (2007), and Reinhart and Rogoff (2009).

parliamentary reforms and public debts.[14] In turn, it tends to overlook the direct impacts of institutional reforms on state budgets. This book analyzes two key channels through which political changes reduced credit risk: increases in government revenues per head and improvements in fiscal prudence. The investigation thus accounts for the precise ways in which fiscal centralization and limited government transformed public finances.

1.3. Overview of Contents

Chapter 2 examines the shift from fiscally fragmented to fiscally centralized regimes, the first fundamental transformation that European states underwent. Tax centralization granted new fiscal authority to national governments. However, the problem of executive discretion remained, since rulers could still use public funds as they pleased (e.g., on foreign military adventures). Chapter 3 examines the second fundamental transformation, the shift from absolutism to limited government.

Taken in combination, these two chapters demonstrate how institutional transformations resolved the Old Regime political problems of fiscal fragmentation and absolutism. European states gained tax force through fiscal centralization, and restricted executive power through limited government. The end result was a set of balanced fiscal and political institutions that had major implications for public finances. The rest of the book pursues this argument using a combination of qualitative and statistical methods.

The set of sample countries is inspired by, and overlaps with, those used in previous studies of European fiscal history.[15] For clarity, sample states are divided into two distinct groups. Group 1 countries were typically core powers. They are also characterized by long data series over a variety of political regimes. The Group 1 countries are Austria, England, France, the Netherlands, Prussia, and Spain. Group 2 countries, by contrast, were generally peripheral players, with relatively short data series. They are Belgium, Denmark, Italy, Portugal, and Sweden. In total, this set of sample states well captures the diversity of the European historical experience.

---

[14] See Epstein (2000, ch. 2), Sussman and Yafeh (2000, 2006), Quinn (2001), Stasavage (2003, 2005, 2011), and Summerhill (2011), as well as the citations listed in the preceding note.

[15] These works typically focus on Western Europe. See Hoffman and Norberg (1994a), Bonney (1995, 1999), Bordo and Cortés-Conde (2001), and Cardoso and Lains (2010a).

Chapter 4 examines sovereign credit, a vital statistic of the fiscal health of nations. The descriptive and case study evidence suggests that political transformations typically led to notable improvements in yield levels on government bonds. But by what means? Chapter 5 identifies two precise mechanisms by which fiscal centralization and limited government generated credit gains. It examines the evolution of public revenues and budget deficit-to-revenue ratios, where the latter measure fiscal prudence. Here the descriptive and case study evidence suggests that improvements in revenue collection and fiscal prudence were important channels through which political transformations reduced sovereign credit risk. Both fiscal centralization and limited government generally led to notable increases in government revenues and reductions in deficit ratios.

The findings in these two chapters are then subjected to a battery of rigorous statistical tests. Chapter 6 describes the results of structural breaks tests, which assume no a priori knowledge of key turning points in the different fiscal series. When the data speak for themselves through the breaks methodology, they typically identify political transformations as major turning points. These breaks generally led to significant increases in government revenues and improvements in fiscal prudence, coupled with significant reductions in sovereign credit risk.

Historical factors beyond political transformations, however, also affected public finances. To account for the impacts of conflict, growth, fiscal and monetary policies, country- and time-specific effects, and other elements, a regression analysis is undertaken in Chapter 7. The key strength of this approach is the ability to systematically disentangle the role of political regimes from other potentially relevant factors through the use of control variables. The econometric evidence confirms that political transformations led to significant improvements in public finances even after accounting for other important historical factors.

Overall, the qualitative and quantitative findings provide robust support for the argument that political transformations enhanced public finances. The final chapter examines the implications of fiscally centralized and politically limited regimes for the changing economic role of the state. It also draws historical lessons for today's emerging and advanced economies.

2

Gaining Force

From Fragmentation to Centralization

Fiscal fragmentation and absolutism plagued Old Regime states. This chapter examines fiscal centralization, the first fundamental political transformation that European states underwent. It begins by characterizing the problem of fiscal fragmentation in both qualitative and quantitative terms. It then describes the coding process for institutional reform and identifies the dates for fiscal centralization for each sample country.

2.1. The Fragmented Old Regime

Most polities in Europe were fiscally fragmented before the nineteenth century. Contrary to the conventional wisdom, early modern monarchs confronted a host of incumbent local institutions that reduced their fiscal powers.[1] To illustrate, this section examines France, Spain, the Netherlands, and England, four of the most celebrated cases in the literature on state formation in Europe.

Modern France inherited the territorial borders set under Louis XI during the late 1400s. As the state expanded, it was forced to superimpose control on top of entrenched regional institutions. The fiscal implications of this political arrangement, which Brewer (1989, p. 6) describes as "particularistic," were harsh. Since the French Crown had to negotiate independently over tax amounts with local authorities, tax rates were

---

[1] In the words of Epstein (2000, p. 13): "[D]ecades of research on pre-modern political practices ... has shown how 'absolutism' was a largely propagandistic device devoid of much practical substance." Also see Henshall (1992), Hoffman and Norberg (1994b), Hoffman and Rosenthal (1997), Rosenthal (1998), O'Brien (2001, pp. 14–24), and Magnusson (2009, ch. 2).

uneven. Whole towns and provinces avoided certain duties. From the fifteenth century onward, nobles in central and northern France were exempt from the land tax (*taille*), the most valuable direct tax. Nobles in the south paid the *taille* for only certain holdings. Fiscal fragmentation, moreover, was persistent.[2] The ultimate "success" of Finance Minister Colbert's reforms in the 1660s, for instance, was to carve France into eight distinct tariff areas. In the aftermath, there were still local excises, including five within the Five Great Farms, the largest French customs zone.[3] Shapiro and Markoff (1998) argue that the bewildering variety of taxes, levied at diverse local rates, was a key complaint on the eve of the French Revolution.[4]

The Spanish kingdoms of Castile and Aragon (including Catalonia and Valencia) were united in 1497. The subsequent conquest of a large portion of the Basque Country gave Spain its modern contours by the start of the sixteenth century. Repeated attempts to forge tax agreements among the five kingdoms united under the Spanish Crown were unsuccessful. Seventeenth-century efforts by Count-Duke Olivares to implement structural fiscal changes were a failure, for instance, and so the national government had to impose new royal taxes on top of traditional local ones. The Bourbon tax reforms of the early 1700s also fell short. Unable to extend the Castilian tax system eastward, the Crown was again forced to superimpose additional duties. The incongruous names of the new tax, called the *contribución única* in Aragon, the *catastro* in Catalonia, and the *equivalente* in Valencia, reflected the disparities in tax rates that remained. As in France, fiscal fragmentation in Spain was chronic. Comín (1990, p. 86) claims that the first genuine reform of the Spanish tax system did not take place until the middle of the nineteenth century.[5]

---

[2] In the words of White (2001, p. 66): "Several times an invigorated Crown initiated new reforms to centralize and simplify the tax system, but in the long run the government had limited success in altering the basic tax structure."

[3] Johnson (2006) analyzes the fiscal effects of Colbert's reforms.

[4] Also see Sutherland (1986), Rosenthal (1992), Hoffman (1994), Major (1994), and Sargent and Velde (1995).

[5] In the words of Tortella (2000, pp. 174–5): "Until 1845 the Spanish taxation system was a disorganized and unsystematic mosaic … not only were the privileged classes virtually exempt from taxation, but the Church and the nobility often had quasi-fiscal prerogatives, since they collected in their own names rents which looked very much like taxes. The tax burden varied from region to region and there were even specific taxes for particular cities or districts…. The total taxation picture was a hodgepodge of incomplete and variable components." Also see Elliot (1986), Lynch (1989), and Tortella and Comín (2001).

The borders of the Dutch Republic, which officially declared its independence from Spain in 1581, correspond to those of the modern Netherlands. The Republic was a confederation composed of seven sovereign provinces.[6] Each province had separate public finances, and no unified tax system was ever implemented. To fund common costs of warfare and administration, there was a quota system in which the seven provinces promised to pay fixed amounts.[7] The largest share of the burden (almost 60 percent of the total) fell to Holland, the most populated and wealthiest province. Van Zanden and van Riel (2004, chs. 1, 2) argue that fiscal fragmentation weakened the Republic's ability to raise funds and service debts, since other provinces typically shirked their obligations and free-rode on Holland's payments. Provincial elites, moreover, resisted calls for fundamental tax reforms. Van Zanden and van Riel claim that, over the long term, this political stalemate created an untenable fiscal situation.

One general feature of fragmented states, whether in France, Spain, or the Dutch Republic, was the close relationship between local tax control and political autonomy. Provincial elites had strong incentives to oppose fiscal reforms that threatened traditional tax rights. The result was a classic public goods problem. Since each local authority attempted to free-ride on the tax contributions of others, the revenues that national governments could gather on a per capita basis were low.

England was exceptional in this regard. The Norman Conquest of 1066 established a uniformity of laws and customs that other European states did not achieve until much, much later.[8] Furthermore, Brewer (1989, p. 4) argues that the development of a strong national parliament paralleled the emergence of a powerful, centralized monarchy. The English king thus avoided costly, drawn-out tax negotiations with provincial elites.[9]

---

[6] The Republic also included the sparsely populated rural lordship of Drenthe and, after the Peace of Westphalia in 1648, the Generality Lands.

[7] See t'Hart (1997) and Fritschy (2007).

[8] See Brewer (1989, pp. 3–7), Sacks (1994, pp. 14–23), and Hoffman and Norberg (1994b).

[9] Also see Epstein (2000, ch. 2) and O'Brien (2001, pp. 14–24). We must distinguish between English fiscal and political institutions and those for the British Isles as a whole. In the words of Brewer (1989, pp. 5–6): "There was certainly an English medieval state, made from a Norman template, but not a British one.... Nevertheless the English core of what was eventually to become the British state was both geographically larger and better administrated than its French equivalent." For consistency, the term "England" is used throughout the text. Appendix 2 documents the construction methods of the English time series for the various fiscal indicators.

To resolve the problem of local tax free-riding elsewhere in Europe, executives had to gain the fiscal authority to impose standard tax menus rather than bargain place by place over individual rates. So long as states equalized rates across provinces at relatively high levels, government revenues per head rose. Hoffman and Rosenthal (2000) argue that both executives and local elites may have preferred centralized fiscal regimes as part of power-sharing agreements in which the former received larger funds and the latter, which coordinated efforts through representative bodies, could finance a larger portion of the public services that they desired. Chapter 3 further examines this possibility.

2.2. Quantitative Analysis

2.2.1. *Research Design*
A simple quantitative analysis that examines changes in fragmented authority over time complements the qualitative accounts of fiscal fragmentation. The focus is again on France, Spain, the Netherlands, and England, four of the most prominent cases in the historical literature on state formation in Europe.[10] The sub-period under study, from 1700 to 1815, captures the critical institutional crossroads that occurred with the French Revolution (1789–99).

Although an ideal test of fiscal fragmentation would be to measure the size of fiscal zones within states and record institutional changes one by one as they occurred over time, data sufficiently comprehensive for such a study to be undertaken do not exist. Given the lack of systematic information that is available prior to the nineteenth century, any alternative indicator should provide a succinct measure of institutional fragmentation that is comparable across states.

Internal customs borders are one unique source of data that satisfy this condition. Domestic tariffs, in the words of Adam Smith, obstructed the most important branch of commerce, the interior trade of a country.[11] Trade barriers hampered the legitimate market exchange of goods and services. Major rivers and roads typically crossed multiple customs frontiers where holdups occurred and tariffs had to be paid. In this way, trade barriers encouraged black market traffic. The administration of customs was also expensive and prone to inefficiency. Epstein

---

[10] Dincecco (2010b) examines a larger set of sample states.

[11] See Smith (2003, p. 1135). The description attributed by Henderson (1939, pp. 22–3) to an influential merchant union was more vivid: customs barriers "cripple trade and produce the same effect as ligatures which prevent the free circulation of blood."

(2000, chs. 1, 2) argues that the total effect of internal barriers was to impose costs, delays, and risks that atomized domestic economies and restricted growth.

Domestic tariffs were also part of a larger problem of fragmented sovereignty. As described in the preceding section, towns and provinces often had distinct economic and political institutions, including local customs, tax privileges, weights and measures, and monopolist guilds. Furthermore, centralizing reforms like the unification of domestic tariffs, the establishment of national tax systems and central banks, the standardization of weights and measures, and the abolition of guilds often took place in one fell swoop.[12]

A focus on major internal customs facilitates the analysis. This simplification suggests that some of the smaller steps toward centralization were missed. For instance, for tractability the Five Great Farms in France is recorded as a unified zone from the 1660s onward, though at least five local tariffs remained. Systematic underestimation of the true extent of divided authority biases the analysis against finding evidence of institutional fragmentation. Any results that still indicate the presence of divided authority will thus be stronger than otherwise.

As described in the preceding section, sovereign borders for France, Spain, and the Netherlands were put in place by the 1600s and remained relatively stable thereafter. Net growth in physical size from 1700 to 1815 was small. Though France conquered the Netherlands in 1795, it became independent by the end of the Napoleonic era. Since the analysis focuses on changes in fragmented authority in 1815 relative to the Old Regime, this set of events did not have a significant effect.

Across the English Channel, however, we must discriminate between English and British customs institutions.[13] As described in the preceding section, the unification of internal tariffs in England occurred during the eleventh century. England conjoined with Wales in 1536. The Scottish and English Crowns were united in 1603, but it was not until the 1707 Act of Union that the internal customs border separating the two territories was eliminated. A similar Act of Union conjoined Ireland in 1800.[14] Although net gains in physical size for countries like France were small from 1700 to 1815, growth in the size of the British state was large and permanent. The present investigation concerns fragmented authority within polities rather

---

[12] See Dincecco (2010b, table 1).
[13] See Brewer (1989, pp. 3–7) for a general discussion of this point.
[14] The Irish Free State was established in 1922.

than state consolidation. To avoid confounding the effects of internal and external fragmentation, the analysis is restricted to England (including Wales).[15] However, the use of Britain (England, Scotland, and Wales), which was already established and was free of internal customs by the start of the 1700s, generates results similar to those obtained for England itself.

The sample consists of all 175 cities in England, France, the Netherlands, and Spain with at least 10,000 inhabitants in 1800 from De Vries (1984, app. 1). Each polity is well represented: there are 44 English, 19 Dutch, 78 French, and 34 Spanish sample cities. Since the investigation focuses on the Continent, where rapid urbanization did not begin until after the end of the Napoleonic Wars (1803–15), the use of 1800 as the base year mitigates problems of sample bias.[16]

Although it would be useful to evaluate the economic impact of differences in marginal tax rates across internal customs zones, systematic information does not exist. Data for physical sizes and urban populations, however, are available. Employing both measures ensures that the results are not contingent upon a particular approach. The first method estimates the sizes of the regions in square kilometers within which goods from sample cities could travel duty free. Historical accounts were used to characterize major internal customs borders for each country. Dincecco (2010b) documents the sources and construction methods. Since the analysis concerns the centralization of authority within European states themselves, only domestic sovereign areas are considered.[17]

The analysis used changes (if any) in internal tariff borders to calculate the area of the customs zone that surrounded each sample city at different points in time. Dincecco (2010b) provides the details. The chosen breaks were 1700, 1750, 1788 (just before the French Revolution), and 1815 (marking the end of the Napoleonic era). The unification of domestic customs took place when the final internal tariff barrier was eliminated. To compare levels of internal fragmentation across countries of different physical sizes, customs zones were calculated as percentages of total sovereign areas.

De Vries (1984, app. 1) provides urban populations at 50-year intervals over the eighteenth century. The second method summed the populations

---

[15] By the same logic, territories east of the Rhine River, which constitutes part of the eastern border of France, were not examined, since there were major changes in sovereign borders over time. Dincecco (2010b) tests state consolidation in the German and Italian territories over the nineteenth century.

[16] See Hohenberg and Lees (1985), Bairoch (1988), and Mokyr (1998).

[17] Colonial goods typically faced customs taxes at home ports. See Bordo and Cortés-Conde (2001).

TABLE 2.1. *Average Internal Customs Zones as Percentages of Sovereign Areas, 1700–1815*

	1700 (%)	1750 (%)	1788 (%)	1815 (%)
England	100	100	100	100
France	22	22	22	100
Netherlands	14	14	14	100
Spain	61	94	94	94

Note: For example, the size of the average customs zone in France in 1700 was 22% of total sovereign area.
Source: Dincecco (2010b).

of all sample cities contained within each customs zone in 1700, 1750, and 1800. These sums were then divided by total urban populations among sample cities within each country. Dincecco (2010b) describes the details. This technique produces reliable estimates so long as one assumes that internal tariffs had the largest effect on urban merchants, since rural populations typically produced subsistence goods.

2.2.2. Results

Table 2.1 indicates that, notwithstanding England, which was centralized from medieval times, there was a remarkable difference between the size of internal customs zones surrounding sample cities and total sovereign areas under the Old Regime. The average customs zone in France constituted just 22 percent of its total area. This result is consistent with Nye (2007, pp. 56–7), who argues that cumbersome tariffs created a virtual autarky between French regions. Similarly, the average customs zone in the Dutch Republic was only 14 percent of its total area. This finding concurs with Griffiths (1982, pp. 514–17), who claims that internal barriers created isolated economic Dutch sub-units. Finally, note that the use of the median or the largest customs zones was also indicative of internal fragmentation.

Spain was exceptional in this regard. The average Spanish customs zone, at 61 percent of total sovereign area in 1700, increased to 94 percent by 1750 due to the abolition of internal customs by Bourbon reformers in the 1710s. Prior to the eighteenth century, there were internal customs borders between Castile, Aragon, Catalonia, Valencia, and the Basque Country. Basque customs were restored in 1722 and lasted until 1839, when internal tariffs were finally abolished.[18]

---

[18] See Tortella and Comín (2001, pp. 155–65).

TABLE 2.2. *Cumulative Percentage of Sample Cities Surrounded by Internal Customs Zones of Various Sizes, 1700–1815*

Size (km²)	1700 (%)	1750 (%)	1788 (%)	1815 (%)
< 50,000	32	29	29	11
< 100,000	39	36	36	11
< 150,000	39	36	36	11
< 200,000	65	61	61	37
< 250,000	85	81	81	37
< 300,000	85	81	81	37
< 350,000	85	81	81	37
< 400,000	100	81	81	37
< 450,000	100	81	81	37
< 500,000	100	100	100	55
< 550,000	100	100	100	100

Note: 175 cities with at least 10,000 inhabitants in 1800 in England, France, the Netherlands, and Spain were included. For example, 32% of sample cities in 1700 were surrounded by a customs zone of less than 50,000 square kilometers.
Source: Dincecco (2010b).

By nearly all other fragmentation measures, however, Spain was worse off than other Old Regime states. Centralizing reforms like the establishment of a national tax system and central bank, the standardization of weights and measures, and the abolition of local guilds did not occur until the 1830s or later.[19] Poor transportation networks also hindered economic development. In 1800, there were nearly 30,000 kilometers of English roads but fewer than 5,000 kilometers of Spanish ones, though Spain was more than three times as large as England.[20] The calculations that use internal customs are thus strong underestimates of the true extent of divided authority in early modern Spain.

Other measures also suggest that internal customs zones were generally small before 1789. Table 2.2 indicates that more than 25 percent of sample cities were surrounded by a customs zone of less than 50,000 square kilometers, more than 60 percent were surrounded by a customs zone of less than 200,000 square kilometers, and more than 80 percent were surrounded by a customs zone of less than 250,000 square kilometers. Furthermore, Table 2.3 indicates that the average customs zone in

[19] See Dincecco (2010b, table 1).
[20] The Spanish estimate is from Vicens Vive (1969, pp. 679–81). Also see Ringrose (1968, 1970) and Tortella (2000, pp. 115–20). The English estimate is from Bogart (2005, p. 440).

TABLE 2.3. *Average Sizes of Internal Customs Zones, 1700–1815*

Size (km²)	1700	1750	1788	1815
England	151,000	151,000	151,000	151,000
France	118,000	118,000	118,000	544,000
Netherlands	5,000	5,000	5,000	34,000
Spain	302,000	467,000	467,000	467,000
Overall	150,000	182,000	182,000	375,000

Source: Dincecco (2010b).

1788 was just 182,000 square kilometers. A comparison of France and England is particularly noteworthy, since the average pre-1789 French customs zone was 33,000 square kilometers smaller than England, the only sample polity free of internal tariffs. If France had been centralized, its free customs area would have been more than three and a half times as large as that of its English counterpart.

Table 2.4, which displays the results of the calculations for urban populations within customs zones as percentages of total urban populations over time, also indicates that domestic free-trade areas were fragmented under the Old Regime. The number of urban residents within customs zones was typically less than 10 percent of total urban populations. Exceptions included the Five Great Farms in France, where urban inhabitants made up 55 percent of the total, and the Dutch province of Holland, where they were 75 percent. However, at least five local customs remained within the Five Great Farms after Colbert's 1660s reforms. By restricting the analysis to major internal borders, the French calculations systematically underestimate the true extent of fragmented authority. The same logic holds for the Dutch Republic, where cities, towns, and provinces were largely autonomous.[21] In Spain, urban residents of the Kingdom of Castile constituted 77 percent of the total urban population in 1700, and 98 percent by 1750. As already described, however, the use of internal customs significantly underestimates eighteenth-century institutional fragmentation in Spain.

2.3. Centralization after 1789

Although the process of fiscal centralization in Europe took centuries, the evidence shown in the preceding two sections indicates that it was largely unfinished through the late 1700s. Fundamental changes to tax systems

---

[21] See van Zanden and van Riel (2004, pp. 32–40).

TABLE 2.4. *Urban Populations within Internal Customs Zones as Percentages of Total Urban Populations, 1700–1800*

Customs Zone	1700 (%)	1750 (%)	1800 (%)
Panel A: France			
Effectively Foreign 1	4	5	
Effectively Foreign 2	1	1	
Five Great Farms	55	55	
Reputedly Foreign 1A	8	7	
Reputedly Foreign 1B	6	7	
Reputedly Foreign 1C	8	8	100
Reputedly Foreign 1D	7	7	
Reputedly Foreign 2	3	3	
Reputedly Foreign 3	1	1	
Reputedly Foreign 4	6	6	
Panel B: Netherlands			
Friesland	2	2	
Gelderland	3	3	
Generality Lands	6	5	
Groningen	3	4	
Holland	75	75	100
Overijssel	2	2	
Utrecht	5	4	
Zeeland	4	4	
Panel C: Spain			
Aragon	5		
Castile	77	98	99
Catalonia	8		
Valencia	9		
Basque Country	1	2	1

Source: Dincecco (2010b).

were in several cases the result of radical, exogenously imposed administrative reforms by French revolutionary or Napoleonic armies.[22] More generally, fiscal reforms often took place in the context of large-scale administrative reforms that established new government bureaucracies. We may thus typically identify fiscal centralization as part of a structural shift in the institutional basis of states that occurred from 1789 onward.

The quantitative analysis supports this interpretation of the timing of fiscal changes. Whether measured by physical area or urban population, there

---

[22] See Godechot et al. (1971), Woolf (1991), Grab (2003), and Acemoglu et al. (2009a).

was a significant increase in the size of internal customs zones after the fall of the Old Regime. The Revolution eliminated major internal customs in France. In the Netherlands, customs unification occurred after the French conquest in 1795. Table 2.1 indicates that domestic customs zones and total sovereign areas coincided in both countries by 1815, and Table 2.4 suggests a one-to-one correspondence between urban populations within customs zones and urban population totals by the start of the 1800s.

Furthermore, Tables 2.2 and 2.3 indicate that internal customs unification took place from 1789 onward. Neither the cumulative percentage of cities surrounded by customs zones of various sizes nor the average size of customs zones in Europe changed much from 1700 to 1788. However, Table 2.2 shows that customs zones grew quickly over the next two and a half decades. Nearly 30 percent of cities were surrounded by a customs zone of 50,000 square kilometers or less in 1788, whereas in 1815 only about 10 percent of cities were surrounded by one of that size. More than 80 percent of cities were surrounded by a customs zone smaller than 450,000 square kilometers in 1788, while in 1815 this figure was less than 40 percent. Likewise, Table 2.3 indicates that the overall average customs zone surrounding sample cities more than doubled in size, from 182,000 square kilometers in 1788 to 375,000 square kilometers in 1815.[23]

2.4. Coding Centralization

A clear and simple definition of fiscal centralization facilitates comparison across states. The process of fiscal centralization was completed the year that the national government first secured its revenues through a standard tax system with uniform rates throughout the country.[24] All pre-centralized regimes were classified as entirely fragmented, even for states where fiscal divisions were relatively small. This choice implies that some regimes counted as fully fragmented will encompass data associated with

---

[23] These results are consistent with the literature on the integration of domestic European grain markets. Persson (1999), Jacks (2005), and Keller and Shiue (2007) find that Old Regime markets were inefficient but that there were significant reductions in price dispersions after 1815. British markets, which were efficient by the late 1700s, were exceptional.

[24] This definition does not imply that central governments became tax monopolists. The history of the United States just after the Revolution of 1776 illustrates this point. Under the Articles of Confederation, the first U.S. constitution, Congress could only request tax funds from states. Fiscal centralization took place in 1788, when the new constitution granted Congress the legal power to ensure that states complied with national tax standards. However, states could still levy local taxes. Also see Edling (2003).

better fiscal outcomes (e.g., higher per capita revenues). Average improvements after fiscal centralization will therefore be smaller than otherwise. Systematic underestimation of the fiscal effects of centralization biases the data against the hypothesis that fiscal centralization improved public finances. The results of the empirical analysis in Chapters 4 to 7 will thus be stronger than otherwise if they still indicate that fiscally centralized regimes had significant positive effects on the various fiscal indicators.

Table 2.5 displays the dates of fiscal centralization for Group 1 and Group 2 countries. As described in Section 2.1, England had centralized institutions from very early on. In many parts of continental Europe, structural fiscal changes took place swiftly and permanently after the fall of the Old Regime. With the start of the Revolution (1789–99), the National Assembly transformed the tax system in France by eliminating traditional privileges. Napoleon completed this process upon taking power in 1799. The First French Republic conquered the Low Countries in 1795, and the Southern Netherlands including Belgium became standard French departments. The Batavian Republic, the successor to the Dutch Republic, established a national system of taxation under French rule in 1806. Napoleonic conquest at the start of the 1800s was also the major catalyst for fiscal change on the Italian peninsula. However, the unification of tax systems among pre-unitary Italian states did not occur until after the establishment of the Kingdom of Italy in 1861. Finally, Prussia undertook major administrative reforms, including fiscal centralization, after its loss to France in the Battle of Jena-Auerstedt in 1806.[25]

Although Napoleon defeated Austria in 1805 and invaded Portugal in 1807 and Spain in 1808, he failed to implement lasting administrative changes in those territories. Fiscal centralization did not take place in the Austrian Empire until after the Revolutions of 1848, which had important implications for bureaucratic structures. Most notably, the central government in Vienna began to implement an effective Cisleithanian tax system in Hungary.[26] Fiscal centralization also occurred in the 1840s in

---

[25] For France, see Bordo and White (1991, pp. 314–16) and White (1995, pp. 234–41). For Belgium, see Holtman (1967, p. 100) and Sutherland (1986, pp. 344–6). For the Netherlands, see Fritschy and van der Voort (1997, pp. 78–82) and van Zanden and van Riel (2004, pp. 40–51). For Italy, see Cohen and Federico (2001, ch. 3) and Federico (2010, pp. 192–3). For Prussia, see Kiser and Schneider (1994, pp. 200–1), Breuilly (2003, pp. 131–2), and Ziblatt (2006, pp. 114–15).

[26] Austria and Hungary were the largest territories of the Austrian Empire (1804–67). The Compromise of 1867 led to the establishment of the Austro-Hungarian Empire (1867–1918). For consistency, the term "Austria" is used throughout the text. Also see Pammer (2010, pp. 132–3).

TABLE 2.5. *Dates of Fiscal Centralization in Europe*

	Year	Event
Group 1		
England	1066	Norman Conquest and erosion of provincial authority
France	1790	Administrative reforms after Revolution of 1789
Netherlands	1806	Administrative reforms under French control
Prussia	1806	Administrative reforms after French defeat in battle
Spain	1845	Administrative reforms during Moderate Decade
Austria	1848	Administrative reforms during Year of Revolutions
Group 2		
Belgium	1795	Administrative reforms after French annexation
Portugal	1859	Centralization and regulation of government accounts
Italy	1861	Establishment of kingdom and tax unification
Sweden	1861	Abolition of pre-modern tax system
Denmark	1903	Abolition of pre-modern tax system

Note: Group 1 includes core powers and has long data series over diverse political regimes. Group 2 includes peripheral powers and has shorter data series. The second column indicates the year that the process of fiscal centralization as defined in the text was completed. The final column offers brief explanations for these dates, which the text elaborates upon.
Source: See text.

Spain during a decade of major institutional reforms. Significant changes in public finances in Portugal took place in the 1850s, after the end of the revolutionary era (1820–51). The 1859 reform led to the centralization and regulation of government accounts.[27]

Pre-modern fiscal structures remained in Scandinavia through much of the 1800s. Major tax changes did not occur until the second half of the nineteenth century or later. The 1861 reform in Sweden abolished the ancient system of dividing tax subjects into different classes, with many sub-groups and different rules for fixed contributions for each of

[27] For Austria, see Pammer (2010, pp. 136–9, 156–7). For Spain, see Tortella (2000, pp. 173–92) and Comín (2010, pp. 220–6). For Portugal, see Cardoso and Lains (2010b, pp. 261–4). Because of new evidence published in Cardoso and Lains (2010a), the coding for Denmark, Portugal, Spain, and Sweden was updated from Dincecco (2009a).

them. Similarly, the 1903 reform in Denmark eliminated traditional tax structures and introduced a modern income tax with standard, country-wide rates.[28]

Fiscal prowess is a key factor that characterizes today's rich countries. Yet many advanced economies were not "born" with strong tax institutions. To understand how wealthy states gained tax force, we must look to the past. This chapter has examined fiscal centralization, the first fundamental political transformation that European states underwent. Both the qualitative and quantitative evidence indicates that the establishment of national tax systems was the result of a long and difficult historical process and was not typically completed until after the fall of the Old Regime at the end of the eighteenth century.

Although fiscal centralization granted new fiscal authority to European states, the problem of executive discretion remained, since rulers could still use government funds as they wished (e.g., on foreign military adventures). The focus now turns to the second fundamental political transformation in European fiscal history, the shift from absolutist to parliamentary regimes.

---

[28] For Sweden, see Schön (2010, pp. 169–78). Hans Christian Johansen provided the account for Denmark. Also see the preceding footnote.

3

Restricting Power

From Absolutism to Limited Government

By eliminating local tax free-riding, fiscal centralization should have increased the ability of national governments to collect greater revenues. Since rulers retained control over state expenditures, however, the consolidation of fiscal powers may have exacerbated problems of executive discretion. Spending constraints were thus necessary.

This chapter examines the second fundamental political transformation that European states underwent, from absolutism to limited government, which restricted the ways in which rulers could use public funds. It begins by characterizing the problem of unconstrained absolutism. It then describes the coding process for political change and identifies the dates for constitutional reform across sample countries.

3.1. Predatory Kings

Two well-known cases illustrate the importance of regular institutional limits on executive spending: King William I of the Netherlands and King Charles I of England.

The Kingdom of the United Netherlands (including Belgium) was established at the end of the Napoleonic Wars (1803–15).[1] Its new constitution bestowed hereditary autocratic powers on the new king, William I (r. 1815–40). Although a national parliament was granted the constitutional right to audit state finances, there were 10-year budgets for recurrent expenditures. Parliament could therefore exercise its authority only

---

[1] The account of William I is based on van Zanden and van Riel (2004, pp. 85–106, 171–8). Also see van Zanden (1996), Fritschy, t'Hart, and Horlings (2002, pp. 22–3), and van Zanden and van Riel (2010, pp. 58–72).

once per decade. The consequences of repeated budget rejections were also vague, in part because finance ministers were not forced to step down if their proposals were not approved. For these reasons, parliamentary oversight was greatly diminished.

William I spent heavily on the military, on infrastructure, and on the monarchy itself. Although fiscal centralization in 1806 had roughly doubled the size of the Dutch tax base, interest payments had fallen, and Europe was politically stable, the king could not balance the national accounts. By 1840, public debt had risen to more than 200 percent of GDP, a ratio comparable to that during the height of the Napoleonic Wars. William I also resorted to semi-legal means to hide the true state of public finances.[2]

William I's reckless fiscal policy came apart at the end of the 1830s. Parliamentary debate and a special inquiry made clear that the state was bankrupt, and the constitution was amended in 1839 to limit executive fiscal powers. Two-year budgets took the place of 10-year ones. Public finances also became more transparent. It is likely that William I abdicated in 1840 at least in part because of the greater institutional limits that had been imposed on him. A new constitution, promulgated in 1848, marked the establishment of a truly liberal era in the Netherlands. Now the king had to submit annual budgets to parliament for approval. By implementing a firm check on executive spending, this reform became what van Zanden and van Riel (2004, p. 175) call the "cornerstone" of parliamentary power.

Although rulers spent government revenues as they pleased, representative bodies exercised tax authority.[3] Executives thus made attempts to evade parliament in the never-ending search for greater funds. The familiar example of King Charles I of England (r. 1625–49) demonstrates this phenomenon.[4] One major source of revenues for Charles I was forced loans, which he repaid in ways that were unpredictable and in terms that were altered

---

[2] In the words of van Zanden and van Riel (2004, p. 97): "The perhaps most striking aspect of William's financial policy consisted of his attempts to reduce the influence of parliament on fiscal policy and to suppress public debate in general on issues of government finance ... he unchangingly found himself in the situation where the creation of one fiscal hole was used to fill the next, leading to a situation that became more and more difficult to control. As a result, it became increasingly less attractive to be candid about the true state of government finance."

[3] With the exception of England, representative bodies in Old Regime Europe were not national parliaments, but culled delegates from particular provinces and social groups. Also see Chapter 2. Stasavage (2011) and van Zanden, Buringh, and Bosker (2011) examine the fiscal and economic effects of medieval parliaments.

[4] This account is based on North and Weingast (1989, pp. 808–17). Also see Ashton (1960, pp. 31–67, 154–84), Hirst (1986, pp. 126–59), Cust (1987, pp. 39–71, 99–149), and Sacks (1994, pp. 53–6).

from the original agreements. Other measures to skirt parliament included customs impositions and the sale of government lands, monopolies, and offices. The king also seized private goods such as bullion. Finally, Charles I kept parliament in the dark about the true state of public finances.

Predatory fiscal practices by English rulers continued through the Glorious Revolution of 1688, in which King James II (r. 1685–8) was overthrown. The Revolution Settlement reaffirmed parliament's exclusive authority to levy new taxes and curtailed the executive's capacity to pursue independent revenue sources. Soon after, parliament gained for the first time the annual right to veto expenditures and audit government finances. The ability to monitor the budget at regular intervals established what North and Weingast (1989, p. 816) call parliament's "supreme" role in fiscal matters.

3.2. The Fiscal Supremacy of Parliament

The type of equilibrium that we observe in England before 1688 and the Netherlands before 1848, which Hoffman and Rosenthal (1997, 2000) characterize as "divided fiscal authority," left states locked in a vicious circle.[5] Since parliamentary elites feared that executives would spend additional funds in wasteful ways (e.g., on foreign military adventures), they demanded the power of budgetary oversight before raising new taxes.[6] Rulers thus resorted to fiscal predation, which reinforced parliaments' worry that they could not be trusted. In turn, parliaments fervently resisted tax requests and revenues were low.

Regular parliamentary control over state budgets, which typically emerged over the nineteenth century, firmly established the fiscal supremacy of national parliaments. In turn, the likelihood of poor spending choices by executives fell. Just as rulers and parliaments each had reasons to favor fiscal centralization (see Chapter 2), they both had incentives to set new rules over government expenditures. Structural tax reforms implied that rulers would receive greater revenues. The surrender of budgetary control, however, was the only credible way for executives

---

[5] Also see Rosenthal (1998).

[6] Hoffman (2009) and Cox (2011) examine the royal moral hazard problem in warfare. In the words of Hoffman (2009, p. 24), monarchs "overspent on the military and provided more defense than their citizens likely desired. But they had little reason not to. Victory.... won them glory, enhanced reputations, and resources.... Losses never cost them their throne, at least for the major powers and as long as they faced no civil war." Cox (2011) argues that the establishment of ministerial responsibility after the Glorious Revolution in England resolved the Crown's moral hazard problem.

to guarantee that a portion of the new funds would be spent on public services that parliamentary elites desired. So long as rulers and parliaments struck deals, regimes with low taxation and expenditures were less attractive.[7] It is a well-established fact that tax burdens in polities with representative institutions like eighteenth-century England or Holland were notably higher than in absolutist ones like France and Spain.[8]

Hoffman and Rosenthal (2000) argue that limited government emerged after 1800 due to an important change in the nature of warfare. For the first time, kings who were defeated on the battlefield also faced the risk of losing their thrones. The advantages of greater tax revenues to wage successful wars thus began to outweigh the benefits of absolute control over spending. Furthermore, Acemoglu and Robinson (2000) claim that rulers also gained from expenditures on non-military public services that prevented social unrest.

Hoffman and Rosenthal (2000) explain the shift from absolutist to parliamentary regimes in broad strokes. They suggest that fiscal centralization and limited government took place simultaneously. Although it is true that each political transformation complemented the other (see Chapter 1), political transformations did not typically occur in one fell swoop. Structural changes in tax systems, which were in several cases imposed "exogenously" by French revolutionary or Napoleonic armies, generally took place decades before the establishment of stable national parliaments. The present analysis thus distinguishes between the fiscal effects of fiscal centralization and those of limited government.

Political transformations, moreover, were typically the result of a conflux of diverse economic, geographical, political, and social factors.[9] There was also a crucial element of chance. The establishment of the 1848 constitution in the Netherlands, for instance, took place during an economic downturn and related wave of political revolutions across Europe. Similarly, the Glorious Revolution in England occurred in the context of international tensions and the start of the War of the Grand Alliance (1688–97). Critical junctures in history exerted a significant influence on the precise scope and timing of institutional reforms that most likely dominated any premeditated bargains between rulers and elites. The discussion of the regression framework in Chapter 7 further examines this point.

---

[7] Van Zanden and Prak (2006) also make an argument for the economic role of citizenship along such lines in the context of the Dutch Republic.

[8] See Mathias and O'Brien (1976) and Hoffman and Norberg (1994b).

[9] See Moore (1966), Acemoglu et al. (2009b), and Dincecco, Federico, and Vindigni (2011).

3.3. Coding Limited Government

A valid depiction of parliamentary authority must capture parliament's real power to act on the budget. It must also be clear and simple enough to apply across states. The substance of the definition used here derives from the original spirit of constitutional reform as expressed by North and Weingast (1989). Limited government was established the year that parliament gained the stable constitutional right to control the national budget on an annual basis. The requirement that parliament's power of the purse held for at least two consecutive decades ensures the stability condition. To make the coding as objective as possible, years and regimes for which there are widespread academic consensus were selected. There is a close correspondence between the present classification scheme and those of De Long and Shleifer (1993), Acemoglu et al. (2005), and the Polity IV Database of Marshall and Jaggers (2008), though none of them fit the particular demands of this analysis.[10] In total, these three features – a regular right by parliament to manage budgets, regime stability, and scholarly agreement – imply that the coding of limited government parallels the standard that North and Weingast first introduced.

Selecting early dates to define political regimes as limited implies that average outcomes under parliamentary regimes will be worse than otherwise. For example, say that a stable form of limited government did not truly emerge in Germany until after World War II (recall that the Weimar Republic endured for only 14 years, from 1918 to 1933) or in Spain until after the death of Franco in 1975. If that were the case, then the correct coding would be to categorize pre-twentieth-century Prussian and Spanish regimes as absolutist. Since public finances in Europe have typically improved over time, the selection of early dates implies that some regimes classified as limited will encompass data associated with poorer fiscal outcomes. Average improvements after parliamentary reforms will therefore be smaller than otherwise. Systematic underestimation of the fiscal impacts of limited government biases the data against the hypothesis

---

[10] De Long and Shleifer (1993) use three measures: a binary indicator of absolutist versus non-absolutist regimes, an eight-point constitutional scale, and Tilly's (1990) categories of capital versus coercion. However, they code political regimes at 150-year intervals. Acemoglu et al. (2005) use two measures: categories of executive constraints and protection for capital, both from the Polity IV Database. However, they code political regimes at 50- or 100-year internals. Though Marshall and Jaggers (2008) classify executive constraints at yearly intervals, their database does not start until the 1800s.

that parliamentary reforms improved public finances. Any results of the empirical analysis in Chapters 4 to 7 that still indicate that limited government had significant positive effects on the fiscal variables of interest will thus be stronger than otherwise.

There were also some instances of switching back and forth between absolutism and limited government over the 1800s. As described earlier, the definition sets a stability threshold by requiring that parliamentary budgetary authority held for at least two straight decades. Furthermore, the regression analysis in Chapter 7 allows for uncertainty among investors and taxpayers over how long newly established limited regimes would last by lagging the start dates by five years.[11]

Nineteenth-century France illustrates the coding methodology.[12] The Bourbon monarchy was restored after the final defeat of Napoleon in 1815. This regime was constitutional, though in name only. In 1830, King Charles X (r. 1824–30) dissolved parliament, manipulated the electorate in favor of his supporters, placed the press under government control, and called for new elections. These measures incited the July Revolution the next day. King Louis Philip (r. 1830–48), the replacement for the deposed monarch, agreed to follow constitutional principles, but his tenure was beset by the economic crisis of the mid-1840s and ended with the Revolution of 1848. Since the reign of Louis Philip endured for less than two decades, the benchmark scheme does not code the July regime as limited. However, the empirical analysis undertaken later in the book explicitly accounts for its fiscal effects. Napoleon III, who was elected president of the Second Republic in 1848, staged a successful coup in 1851 and established an authoritarian regime (called the Second Empire) that lasted nearly 20 years.[13] The emperor was captured during the Franco-Prussian War (1870–1), and the provisional government of the Third Republic was quickly formed. This regime was consolidated in the aftermath of the conflict, which France lost, and endured for 70 years until the German invasion of 1940. Since the Third Republic best satisfied the triple criteria of parliamentary regularity, stability, and scholarly consensus described earlier, the coding methodology dated the emergence of limited government in France to 1870.

---

[11] Neal (2010, pp. 289, 299) also argues that parliamentary fiscal control had to persist long enough to create legitimacy.

[12] This account is based on Jackson (1974, pp. 143–4, 150–1) and Price (1993, pp. 157–65, 177–9, 188–91).

[13] The First Republic endured from 1792 to 1804, and the First Empire from 1804 to 1815.

Table 3.1 displays the dates of limited government for Group 1 and Group 2 countries. As described in the preceding section, parliamentary reforms typically occurred decades after fiscal centralization. Modern Belgium was established as a constitutional monarchy after declaring independence from the Netherlands in 1830. In Prussia, King Frederick William IV granted a liberal constitution after the political revolutions of 1848. Tilly (1966, 1967) argues that there were binding fiscal constraints from that year onward, although the government operated without legislative approval of its military budgets during the 1860s. Chapter 5 examines the Prussian case in detail. In Italy, the constitution first endorsed by King Charles Albert of Piedmont during the political revolutions of 1848 was extended to the entire kingdom in 1861. In Austria, the Compromise of 1867, which established Austria and Hungary as distinct political entities, marked the start of the constitutional era. Spain fought several civil wars over the 1800s. After decades of failed attempts, a stable parliamentary regime was established in 1876.[14]

By contrast, limited government and fiscal centralization took place within a decade of each other in Sweden and Portugal. Although Sweden enacted a constitution in 1809, the executive retained absolute veto authority, and parliament met only once every five years. The parliamentary reform of 1866, which replaced the traditional Diet of Estates with a modern bicameral legislature, established limited government in Sweden. This institutional change occurred five years after fiscal centralization in 1861. Like Spain, Portugal fought a series of civil wars over the nineteenth century. A stable constitutional regime was established in 1851, eight years before fiscal centralization in 1859.[15]

Finally, there are two cases in which limited government was implemented well in advance of fiscal centralization. In Denmark, King Frederick VII renounced his absolutist powers and established a two-chamber parliament after the political revolutions of 1848. Fiscal centralization did not take place in Denmark until 1903.[16] Although

---

[14] For Belgium, see Cook (2002, pp. 49–50). For Prussia, see Tilly (1966, 1967), Ziblatt (2006, pp. 113–16), and Spoerer (2010, p. 107). For Italy, see Federico (2010, pp. 186–93, 199–203). For Austria, see Pammer (2010, pp. 132–3). For Spain, see Tortella (2000, pp. 27–32) and Comín (2010, pp. 214–15).

[15] For Sweden, see Magnusson (2000, pp. 67–70), Nordstrom (2002, pp. 66–7), and Schön (2010, pp. 176–7). For Portugal, see Cardoso and Lains (2010b, pp. 261–4).

[16] However, the constitutional revision of 1866 restricted the suffrage in ways that favored the conservative and the wealthy. Hans Christian Johansen provided the basis for the Danish account. Also see Carstairs (1980, pp. 75–8). In light of that work, the coding for Denmark was updated from Dincecco (2009a).

TABLE 3.1. *Dates of Limited Government in Europe*

	Year	Event
Group 1		
Netherlands	1572	Establishment of Dutch Republic (1572–1795)
	1848	Implementation of new constitution
England	1688	Establishment of constitutional monarchy
Prussia	1848	Establishment of constitutional monarchy
Austria	1867	Establishment of constitutional monarchy
France	1870	Establishment of stable constitutional regime
Spain	1876	Establishment of stable constitutional monarchy
Group 2		
Belgium	1831	Established as constitutional monarchy
Denmark	1848	Establishment of constitutional monarchy
Portugal	1851	Establishment of stable constitutional monarchy
Italy	1861	Established as constitutional monarchy
Sweden	1866	Introduction of bicameral legislature

Note: Group 1 includes core powers and has long data series over diverse political regimes. Group 2 includes peripheral powers and has shorter data series. The second column displays the year that limited government as defined in the text was established. The final column offers brief explanations for these dates, which the text elaborates upon.
Source: See text.

the Dutch Republic (1572–1795) was not limited in the sense of a parliament that monitored executive spending, Tilly (1990), De Long and Shleifer (1993), Acemoglu et al. (2005), and Stasavage (2005) code it as constitutional. Recall from Chapter 2, however, that the Republic was fiscally fragmented at the national level. Chapters 4 and 5 examine the Dutch case in detail.

Representative government is a key feature of today's wealthy countries. Although the link between parliaments and prosperity may seem obvious in hindsight, the establishment of constitutional regimes took a very long time. To understand how rich states restricted executive power, we must turn to history. This chapter has examined limited government, the second fundamental political transformation that European states underwent. The evidence indicates that the establishment of spending constraints on rulers by national parliaments was the result of a deep process of institutional change and did not typically occur until the nineteenth century. After this point, most states were fiscally centralized and politically limited. The remainder of the book tests the effects of political transformations on public finances.

4

Political Regimes and Credit Risk

Fiscal fragmentation and absolutism characterized the Old Regime. Fundamental political transformations resolved weak- and strong-state fiscal problems: European states gained tax force through fiscal centralization, and restricted executive power through limited government. The final result was institutional balance. By the eve of World War I in 1913, states could gather large tax revenues, and rulers faced parliamentary spending constraints. This claim guides the rest of the inquiry, which the book now pursues through a rigorous examination of the new database, using a combination of descriptive, case-study, and statistical methods.

The empirical investigation of the effects of political transformations on public finances starts with sovereign credit. The ability of governments to tap the resources of society to fund expenditures through borrowing is important in its own right. Furthermore, like an electrocardiogram, which documents the activity of the human heart, we may think of free-market long-term rates of interest on government bonds as vital signs of the fiscal health of nations.[1] When these rates are charted as time series, the impacts of political reforms, wars, revolutions, defaults, and other events are evident. This chapter first characterizes the theoretical links between political change and credit risk. It then describes the yield data and examines the times series for select Group 1 countries. In turn, we gain a basic understanding of the fiscal effects of political transformations.

[1] See Homer and Sylla (2005, p. 3).

4.1. Regimes and Risk: Theory

By establishing parliament's power of the purse, limited government reduced the likelihood of poor spending decisions by executives. Rather than using funds for foreign military adventures or other ill-advised items, states should have devoted greater amounts to fiscally prudent policies like debt service. Limited government should have thus improved sovereign credit risk relative to absolutist regimes. Chapter 5 considers two explicit mechanisms through which credit reductions may have occurred.

The relationship between fiscal centralization and sovereign credit risk is more ambiguous than that of limited government. By resolving the problem of local tax free-riding, centralization enabled states to gather larger revenues. It should have thus been easier for responsible governments to follow sound fiscal policies, decreasing credit risk. However, there was always the chance that rulers would waste the new funds on reckless wars or the monarchy itself. The consolidation of fiscal powers may have thus exacerbated problems of executive control. If so, then credit risk should have risen after fiscal centralization.

Table 4.1 summarizes the sovereign credit risk characteristics of the four possible political regimes: fragmented and absolutist, centralized and absolutist, fragmented and limited, and centralized and limited. Credit risk under centralized and limited regimes should have been lower than that under fragmented and absolutist ones. By eliminating local tax free-riding, fiscal centralization implied an increase in public funds. Similarly, limited government placed spending constraints on executives, suggesting an improvement in fiscal prudence. The combination of greater revenues and parliamentary control should have improved credit risk.

By this logic, sovereign credit risk should have decreased under fragmented and limited regimes relative to fragmented and absolutist ones. Theory cannot predict whether there was an improvement in credit risk under centralized and absolutist versus fragmented and absolutist regimes, since fiscal centralization generated new funds that executives could have used to repay debts responsibly or spent recklessly. We may definitively say, however, that credit risk under centralized and limited regimes should have been the lowest of all, since both weak- and strong-state fiscal problems had been resolved.

A final point: although the theoretical predictions are in ceteris paribus terms, factors beyond political regimes also influenced sovereign credit

TABLE 4.1. *Sovereign Credit Risk Characteristics of Political Regimes*

Fragmented and absolutist	High due to free-riding and lack of credible commitment
Centralized and absolutist	Fall due to resolution of free-riding, but rise due to executive consolidation of fiscal powers
Fragmented and limited	Fall due to credible commitment, but still-free riding
Centralized and limited	Low due to resolution of free-riding and credible commitment

risk. The regression analysis in Chapter 7 explicitly controls for the yield effects of a wide variety of political and economic variables, including large debt burdens.

4.2. The Data

The analysis uses a new database for free-market yields on long-term government bonds from 1750 to 1913. Unlike nominal yields, which simply report the government's stated rate of interest, market-determined yields provide direct measures of investor perceptions of sovereign credit risk. Appendix A.1 displays the time series data.

These data are from a variety of primary and secondary sources. Appendix A.2 describes the data sources and construction methods. One key source was the Global Financial Database (GFD), which offered high-frequency (i.e., weekly or monthly) data. Comparison of the GFD time series with data, typically low frequency (i.e., yearly), from Homer and Sylla (2005) indicate that these series were generally similar.

Since bond prices often exhibited high volatility, the use of annual data (one observation per year) increased the likelihood of misrepresenting yield trends. To mitigate this possibility, yearly averages of weekly or monthly data were calculated. Appendix A.2 documents the details.

Homer and Sylla (2005, pp. 1–13) discuss the limitations of the historical yield data. Demand for sovereign bonds was not integrated or elastic, and governments faced different domestic and foreign opportunities to market their debts. Bonds for Group 1 countries were typically traded on home exchanges, while those for Group 2 countries were traded in London. Before the nineteenth century, moreover, most governments did not offer a public asset comparable to the British consol, which was perpetual, widely used, easily negotiated, and relatively risk free, but issued a multitude of debt instruments, each subject to different terms and conditions. In these cases, the sovereign bond that best captured long-term yield levels was chosen. Appendix A.2 provides the details.

Table 4.2 displays the descriptive statistics for the panel of government bond yields. There are 1,027 observations: 108 for fragmented and absolutist regimes, 186 for centralized and absolutist ones, 74 for fragmented and limited ones, and 659 for centralized and limited ones. Average yields for centralized and absolutist (5.77 percent), fragmented and limited (4.26 percent), and centralized and limited (4.24 percent) regimes were low relative to those for fragmented and absolutist ones (6.59 percent).[2] These trends also hold within Groups 1 and 2, and within individual countries. In France, for instance, average yields fell from 6.11 percent under the fragmented and absolutist regime to 5.30 percent under the centralized and absolutist one and to 3.57 under the centralized and limited one.

4.3. Regimes and Risk: Case-Study Evidence

To see how sovereign credit risk evolved with political regimes, this section examines the time series for three Group 1 countries: France, the Netherlands, and Spain. Austria is omitted from the analysis, because the available yield data do not start until 1874, seven years after the establishment of a centralized and limited regime.[3] Due to the unusual fiscal patterns that it displays, the investigation of credit risk in Prussia is postponed until the next chapter, when Prussian revenues and deficits are also examined.

---

[2] Following Ferguson and Schularick (2006), 16 observations with yields of 20% or more were excluded. These were the Netherlands, 1811 and 1813, and Spain, 1824–33 and 1876–9. However, the inclusion of such observations only strengthened the regression results described in Chapter 7.

[3] Homer and Sylla (2005, p. 529) note that the history of Austrian interest rates over the nineteenth and early twentieth centuries resembled that of Germany but was comparatively brief. Ferguson (2006, fig. 1) collected yield data for Austria from 1843 onward. Those data, which are discontinuous, reveal that yield spreads were around 100 basis points at the start of the 1840s but rose to 200 to 400 points during the late 1840s, when Austria fought the First Italian War of Independence (1848–9). Spreads rose even further with the Franco-Austrian War (1859), the Second Italian War of Independence (1859–61), the Second Schleswig-Holstein War (1864), and the Austro-Prussian War (1866). The GFD series that begins in 1874 indicates that spreads also spiked with the Austrian conquest of Bosnia in 1878. Thereafter, spreads fell to around 100 basis points through 1913. Pammer (2010, p. 152) notes that the major increase in public debt in Austria took place during the 1850s, just after fiscal centralization in 1848. In response to the new loan (called the National Loan), the long-term public debt grew by half of its previous value.

TABLE 4.2. *Descriptive Statistics for Sovereign Bond Yields*

		All Regimes	Fragmented and Absolutist	Centralized and Absolutist	Fragmented and Limited	Centralized and Limited
Totals	Obs	1,027	108	186	74	659
	Mean	4.76	6.59	5.77	4.26	4.24
	St dev	1.95	2.92	2.16	1.25	1.39
	Min	2.41	3.27	3.45	2.41	2.45
	Max	16.19	15.65	16.19	8.93	16.15
Group 1						
Totals	Obs	670	54	186	16	414
	Mean	4.74	7.65	5.77	3.09	3.95
England	Obs	164				164
	Mean	3.58				3.58
France	Obs	157	40	73		44
	Mean	5.02	6.11	5.30		3.57
Netherlands	Obs	131		49	16	66
	Mean	4.36		5.60	3.09	3.74
Spain	Obs	79	14	31		34
	Mean	7.98	12.06	8.52		5.80
Austria	Obs	40				40
	Mean	4.67				4.67
Prussia	Obs	99		33		66
	Mean	4.14		4.50		3.96
Group 2						
Totals	Obs	357	54		58	245
	Mean	4.82	5.53		4.58	4.72
Belgium	Obs	82				82
	Mean	3.96				3.96
Denmark	Obs	88	27		50	11
	Mean	4.16	4.34		4.16	3.71
Italy	Obs	52				52
	Mean	5.32				5.32
Portugal	Obs	89	27		8	54
	Mean	6.44	6.71		7.20	6.19
Sweden	Obs	46				46
	Mean	3.91				3.91

Note: Sovereign bond yields are expressed as percentages per year.
Source: See Appendix A.2.

Recall from Chapters 2 and 3 that England had a centralized and limited regime from 1688 onward. British consols thus function as the benchmark bond.[4] For each case, yield spreads over consols, the difference between the yield on a country's bonds and that of consols, were computed. This method is standard for historical financial market investigations.

The case studies of France, the Netherlands, and Spain provide a first test of the theoretical predictions that relate political transformations to improvements in sovereign credit risk. The findings suggest that fiscal centralization and limited government alike typically led to notable reductions in yield spreads. They also highlight the impacts of external and internal conflicts and other factors on credit risk.

4.3.1. *France*

Figure 4.1, which plots French yield spreads from 1750 to 1913, indicates that spreads averaged more than 150 basis points under the fragmented and absolutist regime that lasted through 1789. The two peaks, occurring around 1760 and 1770, represent default episodes.[5] The French Revolution led to the establishment of a national tax system with uniform rates. In the short run, domestic upheaval reduced the tax base, and the government turned to confiscation, capital levies, and an inflation tax to fund expenditures, including the War of the First Coalition (1792–7). At war's end, the government reduced the value of interest payments on the public debt by two-thirds, ruining France's reputation as a borrower. Though Napoleon lacked access to credit, Bordo and White (1991) argue that major tax reforms like fiscal centralization enabled him to gather enough in revenues to fund war efforts. Indeed, France never again defaulted on its public debt.[6]

French yield spreads remained high through the end of the Napoleonic Wars in 1815, but fell in the aftermath. Though the Bourbon monarchy was restored, the next decades saw intense fights between liberal and royal forces (see Chapter 3). The July Revolution of 1830 established a short-lived constitutional regime. After an initial spike, spreads stayed around 60 basis points or fewer. Spreads peaked once more during the Year of Revolutions in 1848 and the start of the First Italian War of

---

[4] The British consol was created in 1751 (Ferguson, 2006, p. 76).
[5] See Sargent and Velde (1995). According to Reinhart et al. (2003, table 2), France defaulted eight times on its external debt from 1500 to 1789: in 1558, 1624, 1648, 1661, 1701, 1715, 1770, and 1788.
[6] See Bonney (2010a, pp. 88–9, 98–9).

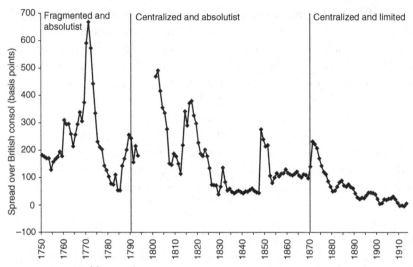

FIGURE 4.1. Yield spreads, France, 1750–1913.
Source: See Appendix A.2.

Independence (1848–9). Under Napoleon III, who established an author-itarian regime in 1851, spreads doubled from July regime levels to more than 100 basis points.

Yield spreads spiked again during the Franco-Prussian War (1870–1), which France lost. In the aftermath, Napoleon III was deposed, and the Third Republic, a stable centralized and limited regime, was established. Spreads fell steadily over the 1870s and 1880s. By the start of the 1890s, French yields had reached near parity with those of the British consol, where they stayed through 1913.

The evolution of sovereign credit risk over French political regimes fits with the theoretical predictions. The evidence suggests that both fiscal centralization and limited government led to fiscal improvements. Wars and political turmoil also affected French credit risk.

4.3.2. *The Netherlands*
The Dutch Republic (1572–1795) is typically classified as a constitutional regime, although it was not limited in the nineteenth-century sense of a parliament that regularly monitored executive spending.[7] By investing heavily in government bonds, ruling elites aligned lender and borrower

---

[7] For instance, the coding schemes of Tilly (1990), De Long and Shleifer (1993), Acemoglu et al. (2005), and Stasavage (2005) characterize the Dutch Republic as constitutional.

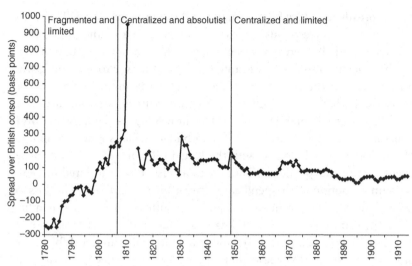

FIGURE 4.2. Yield spreads, Netherlands, 1780–1913.
Source: See Appendix A.2.

incentives and provided a credible commitment to repay debts.[8] Figure 4.2, which plots Dutch yield spreads from 1780 to 1913, highlights the success of this mechanism. Since the Republic received loans at lower rates of interest than England, spreads were negative through the 1790s.

Fiscal institutions in the Dutch Republic were fragmented, however, because each of the seven provinces had separate tax systems. As described in Chapter 2, van Zanden and van Riel (2004, chs. 1–2) argue that fiscal fragmentation weakened the Republic's ability to raise funds and service debts over the long term. Although each province was required to pay a fixed amount toward collective military and administrative expenditures, other provinces typically shirked their obligations and free-rode on Holland, the most populated and wealthiest province, whose quota was almost 60 percent of the total burden. This institutional deficiency not only created an unsustainable financial situation, but weakened the Dutch military. Indeed, spreads rose rapidly in the years before French conquest in 1795.

Dutch yield spreads rose once more with the start of the War of the Second Coalition (1798–1801). Though fiscal centralization occurred in

[8] See Tracy (1986), t'Hart (1997), van Zanden and van Riel (2004, chs. 1, 2), and Fritschy (2007). Gelderblom and Jonker (2011) highlight the role of private savings as a necessary complement to credible fiscal institutions in the Republic.

1806, spreads remained high throughout the Napoleonic Wars. The major spike in 1810 corresponds to Napoleon's tiërcering of the public debt, which reduced all interest payments to one-third of previous amounts.

The Constitution of 1815 granted absolutist power to William I, who became king at the end of the Napoleonic era. Promulgated at 10-year intervals, parliamentary authority over government expenditures was ineffective (see Chapter 3). William I spent heavily on the military, infrastructure, and the monarchy itself, and budget deficits rose through the 1820s. Yield spreads spiked with the Belgian Revolt of 1830 and subsequent War of Independence. Though an armistice was declared in 1833, William I continued to spend large sums on the military. The loss of tax revenues from the now-independent southern provinces, including Belgium, also aggravated Dutch finances.[9] During the late 1830s, spreads were nearly three times those of the constitutionally limited July regime in France. This result suggests that, in the absence of effective parliamentary constraints, fiscal consolidation may have exacerbated problems of executive control.

Throughout his reign, William I used a variety of semi-legal tactics to hide the true state of public finances. When fiscal troubles finally became public in 1839, the parliament vetoed the upcoming 10-year budget, and William I was forced to abdicate. The constitutional reform of 1840 granted parliament the right to monitor the budget every two years. Dutch yield spreads fell by the mid-1840s. The Year of Revolutions in 1848 led to the establishment of a stable centralized and limited regime, with parliamentary budget authority coming at annual intervals. After an initial spike, spreads averaged fewer than 70 basis points through 1913.

The ways in which sovereign credit risk evolved with political transformations in the Netherlands are also consistent with the theoretical predictions, though with a twist. As for France, the evidence suggests that limited government reduced Dutch yield spreads. This finding bolsters the case that parliamentary reforms had positive effects on credit risk.

Recall from Section 4.1 that theory could not predict with certainty how fiscal centralization would affect yield spreads. If the ruler spent the new revenues generated by centralization on responsible debt service, then sovereign credit risk should have fallen. The evidence described in the preceding section suggests that the establishment of a national tax system in France had a positive fiscal effect by curtailing the likelihood of default. If the ruler impulsively spent the new funds, however, then centralization

---

[9] See Fritschy et al. (2001, pp. 20–2).

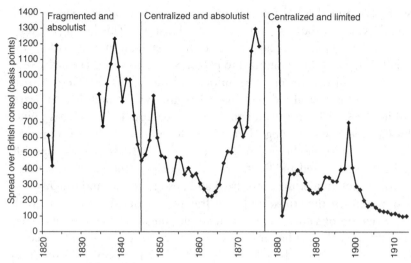

FIGURE 4.3. Yield spreads, Spain, 1821–1913.
Source: See Appendix A.2.

should have increased credit risk. The evidence for the Netherlands suggests that this outcome occurred during the reign of William I, when yield spreads rose dramatically as a result of reckless fiscal policies. The Dutch case thus illustrates a diverse theoretical implication of fiscal centralization.

4.3.3. Spain

In contrast to France or the Netherlands, Spain saw three major civil conflicts over the nineteenth century: the First (1833–9), Second (1847–9), and Third (1872–6) Carlist Wars. Figure 4.3, which plots Spanish yield spreads from 1821 to 1913, indicates that each of these conflicts led to large spikes in yield spreads of 1,000 basis points or more.

Nonetheless, we may still characterize the impact of political transformations on Spanish sovereign credit risk. Unlike France or the Netherlands, fiscal centralization did not take place in Spain until the mid-1840s (see Chapter 2). Although Spanish absolutists had often previously neglected responsible debt payments, Comín (2010, pp. 236–7) shows that debt service soon became a key spending item. Debt payments rose from less than 10 percent of total state expenditures during the first half of the 1800s to more than 50 percent from the end of the 1840s to 1870. After peaking with the Second Carlist War, yield spreads fell steadily to a little more than 200 basis points by the mid-1860s. Overall, average spreads under the centralized and absolutist regime were more than 300 basis points fewer than those under the fragmented and absolutist one. This finding suggests that fiscal centralization had a positive effect on Spanish credit risk.

Political instability continued to plague Spain, however. The late 1860s saw the Spanish Glorious Revolution, and the 1870s the Third Carlist War. A stable centralized and limited regime was established at war's end in 1876. Yield spreads fluctuated between 200 and 400 basis points through the 1890s. Though large, these levels represented an improvement in Spanish credit risk relative to earlier periods: average spreads under the centralized and limited regime were more than 200 basis points less than those under the centralized and absolutist one, and roughly 600 basis points less than those under the fragmented and absolutist one. With the exception of 1882, moreover, Spain no longer defaulted on its external debt, something it had done six times since the end of the Napoleonic Wars in 1815.[10] Spreads spiked once more during the Spanish-American War (1898), which Spain lost. Thereafter, they fell to around 100 basis points through 1913.

As for the French and Dutch cases, the evolution of sovereign credit risk over Spanish political regimes corresponds to the theoretical predictions. The evidence suggests that limited government led to an improvement in Spanish yield spreads. This result reinforces the argument that constitutional change had positive fiscal impacts. As with France (but not the Netherlands), the evidence suggests that fiscal centralization in Spain also generated a reduction in yield spreads. Taken in combination, these findings suggest that the establishment of national tax systems with uniform rates had positive net effects on credit risk. Finally, the Spanish case highlights the negative impact of prolonged domestic turmoil on yield spreads.

Sovereign credit is a vital sign of the fiscal health of nations. This chapter has examined the effects of political transformations on yield spreads of long-term government bonds. Both the descriptive and case-study evidence indicates that fiscal centralization and limited government typically led to notable improvements in yield spreads. The next chapter takes the empirical investigation further by examining two specific channels through which political reforms actually reduced credit risk.

---

[10] See Reinhart et al. (2003, table 2). Also see Chapter 5.

5

Two Mechanisms

Political transformations had important effects on sovereign credit risk. Both fiscal centralization and limited government typically led to notable improvements in yield spreads. But by what means? So far, the analysis does not identify the precise mechanisms by which institutional changes led to credit gains. This chapter analyzes two channels through which risk reductions occurred: increases in government revenues per head and improvements in fiscal prudence.

Ferguson (2006) argues that there is a dearth of information about European macroeconomic conditions before the 1870s. Budgetary figures are one unique source of data that are readily available across countries. The first mechanism concerns the amount of tax revenues that national governments collected on a per capita basis. The key conceptual reason to scale by population rather than by some measure of national production is to capture the state's ability to extract tax revenues per head, and not government size relative to that of the economy. There is, moreover, an issue of feasibility. As Ferguson (2006) notes, nineteenth-century GDP measures were still in their infancy, and modern reconstructions of pre-1815 GDP levels tend toward educated guesses at best (see Acemoglu et al., 2005).

Data limitations also preclude scaling by wages or export earnings. Furthermore, Rosenthal (2010, pp. 243–4) raises important conceptual issues regarding the use of wage data as proxies for past development levels. It is not obvious, for instance, that high wages in London in 1750 were truly representative of the whole of England or (the even larger) United Kingdom. Similar difficulties arise if wages in Paris are used to stand for the whole of France or those in Madrid to stand for the whole of Spain. Mokyr (2010, p. 513, n. 5) also warns that data on real wages for select workers are dubious proxies for income growth.

The econometric framework in Chapter 7 accounts for income effects in two ways. Since there was a close relationship between city growth and economic performance in European history, urbanization rates are included as a control variable. To mitigate the impact of the Second Industrial Revolution, which took place in continental Europe and North America at the end of the nineteenth century (see Mokyr, 1998), regressions were also performed for the period before 1870.

The second mechanism concerns the state's ability to pursue responsible fiscal policies and incorporates government expenditures to compute budget deficits. The question of scaling also arises in this context. Given the lack of macroeconomic information before the 1870s, Ferguson and Schularick (2006) argue that the main problem of early investors was how to make accurate assessments of fundamental resources within countries. To deflate budget estimates over time, sophisticated analyses of government finances employed public revenues. Indeed, Cain and Hopkins (1994, chs. 4–7) claim that calculating budget deficit-to-revenue ratios was the method most preferred by investors to evaluate macroeconomic policies.[1] Following the "gentlemanly capitalists" of London, this analysis also uses deficit ratios as an effective summary statistic of fiscal prudence.

This chapter first characterizes the theoretical relationships between political regimes and government revenues and fiscal prudence. It then describes the data and investigates the time series for Group 1 countries. In turn, we gain a better understanding of the mechanisms by which political transformations led to improvements in sovereign credit risk.

5.1. Regimes, Revenues, and Prudence: Theory

Since executives could make credible commitments to spend new funds on public services rather than on ill-advised wars or the monarchy itself, limited government made parliaments more willing to submit to greater tax burdens. Hence, it should have increased revenues per capita relative to absolutist regimes. By reducing the likelihood of bad spending choices by executives, parliamentary power of the purse should have also improved fiscal prudence, as measured by a decrease in deficit ratios. It is important to note that, although the theoretical predictions are in ceteris paribus terms, the regression analysis in Chapter 7 explicitly accounts

---

[1] Also see Flandreau and Zumer (2004).

for the effects of warfare and other political and economic variables on government revenues and fiscal prudence.

Fiscal centralization should have increased the amount of revenues that governments collected per head by eliminating local tax free-riding. As for sovereign credit risk, however, the relationship between fiscal centralization and fiscal prudence is more ambiguous than that for limited government. Although larger revenues should have made it easier for executives to pursue responsible fiscal policies, the consolidation of fiscal powers may have had an adverse impact on public finances through wasted spending. Whether deficit ratios ultimately fell or rose under centralized versus fragmented regimes depends on which effect won out.

Table 5.1 summarizes the revenue and deficit ratio characteristics of the four possible types of political regime and (building on Table 4.1) relates the two mechanisms to sovereign credit risk. Revenues should have been higher, and deficit ratios lower, under fragmented and limited regimes in comparison with fragmented and absolutist ones. Sovereign credit risk should have improved as a result. Revenues should have also been greater under centralized and absolutist regimes than under fragmented and absolutist ones. The effect on fiscal prudence, however, was contingent upon the ways in which executives spent new funds (i.e., to balance budgets or recklessly). Credit risk may have thus increased or decreased depending on the relative magnitudes of the impacts of these competing elements. Revenues should have been the largest, and fiscal prudence the best, under centralized and limited regimes, due to the resolution of local tax free-riding and a credible commitment to prudent fiscal policies. Credit risk under this regime type should have therefore been the lowest of all. As already noted, the regression analysis in Chapter 7 explicitly controls for the fiscal impacts of historical factors beyond political regimes.

England, which had a centralized and limited regime from 1688 onward, illustrates these arguments. The next section describes the English data. Figure 5.1, which plots English revenues from 1650 to the end of the Old Regime in 1788, indicates that average revenues more than doubled to nearly six gold grams per head in the years after the establishment of limited government but before the onset of the British Industrial Revolution in 1750 (see Mokyr, 1999).

Figure 5.2, which plots English deficit ratios from 1692 to 1913, resembles a tax-smoothing simulation.[2] Barro (1979, 1987, 1989) argues that, to

---

[2] As first noted by Sargent and Velde (1995).

TABLE 5.1. *Revenue and Deficit Ratio Characteristics of Political Regimes*

Fragmented and absolutist	Low revenues, prudence	High credit risk
Centralized and absolutist	Revenues rise, prudence rises or falls	Credit risk falls or rises
Fragmented and limited	Both revenues, prudence rise	Credit risk falls
Centralized and limited	High revenues, prudence	Low credit risk

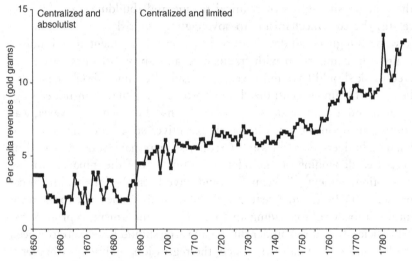

FIGURE 5.1. Per capita revenues, England, 1650–1788.
Source: See Appendix A.2.

minimize supply-side disincentives caused by sudden changes in taxation, governments should finance large temporary increases in spending, such as those for wars, with loans funded by peacetime surpluses. The effect of external conflicts on English public finances is clear. Deficit ratios increased with the War of the Grand Alliance (1688–97), the War of the Spanish Succession (1701–14), the War of the Austrian Succession (1740–8), the Seven Years' War (1756–63), the War of American Independence (1775–83), the Wars of the First and Second Coalitions (1792–1801), and the Napoleonic Wars (1803–15), but they always fell at war's end. In peacetime, the government generated small but effective surpluses. There

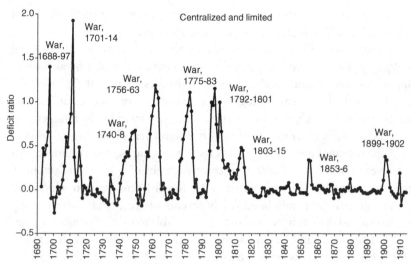

FIGURE 5.2. Deficit ratios, England, 1692–1913.
Sources: See Appendix A.2 for deficit ratios and Clodfelter (2002) for wars.

were no defaults.[3] Although the number of external conflicts fell during the post-Napoleonic period, deficit ratios increased once more with the Crimean War (1853–6) and the South African War (1899–1902).

The sound nature of English public finances was reflected in low sovereign credit risk. Recall from Chapter 4 that the British consol was the standard against which the performance of other European government bonds was measured over the eighteenth and nineteenth centuries. More generally, England played the leading role in the development of modern financial markets.[4]

5.2. The Data

The database on government revenues and expenditures from 1650 to 1913 is from a variety of secondary sources. Appendix A.1 displays the time series data, and Appendix A.2 describes the data sources and construction methods. Two key sources were the European State Finance Database (ESFDB), created by Bonney and administered by Coffman and

---

[3] The last default took place in 1672, sixteen years before the establishment of limited government. See Jones (1994, p. 94) and Reinhart et al. (2003, table 2).

[4] See Homer and Sylla (2005, chs. 11, 13). In their words (p. 178–9): "British supremacy was generally acknowledged.... Many countries imitated British monetary and financial techniques and British interest rate policies.... The rules of the game were set in London."

Murray (2010), for the pre-1800 period, and International Historical Statistics of Mitchell (2003) for the post-1800 period.

Bonney (1995, pp. 423–506) discusses the limitations of the historical budgetary data. European states did not maintain detailed fiscal records during the seventeenth and eighteenth centuries. National governments may have calculated yearly budgets in a variety of ways. For instance, some states computed budgets with revenues that they intended to raise, even if the funds did not enter government coffers until years later. Insofar as possible, the revenues used here were tax receipts for national governments in a given year. Ordinary and extraordinary (when given) figures were summed, and loan incomes were subtracted. Since the different ways in which Old Regime governments tabulated yearly revenues suggest that they typically overestimated the amounts of resources available to them, average revenues under fragmented and absolutist regimes should have been larger (at least on paper) than otherwise. Furthermore, government accounting practices have typically improved over time, reducing the number and magnitude of misestimates. These features thus bias the data against the hypothesis that political transformations led to greater tax incomes.

The expenditures used here were total spending by national governments, including debt service, and incorporated loan amounts when given. By virtue of reducing (at least on paper) budget deficits under fragmented and absolutist regimes, the overestimation of revenues by Old Regime governments also biases the data against the hypothesis that political transformations had positive impacts on fiscal prudence. The fact that early data were more likely to be missing during periods of political instability, when deficits were presumably high, works in the same direction.

To make revenue and expenditure calculations comparable across countries, all currency units were transformed into gold grams. This conversion reduced inflation effects. The cumulative world gold stock was relatively stable through the 1840s, when there were large discoveries of gold in California (1848) and Australia (1851). The regression analysis in Chapter 7 explicitly controls for the fiscal impacts of gold stock changes.

The years between missing revenue observations were interpolated. Population figures were also interpolated between census years. Since there were few major one-off fiscal changes (or population shocks such as plague) from 1650 to 1913 besides the two political transformations, the interpolated data should provide reasonable estimates. The linkages between tax bases and government spending were weaker than those for revenues, particularly during wars. Hence, the years between missing expenditure observations were not interpolated.

Tables 5.2 and 5.3 display the descriptive statistics for the revenue and deficit panels, respectively. For revenues, there are 1,739 observations, 624 for fragmented and absolutist regimes, 260 for centralized and absolutist ones, 123 for fragmented and limited ones, and 732 for centralized and limited ones. Average per capita revenues for centralized and absolutist (7.05 gold grams), fragmented and limited (10.66 gold grams), and centralized and limited (13.33 gold grams) regimes were high relative to those for fragmented and absolutist ones (2.43 gold grams). These trends also hold within Groups 1 and 2, and within individual countries. In France, for instance, average revenues rose from 3.32 gold grams per head under the fragmented and absolutist regime to 11.11 under the centralized and absolutist one, and to 30.19 under the centralized and limited one.

For deficit ratios, there are 1,470 observations, 468 for fragmented and absolutist regimes, 201 for centralized and absolutist ones, 121 for fragmented and limited ones, and 680 for centralized and limited ones. The data, which show that average deficit ratios for centralized and absolutist regimes (0.29) were greater than those for fragmented and absolutist regime ones (0.15), suggest that fiscal centralization exacerbated deficits. Although the difference between average deficit ratios under fragmented and absolutist regimes and centralized and limited ones was negligible for Groups 1 and 2 together, average deficit ratios were smaller under the latter regime type for Group 1 countries (0.18 vs. 0.16). The key outlier was Prussia, which nearly achieved a balanced budget under the fragmented and absolutist regime (average deficit ratios were 0.01). Since it was a regular borrower, this outcome did not occur because Prussia was excluded from credit markets.[5] Section 5.4 considers the Prussian case in detail.

5.3. Regimes, Revenues, and Prudence: Case-Study Evidence

To gain a clearer picture of the ways in which government revenues and deficits changed over political regimes, this section examines the time series for Group 1 countries France, the Netherlands, Spain, Austria, and Prussia. These case studies provide a first test of the theoretical predictions that relate political transformations to improvements in the ability of governments to collect greater funds and pursue prudent fiscal

---

[5] Generally speaking, deficit ratios were not equal to zero simply because governments chose never to borrow any funds. See Homer and Sylla (2005, chs. 11–15).

TABLE 5.2. *Descriptive Statistics for Per Capita Revenues*

		All Regimes	Fragmented and Absolutist	Centralized and Absolutist	Fragmented and Limited	Centralized and Limited
Totals	Obs	1,739	624	260	123	732
	Mean	8.29	2.43	7.05	10.66	13.33
	St dev	7.35	1.54	4.80	3.04	7.78
	Min	0.28	0.28	1.10	0.89	0.99
	Max	42.04	10.07	24.38	15.29	42.04
Group 1						
Totals	Obs	1,245	430	255	76	484
	Mean	8.70	2.64	7.12	12.15	14.38
England	Obs	264		38		226
	Mean	12.18		2.61		13.79
France	Obs	264	140	80		44
	Mean	10.16	3.32	11.11		30.19
Netherlands	Obs	187		45	76	66
	Mean	12.43		10.88	12.15	13.82
Spain	Obs	211	142	31		38
	Mean	1.71	1.00	2.44		3.74
Austria	Obs	93	30	19		44
	Mean	9.07	3.16	5.50		14.64
Prussia	Obs	226	118	42		66
	Mean	6.23	3.66	3.77		12.40
Group 2						
Totals	Obs	494	194	5	47	248
	Mean	7.27	1.98	3.63	8.25	11.29
Belgium	Obs	82				82
	Mean	15.13				15.13
Denmark	Obs	50			39	11
	Mean	10.92			9.75	15.04
Italy	Obs	52				52
	Mean	14.95				14.95
Portugal	Obs	146	83		8	55
	Mean	1.46	0.73		0.94	2.60
Sweden	Obs	164	111	5		48
	Mean	4.95	2.89	3.63		9.85

Note: Per capita revenues are tax revenues collected by national governments and are expressed in gold grams.

Source: See Appendix A.2.

policies. The findings suggest that both fiscal centralization and limited government typically led to notable fiscal improvements. They therefore clarify the precise ways in which political reforms reduced sovereign credit risk.

TABLE 5.3. *Descriptive Statistics for Deficit Ratios*

		All Regimes	Fragmented and Absolutist	Centralized and Absolutist	Fragmented and Limited	Centralized and Limited
Totals	Obs	1,470	468	201	121	680
	Mean	0.17	0.15	0.29	0.16	0.16
	St dev	0.35	0.44	0.45	0.19	0.26
	Min	−0.89	−0.89	−0.41	−0.16	−0.41
	Max	2.93	2.77	2.93	0.93	1.92
Group 1						
Totals	Obs	1,017	311	196	75	435
	Mean	0.19	0.18	0.29	0.19	0.16
England	Obs	249		27		222
	Mean	0.16		0.14		0.16
France	Obs	213	98	71		44
	Mean	0.16	0.29	0.08		−0.00
Netherlands	Obs	186		45	75	66
	Mean	0.38		0.79	0.19	0.30
Spain	Obs	94	28	28		38
	Mean	0.07	0.21	0.06		−0.03
Austria	Obs	133	67	19		47
	Mean	0.34	0.31	0.53		0.31
Prussia	Obs	142	118	6		18
	Mean	0.01	0.01	0.08		−0.03
Group 2						
Totals	Obs	453	157	5	46	245
	Mean	0.13	0.09	0.33	0.10	0.16
Belgium	Obs	81				81
	Mean	0.16				0.16
Denmark	Obs	50			39	11
	Mean	0.09			0.09	0.08
Italy	Obs	50				50
	Mean	0.19				0.19
Portugal	Obs	98	36		7	55
	Mean	0.19	0.13		0.18	0.22
Sweden	Obs	174	121	5		48
	Mean	0.09	0.07	0.33		0.10

Note: Deficit ratios are ratios of budget deficits to tax revenues for national governments.
Source: See Appendix A.2.

5.3.1. *France*

Figure 5.3, which plots French revenues from 1650 to 1913, indicates that revenues were low, averaging slightly more than 3 gold grams per capita, under the fragmented and absolutist regime that lasted through 1789. Deficit ratios, which Figure 5.4 plots, were also high, averaging 0.29 (i.e., deficits were roughly three times greater than revenues). Moreover, unlike

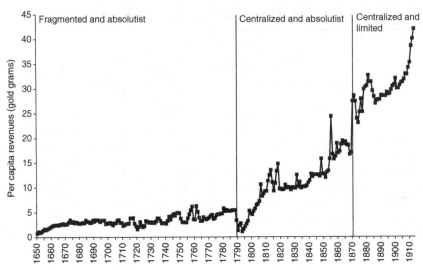

FIGURE 5.3. Per capita revenues, France, 1650–1913.
Source: See Appendix 2.

England, which pursued effective tax-smoothing policies over the 1700s (see Figure 5.2), France defaulted repeatedly (see Chapter 4). Given this combination of weak revenue collection and poor fiscal prudence, it is not surprising that sovereign credit risk was high in Old Regime France (see Figure 4.1).

There was a sharp increase in French revenues, which roughly doubled to 10 gold grams per head, in the two decades after fiscal centralization in 1790. Deficit ratios also fell, even during the Napoleonic Wars (1803–15). This result is consistent with Bordo and White's (1991) claim that tax reforms enabled Napoleon to gather enough to fund war efforts without resorting to major borrowing (see Chapter 4).

French revenues leveled out, but never fell, in the decades just after the Napoleonic era. In the 1840s, they began to increase once more, reaching more than 16 gold grams per capita by the end of the 1860s. The establishment of a stable centralized and limited regime took place in the aftermath of the Franco-Prussian War (1870–1). This set of events was associated with a sharp jump in revenues, which more than doubled to over 40 gold grams per head by 1913. A balanced budget also became the norm. In response, French sovereign credit risk levels came to resemble those of England (see Figure 4.1).

The evolution of revenues and deficit ratios over French political regimes is consistent with the theoretical predictions. The evidence

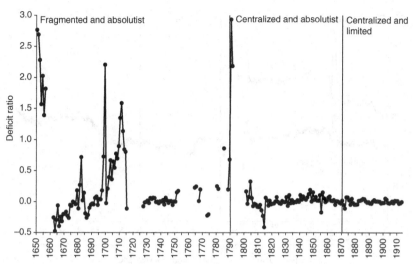

FIGURE 5.4. Deficit ratios, France, 1650–1913.
Source: See Appendix 2.

suggests that both fiscal centralization and limited government led to greater revenues and lower deficits. As a result of political transformations, French sovereign credit risk fell.

5.3.2. *The Netherlands*
Recall from Chapter 4 that the Dutch Republic (1572–1795) was classified as a fragmented and limited regime. The fragmented nature of fiscal institutions at the national level contrasted with fiscal institutions in Holland, the most populated and wealthiest province. By extending common taxes from urban to rural areas in 1574, the Hollandish provincial government established a uniform tax system that reduced local tax free-riding and significantly increased revenues.[6]

Figure 5.5 plots Dutch revenues for both the Republic as a whole and Holland itself from 1720 to 1795, and for the Netherlands from 1796 to 1913. Two points stand out. First, the Republic benefited from limited government: average Dutch revenues at the national level exceeded those of absolutist France by roughly 9 gold grams per capita over the eighteenth century. Second, Holland benefited from fiscal centralization: eighteenth-century Hollandish revenues per head were on average roughly 7 gold grams higher than for the Republic as a whole.

---

[6] See Fritschy (2003) and van Zanden and Prak (2006).

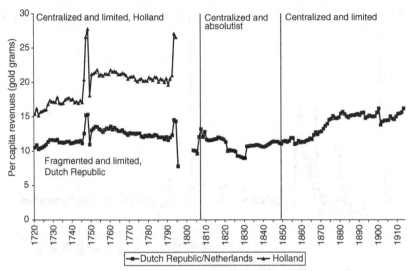

FIGURE 5.5. Per capita revenues, Netherlands, 1720–1913.
Source: See Appendix 2.

How about fiscal prudence? Figure 5.6, which plots Dutch deficit ratios from 1720 to 1913, indicates that ratios were small through the 1770s, though they increased with the War of the Austrian Succession (1740–8).[7] Taken together, large revenues and fiscal prudence help explain why Dutch sovereign credit risk was so low through much of the eighteenth century (see Figure 4.2).

Deficit ratios began to rise from the 1780s onward, however. This finding is consistent with van Zanden and van Riel's (2004) claim that fiscal fragmentation hindered the Republic's long-term ability to raise funds and service debts (see Chapter 4). Although each province was required to pay a fixed amount toward collective military expenditures, most shirked their obligations and free-rode on Holland, which had to cover shortfalls. This institutional deficiency not only created an untenable fiscal situation, but undermined the strength of the Dutch military. Indeed, the rapid increase in Dutch yields in the years before French conquest in 1795 reflected mounting fiscal woes (see Figure 4.2).

Fiscal centralization took place at the national level in 1806, and an absolutist regime led by William I was established at the end of the

---

[7] Since deficit ratios for Holland were similar to those of the Republic, the Hollandish figures are not reported in Figure 5.6.

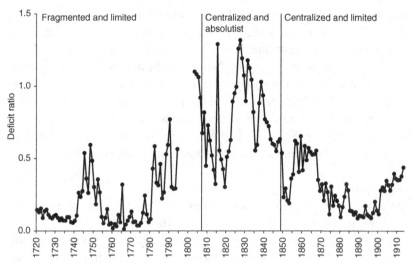

FIGURE 5.6. Deficit ratios, Netherlands, 1720–1913.
Source: See Appendix 2.

Napoleonic Wars in 1815 (see Chapter 4). The shift to absolutism appears to have offset any gains from centralization. Average revenues, at nearly 11 gold grams per head, were about 1 gold gram less than during the eighteenth century. Deficit ratios, moreover, were high throughout William I's tenure, averaging 0.79 (i.e., deficits were roughly eight times greater than revenues). Thus, in contrast to France, the Dutch case suggests that centralization in the absence of parliamentary budget authority had a negative effect on fiscal prudence. The notable increase in Dutch sovereign credit risk during this period likely reflected this concern (see Figure 4.2).

A stable centralized and limited regime was established in 1848. After a lag, Dutch revenues began to grow in the 1860s, reaching roughly 15 gold grams per capita by the following decade. Deficit ratios, which first fell with the abdication of William I and related constitutional reform of 1840, steadily decreased to near zero. Dutch sovereign credit risk levels came to resemble those of England (see Figure 4.2).

As for France, the ways in which revenues and deficit ratios evolved with political transformations in the Netherlands correspond to the theoretical predictions. The evidence suggests that limited government led to greater revenues and lower deficits. This result bolsters the case that constitutional changes had positive fiscal effects.

While fiscal centralization also generated higher revenues in the Netherlands, it increased deficit ratios. Recall from Section 5.1 that the theoretical relationship between fiscal centralization and fiscal prudence depended on two effects. In the French case, the positive impact of the new revenues from fiscal centralization outweighed the negative effect of the consolidation of fiscal powers by Napoleon. In the Dutch case, by contrast, the opposite outcome occurred: the negative impact of fiscal consolidation by William I was greater than the positive effect of the new funds. Thus, the Dutch case again illustrates a diverse theoretical implication of fiscal centralization (also see Chapter 4). Finally, both political transformations had notable implications for Dutch sovereign credit risk.

5.3.3. *Spain*

Figure 5.7 plots Spanish revenues from 1703 to 1913. Revenues were very low, averaging roughly 1 gold gram, through the first half of the nineteenth century.[8] Since expenditure data were not available until 1801, Figure 5.8 plots Spanish deficit ratios from that year onward. Deficit ratios were high, averaging 0.21 (i.e., deficits were more than two times greater than revenues). Spain was also a serial defaulter.[9] It is thus not surprising that Spanish yield spreads were very high under the fragmented and absolutist regime (see Figure 4.3).

There was a steady increase in Spanish revenues after fiscal centralization, which took place in 1845. Under the centralized and absolutist regime, they averaged 2.44 gold grams per capita, more than double those under the fragmented and absolutist one. As for France, centralization also had a positive effect on Spanish deficit ratios, which fell markedly.

Spanish revenues peaked at more than 5 gold grams per head under the centralized and limited regime established in 1876.[10] Surprisingly, given its rocky past, Spain also stayed largely in the black through 1913. In turn, there was a notable improvement in Spanish sovereign credit risk (see Figure 4.3).

---

[8] Drelichman and Voth (2010) argue that short-term liquidity crises led to repeated defaults by King Philip II (r. 1554–98). Divided fiscal authority was an important source of the ruler's fiscal problems. Also see Chapters 2 and 3.

[9] See Reinhart et al. (2003, table 2). However, Spain defaulted only once on its external debts after the establishment of a centralized and limited regime in 1876. Also see Chapter 4.

[10] Though political transformations led to marked increases in per capita revenues in Spain, they were still decidedly lower in absolute levels than those for most other European countries. The fact that Portuguese revenues were also small overall suggests that this phenomenon was particular to the Iberian Peninsula. The econometric framework in Chapter 7 explicitly accounts for geographical factors.

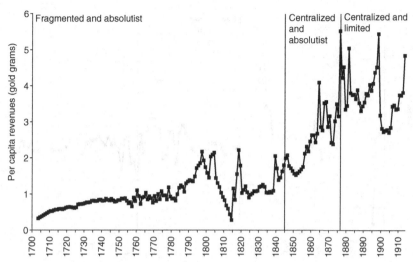

FIGURE 5.7. Per capita revenues, Spain, 1703–1913.
Source: See Appendix 2.

As for the French and Dutch cases, the evolution of revenues and deficit ratios over Spanish political regimes fits with the theoretical predictions. The evidence suggests that limited government led to greater revenues and lower deficits. This finding bolsters the argument that parliamentary reforms had positive impacts on public finances. As with France, the evidence suggests that fiscal centralization in Spain generated higher revenues and (unlike the case of the Netherlands) smaller deficits. These findings provide additional evidence that the establishment of standardized national tax systems had positive net fiscal effects. As a result of both political transformations, Spanish sovereign credit risk fell.

5.3.4. *Austria*

Recall from Chapter 4 that Austrian yield spreads were not analyzed because the available data did not start until after both political transformations had already occurred. Nonetheless, it is useful to examine the Austrian data for revenues and deficit ratios, which span three different political regimes.

Figure 5.9, which plots Austrian revenues from 1818 to 1910, indicates that revenues were low, at slightly more than 3 gold grams per capita, under the fragmented and absolutist regime that lasted through

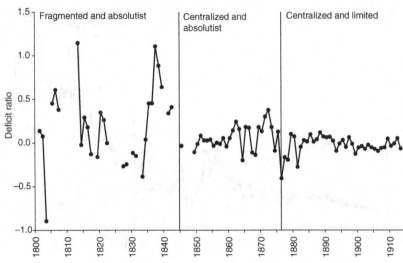

FIGURE 5.8. Deficit ratios, Spain, 1801–1913.
Source: See Appendix A.2.

the 1840s.[11] Moreover, deficit ratios, which Figure 5.10 plots from 1780 onward, were high.

Though a liberal revolution failed in 1848, this event was the catalyst for the creation of uniform fiscal institutions throughout the Austrian Empire. There was a trend break in the Austrian revenue series, which began to increase steadily from that year forward. Revenues averaged 5.50 gold grams per head under the centralized and absolutist regime, nearly double those under the fragmented and absolutist one. Unlike France or Spain (but like the Netherlands), however, deficit ratios in Austria rose with fiscal centralization, increasing from 0.31 to 0.53 (i.e., in the latter case, deficits were more than five times greater than revenues). External conflicts account at least in part for this outcome. Austria, which did not enter any major wars from 1815 to 1847, participated in five such conflicts from 1848 to 1866: the First Italian War of Independence (1848–9), the Franco-Austrian War (1859), the Second Italian War of Independence (1859–61), the Second Schleswig-Holstein War (1864), and the Austro-Prussian War (1866).

[11] Though budgetary figures exist for Austria from the late 1700s, the time series for population did not begin until 1818. Furthermore, the population series ends in 1910 (the Austro-Hungarian Empire was dissolved at the end of World War I in 1918). Pammer (2010, p. 133) provides a brief description of the availability of historical economic and social data for Austria.

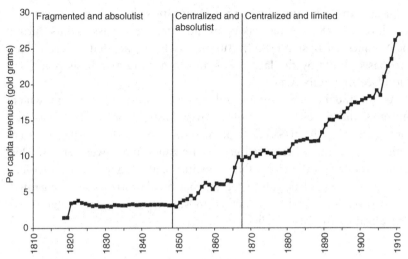

FIGURE 5.9. Per capita revenues, Austria, 1818–1910.
Source: See Appendix A.2.

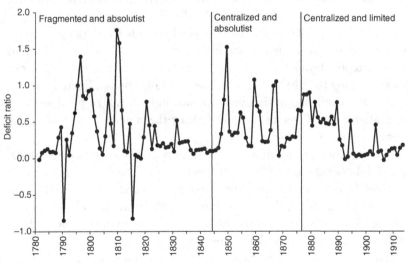

FIGURE 5.10. Deficit ratios, Austria, 1781–1913.
Source: See Appendix A.2.

The 1867 Compromise, which established Austria and Hungary as
distinct political units, signaled the start of the constitutional era. From
that point onward, both states had parliaments that exercised regular
budget authority. Austrian revenues continued to rise, reaching roughly

27 gold grams per capita by 1910. Deficit ratios also fell, achieving near-zero levels by 1890. After spiking at more than 400 basis points during the conquest of Bosnia (1878), Austrian yield spreads fell to fewer than 150 basis points by the late 1880s and to around 100 basis points by 1900 (see Appendix A.1).

As for the French, Dutch, and Spanish cases, the ways in which revenues and deficit ratios evolved over Austrian political regimes are consistent with the theoretical predictions. The evidence suggests that limited government generated greater revenues and lower deficits. This finding reinforces the claim that constitutional change had positive fiscal effects. The evidence also suggests that fiscal centralization generated higher revenues. As with the Netherlands, however, the data suggest that centralization increased deficits in Austria.

5.4. Prussia as an Anomaly

As described in Chapter 4, the unusual nature of public finances in Prussia led to the postponement of the analysis of sovereign credit risk until now, when revenues and deficit ratios could also be examined.

Figure 5.11, which plots Prussian yield spreads from 1815 to 1913, indicates that spreads fell in the aftermath of the Napoleonic Wars in 1815, reaching fewer than 50 basis points by the start of the 1840s, but peaked during the Year of Revolutions in 1848. Though limited government was established in that year, spreads did not fall to previous lows until after 1900. Over the second half of the nineteenth century, they averaged 102 basis points.

External conflicts account for at least part of this discrepancy. Prussia, which did not fight any major wars from 1815 to 1847, entered four such conflicts from 1848 to 1871: the First and Second Schleswig-Holstein Wars (1848–9, 1864), the Austro-Prussian War (1866), and the Franco-Prussian War (1870–1). It is also important to note that, since monthly or weekly data were not available from 1842 to 1869, the present analysis used data from Homer and Sylla (2005), who computed yearly averages over infrequent intervals. There is thus the chance that trends in Prussian yields are not accurately portrayed over this period.

Historical accounts, moreover, suggest a positive role for limited government. Ferguson (1998) claims that Rothschild lenders urged King Frederick William II (r. 1786–97) to implement constitutional reforms as a credible way to reduce sovereign credit risk. Likewise, Tilly (1966, 1967) argues that the establishment of limited government in 1848

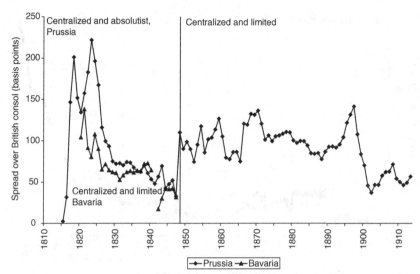

FIGURE 5.11. Yield spreads, Prussia, 1815–1913.
Source: See Appendix A.2.

strengthened the ability of the Prussian parliament to pursue sound fiscal policies.[12]

A quantitative comparison of sovereign credit risk across German polities is also useful here. Figure 5.11 includes yield spreads for Bavaria, which adopted a liberal constitution in 1818, from Homer and Sylla (2005). Through 1848, Bavarian spreads were on average 30 basis points fewer than Prussian ones. This finding suggests that limited government did in fact have a positive effect on credit risk within the German territories.

How about revenues and prudence? Figure 5.12, which plots Prussian revenues from 1688 to 1913, indicates that revenues were low, averaging less than 4 gold grams per capita, under the fragmented and absolutist regime that lasted through the early 1800s. Fiscal centralization took place in 1806, after Prussia's loss to France in the Battle of Jena-Auerstedt. Revenues rose through the end of the Napoleonic Wars in 1815 but were not notably higher over the next three decades than during much of the eighteenth century.

[12] It is also possible that the political regime in Prussia was never truly constitutional, even after 1848. For instance, the Polity IV Database of Marshall and Jaggers (2008) codes nineteenth-century Prussia as absolutist. As described in Chapter 3, however, the selection of early dates to define political regimes as limited biases the data against the hypothesis that constitutional reforms improved public finances. Indeed, the classification of post-1848 Prussia as centralized and absolutist rather than centralized and limited only strengthened the regression results presented in Chapter 7.

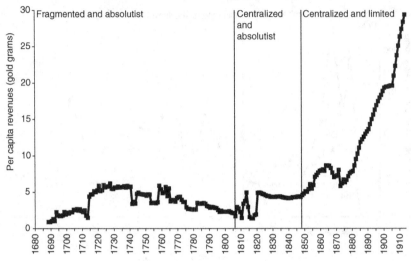

FIGURE 5.12. Per capita revenues, Prussia, 1688–1913.
Source: See Appendix A.2.

Revenues began to increase after the establishment of limited government in 1848, averaging more than 7 gold grams per head over the next two decades. As already noted, Prussia fought four wars from 1848 to 1871. The political unification of Germany took place in the aftermath of Prussia's defeat of France in the Franco-Prussian War (1870–1). Revenues continued to grow rapidly, reaching nearly 30 gold grams per capita by 1913.

As for yields, Prussian deficit ratios also showed surprising features. Figure 5.13, which plots this fiscal indicator from 1688 to 1913, indicates that ratios rose with the War of the Grand Alliance (1688–97) and the War of the Spanish Succession (1701–14). However, Prussia stayed in the black over the tumultuous eighteenth century, even during its participation in major conflicts like the Great Northern War (1700–21), the War of the Austrian Succession (1740–8), the Seven Years' War (1756–63), and the Wars of the First and Second Coalitions (1792–1801). This display of fiscal prudence may have reflected unusual fiscal discipline: Kiser and Schneider (1994) argue that the Prussian tax system was among the most efficient in Europe at the time. Nevertheless, the fact that Prussia made significant tax changes in 1806 suggests that it was aware of the importance of institutional reforms. Though the post-1806 expenditure data are sporadic, the existing observations indicate that Prussia continued to follow prudent fiscal policies through 1913.

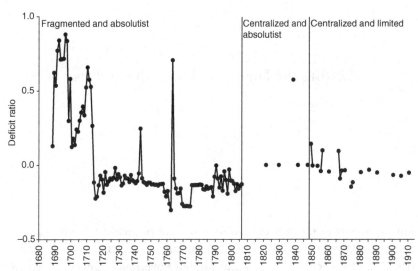

FIGURE 5.13. Deficit ratios, Prussia, 1688–1913.
Source: See Appendix A.2.

Unlike the French, Dutch, Spanish, and Austrian cases, the Prussian case highlights the effects of (idiosyncratic) historical factors beyond political regimes on public finances. Although the evidence suggests that political transformations in Prussia had certain notable fiscal effects, they did not always correspond to the theoretical predictions.

Other anomalies in the fiscal data also bear mention at this juncture. Table 4.2 indicates that yield spreads for Denmark and Portugal fell little from the fragmented and absolutist regime to the centralized and limited one. Similarly, Table 5.3 shows that deficit ratios for Portugal and Sweden actually increased from the fragmented and absolutist regime to the centralized and limited one. The regression analysis in Chapter 7 explicitly accounts for country-specific effects, as well as the impacts of a wide variety of other political and economic variables.

By what means did political transformations improve sovereign credit risk? This chapter has identified two precise mechanisms through which fiscal centralization and limited government led to credit gains: increases in government revenues per head and improvements in fiscal prudence. The findings also indicate the importance of controlling for historical factors besides political regimes. To rigorously characterize the fiscal impacts of political transformations, the next two chapters exploit the data using a set of powerful statistical tools.

6

Letting the Data Speak for Themselves

Improvements in revenue collection and fiscal prudence were two channels through which political transformations reduced sovereign credit risk. Both fiscal centralization and limited government generally led to increases in government revenues and reductions in deficit ratios. To complete the analogy described at the start of Chapter 4, if long-term sovereign bond yields represent the heartbeat of a nation's fiscal health, then revenues and fiscal prudence represent elements of pulmonary circulation like the lungs and blood vessels that underlie its strength.

To fully characterize the fiscal effects of political transformations, the data are now subjected to a battery of rigorous tests. The statistical analysis begins with structural breaks tests, which assume no a priori knowledge of major turning points in the fiscal series, but let the data speak for themselves.[1] So long as these tests identify fiscal centralization and limited government as key breaks, we can have even greater confidence that political transformations improved public finances. In this chapter the breaks setup is first described. Then the results of the breaks tests for sovereign credit risk are reported, followed by those for government revenues and fiscal prudence.

6.1. Structural Breaks Basics

The structural breaks methodology is from Bai and Perron (2003).[2] A program created by Doan (2010) for the Regression Analysis of Time

---

[1] For historical applications, see Willard et al. (1996), Brown and Burdekin (2000), Sussman and Yafeh (2000), Mauro et al. (2002), and Dincecco (2009a).
[2] This methodology identifies multiple structural changes in means while allowing for serial correlation. It thus improves upon the "moving windows" technique that relies upon sequential single structural change methods.

Series (RATS) software implements the Bai–Perron procedure by estimating the following regression equation for each sample country:

$$F_t = \alpha + \Sigma_{l=1,\ldots,L}\ \beta_l\ F_{t-l} + \varepsilon_t, \tag{1}$$

where F_t is the fiscal indicator in year t, β_l through β_L are parameters to be estimated, and ε_t is the disturbance term.[3] Depending on the specification, F_t represents yield spreads (against British consols, in basis points), per capita revenues (in gold grams), or budget deficit-to-revenue ratios. The RATS routine uses a dynamic programming algorithm to evaluate which final partitioning of the time series data achieves a global minimization of the overall sum of squared residuals. It then returns the optimal set of break points.

The RATS procedure requires the user to select a maximum number of "best" turning points in each time series subject to a minimum number of observations between data segments. Willard et al. (1996) discuss the trade-off that occurs when one chooses parameter values. A minimum space of two observations sharply reduces the chance of confounding the effects of different events but ends up analyzing blips (false positives that characterize certain events as "long lasting" that were really not) rather than turning points. Longer periods of analysis, however, increase the likelihood of missing important shifts (false negatives).

Testing a wide variety of parameter values minimizes the likelihood of generating false positives or negatives.[4] Table 6.1 compares the turning points that the RATS routine identifies for yield spreads over different combinations of maximum breaks and minimum observations. Tables 6.2 and 6.3 do the same for per capita revenues and deficit ratios, respectively. The results are very stable. For each fiscal indicator, there is at least one common break (i.e., within 10 years or less) among different sets of parameter values for each sample country nearly 100 percent of the time. There are at least two common breaks around 95 percent of the time and at least three common breaks more than 90 percent of the time. We may thus be confident that the turning points identified by the breaks tests are robust to diverse parameter values.[5]

---

[3] Up to five significant yearly lags of the dependent variable (i.e., $L \leq 5$) were allowed.

[4] Many time series display data gaps before the nineteenth century. For time series that became continuous after 1815, the best one, two, or three structural breaks with at least 5, 10, or 15 observations (i.e., 5, 10, or 15 years) per segment were selected. For time series that were continuous from the seventeenth or eighteenth century onward, the best three, four, or five breaks with at least 15, 20, or 25 observations (i.e., 15, 20, or 25 years) per segment were selected.

[5] The do-file for the structural breaks tests in this chapter is available at the website http://sites.google.com/site/mdincecco/.

TABLE 6.1. *Comparison of Best Breaks in Time Series for Yield Spreads with Different Minimum Observations per Segment*

Best 1			Best 2			Best 3		
5	10	15	5	10	15	5	10	15
Panel A: France, 1816–1913								
1873	1873	1873	1852	1857	1871	1852	1857	1871
			1847	1847	1847	1847	1847	1847
						1824	1825	1831
Panel B: Denmark, 1864–1913								
1900	1900	1878	1900	1900	**1898**			
			1870	1878	1878			
Panel C: Netherlands, 1816–1913								
1830	1830	1830	1829	1830	1830	1829	1829	1830
			1834	**1849**	**1849**	1850	1850	1848
						1834	1839	1885
Panel D: Portugal, 1823–1902								
1836	1848	1848	1895	1849	1848	1849	1848	1848
			1836	1839	1863	1844	1863	1863
						1895	1836	1887
Panel E: Prussia, 1816–1913								
1823	1825	1830	1825	1825	1830	1824	1825	1830
			1849	1849	1897	1847	1847	1847
						1866	1866	1866
Panel F: Spain, 1821–1913								
1831	1832	1835	1831	1832	1835	1833	1832	1835
			1825	1880	1879	1880	1881	1879
						1825	1871	1864

Note: Yield spreads are against the British consol. Panels A to F display the best one, two, or three structural breaks with 5, 10, or 15 minimum observations per segment. Since there were fewer than 50 observations for Denmark, the analysis is limited to the best one or two breaks. Years in boldface identify breaks within 10 years or less of fiscal centralization or limited government. For further details, see Tables 2.5 and 3.1.
Source: See text.

6.2. Sovereign Credit Risk: Results

Table 6.4 shows the findings of the structural breaks tests for yield spreads for Group 1 countries plus select Group 2 ones (Denmark and Portugal) from 1816 to 1913. It displays the combination of the best two breaks with 15 minimum observations per segment, because this set of

TABLE 6.2. *Comparison of Best Breaks in Time Series for Per Capita Revenues with Different Minimum Observations per Segment*

Best 3			Best 4			Best 5		
15	20	25	15	20	25	15	20	25
Panel A: England, 1650–1913								
1797	1797	1797	1802	1797	1797	1802	1797	1797
1816	1817	1822	1817	1817	1822	1818	1818	1822
1898	1893	1888	1898	1893	1888	1898	1893	1888
			1787	1777	1853	1787	1777	1688
						1856	1856	1714
Panel B: France, 1650–1913								
1895	1893	1797	1797	1893	1795	1805	1796	1795
1869	1869	1877	1869	1869	1877	1869	1869	1877
1854	1847	1852	1854	1839	1852	1854	1839	1852
			1895	1818	1820	1820	1818	1820
						1895	1893	1740
Panel C: Portugal, 1762–1913								
1832	1798	1798	1798	1798	1798	1798	1798	1787
1847	1847	1854	1847	1851	1855	1847	1851	1863
1898	1893	1888	1898	1893	1888	1898	1893	1888
			1832	1831	1830	1832	1831	1838
						1880	1871	1812
Panel D: Prussia, 1688–1913								
1713	1713	1713	1713	1713	1713	1713	1713	1713
1765	1765	1765	1764	1764	1771	1771	1771	1771
1740	1740	1740	1819	1819	1820	1819	1819	1819
			1834	1839	1740	1834	1839	1847
						1740	1740	1740
Panel E: Spain, 1703–1913								
1860	1853	1841	1838	1853	1838	1841	1853	1838
1875	1873	1872	1875	1873	1863	1875	1873	1863
1898	1893	1814	1898	1893	1888	1898	1893	1888
			1858	1814	1804	1814	1814	1804
						1860	1779	1779
Panel F: Sweden, 1740–1913								
1802	1864	1864	1802	1864	1863	1864	1867	1863
1787	1789	1787	1787	1789	1787	1787	1789	1787
1817	1812	1812	1817	1812	1812	1817	1812	1812
			1893	1893	1888	1893	1893	1888
						1802	1847	1837

(*continued*)

TABLE 6.2 *(continued)*

Best 1			Best 2			Best 3		
5	10	15	5	10	15	5	10	15
Panel G: Austria, 1818–1910								
1822	1827	1832	1822	1827	1832	1822	1827	1832
			1827	1837	1847	1827	1847	1847
						1832	1837	1862
Panel H: Denmark, 1864–1913								
1874	**1874**	**1883**	**1874**	1873	1879			
			1907	1903	**1894**			
Panel I: Netherlands, 1816–1913								
1873	**1873**	**1873**	1900	1865	1865	1900	**1873**	1881
			1908	1830	1830	1821	1830	1830
						1908	1841	1861

Note: Per capita revenues are tax revenues collected by national governments. Panels A to F display the best three, four, or five structural breaks with 15, 20, or 25 minimum observations per segment. Panels G to I display the best one, two, or three breaks with 5, 10, or 15 minimum observations per segment. Since there were fewer than 50 observations for Denmark, the analysis is limited to the best one or two breaks. Years in boldface identify breaks within 10 years or less of fiscal centralization or limited government. For further details, see Tables 2.5 and 3.1.
Source: See text.

parameter values is representative of the general patterns that the breaks tests identify (see Table 6.1). Austria was omitted, since the available yield data do not begin until after the establishment of a centralized and limited regime (see Chapter 4). However, Portugal was included because the available yield data span both political transformations, and Denmark because they span fiscal centralization.

A gap in the French yield data during the Revolution (1789–99) precluded structural breaks tests near the time of fiscal centralization. The breaks analysis for France thus runs from the end of the revolutionary and Napoleonic era (1789–1815) onward. The 1871 break coincided with the establishment of a stable centralized and limited regime in 1870 and the Franco-Prussian War (1870–1). The fact that this set of events led to a small rise in yield spreads over the following decade suggests that France's loss to Prussia offset the positive effects of constitutional change in the short term. Recall from Figure 4.1, however, that French spreads fell steadily from 1871 onward. The 1847 break coincided with the tumultuous end of the constitutional July regime (1830–48) and the

TABLE 6.3. *Comparison of Best Breaks in Time Series for Deficit Ratios with Different Minimum Observations per Segment*

	Best 3			Best 4			Best 5	
15	20	25	15	20	25	15	20	25
Panel A: Austria, 1781–1913								
1846	1846	1846	1849	1846	1838	1849	1849	1855
1810	1810	1810	1810	1810	1810	1810	1809	1805
1889	1889	1888	1889	1889	1888	1889	1889	1880
			1834	1868	1863	1834	1869	1830
						1795	1829	1880
Panel B: England, 1692–1913								
1711	1711	1716	1711	1711	1716	1711	1711	1716
1738	1738	1741	1737	1739	1741	1737	1739	1741
1797	1797	1797	1797	1797	1797	1797	1797	1797
			1753	1759	1766	1753	1759	1766
						1814	1817	1869
Panel C: Sweden, 1740–1913								
1856	1856	1853	1853	1831	1853	1853	1856	1853
1785	1781	1785	1779	1788	1785	1779	1788	1775
1800	1801	1810	1809	1811	1810	1809	1810	1800
			1794	1763	1879	1763	1763	1825
						1794	1879	1879

	Best 1			Best 2			Best 3	
5	10	15	5	10	15	5	10	15
Panel D: Denmark, 1864–1913								
1876	1876	1878	1893	1887	1878			
			1898	1898	1895			
Panel E: France, 1816–1913								
1864	1864	1864	1839	1839	1839	1839	1861	1870
			1856	1856	1856	1856	1851	1854
						1851	1839	1839
Panel F: Netherlands, 1816–1913								
1820	1825	1839	1838	1838	1848	1840	1838	1853
			1821	1825	1833	1822	1858	1831
						1833	1825	1868
Panel G: Spain, 1849–1913								
1873	1873	1873	1873	1873	1873	1873	1873	1880
			1868	1883	1888	1882	1883	1898
						1868	1859	1865

Note: Deficit ratios are ratios of budget deficits to tax revenues for national governments. Panels A to C display the best three, four, or five structural breaks with 15, 20, or 25 minimum observations per segment. Panels D to G display the best one, two, or three breaks with 5, 10, or 15 minimum observations per segment. Since there were fewer than 50 observations for Denmark, the analysis is limited to the best one or two breaks. Years in boldface identify breaks within 10 years or less of fiscal centralization or limited government. For further details, see Tables 2.5 and 3.1.

Source: See text.

TABLE 6.4. *Major Breaks in Time Series for Yield Spreads*

Year	Percent Change	Event
Panel A: France, 1816–1913		
1847	+198%***	End of constitutional regime
	(3.97)	(1830–48) / start of First Italian War of Independence (1848–9)
1871	+26%	**Limited government (1870)** /
	(1.38)	Franco-Prussian War (1870–1)
Panel B: Denmark, 1864–1913		
1878	–19%***	Railway nationalizations (1878–82)
	(3.04)	
1898	–5%	**Fiscal centralization (1903)**
	(0.61)	
Panel C: Netherlands, 1816–1913		
1830	+56%***	Start of Belgian War of Independence
	(3.20)	(1830–3)
1849	–30%***	**Limited government (1848)**
	(2.69)	
Panel D: Portugal, 1823–1902		
1848	+10%	Third Civil War (1846–7) / **limited**
	(0.50)	**government (1851)**
1863	+20%	**Fiscal centralization (1859)**
	(1.69)	
Panel E: Prussia, 1816–1913		
1830	–53%***	First *Zollverein* Customs Union
	(4.92)	(1834)
1897	–29%**	*Weltpolitik* of Emperor Wilhelm II
	(2.42)	(1890s)
Panel F: Spain, 1821–1913		
1835	–72%***	End of First Carlist War (1833–9) /
	(5.82)	**fiscal centralization (1845)**
1879	–56%***	**Limited government (1876)** / end of
	(2.73)	Third Carlist War (1872–6)

Note: Yield spreads are against the British consol. The first column shows the years for the two best structural breaks with 15 minimum observations according to the algorithm described in the text. The second column shows the percent change in average yield spreads for the decades before and after each break. *T*-statistics in absolute values are in parentheses. The final column offers brief explanations for the turning points, which the text elaborates upon. Breaks are counted for fiscal centralization or limited government (in boldface) if they coincide by 10 years or less.

*Significant at 10%; **Significant at 5%; ***Significant at 1%.
Source: See text.

start of the First Italian War of Independence (1848–9). This set of events led to a significant increase in yield spreads of nearly 200 percent.

As for France, a data gap during the Napoleonic Wars (1803–15) precluded structural breaks tests near the time of fiscal centralization for the Netherlands. The breaks analysis for Dutch yield spreads thus runs from 1816 onward. The 1849 break coincided with the establishment of a centralized and limited regime in 1848. Over the following decade, there was a significant decrease in spreads of 30 percent. The 1830 break coincided with the Belgian Revolt (1830) and subsequent War of Independence (1830–3). This set of events led to a significant increase in yield spreads of more than 50 percent.

A lack of continuous Danish yield data before 1864 precluded structural breaks tests near the time of the establishment of limited government. The breaks analysis for Denmark thus runs from that year onward. The 1898 break coincided with fiscal centralization in 1903. There was a small decrease in spreads of 5 percent over the following decade. The 1878 break coincided with railway nationalizations during the late 1870s and early 1880s. Surprisingly, these nationalizations led to a significant decrease in yield spreads of 20 percent.

Since the available yield data for Spain start before fiscal centralization and limited government took place, structural breaks tests for both political transformations can be performed.[6] The 1835 break coincided with internal conflict (the First Carlist War, 1833–9) and came 10 years before fiscal centralization in 1845. With the notable exception of the Second Carlist War (1847–9), Spanish spreads fell steadily through the 1850s and 1860s (see Figure 4.3). The 1879 break coincided with the establishment of a stable centralized and limited regime in 1876 and the end of the Third Carlist War (1872–6). This set of events led to a significant decrease in yield spreads of more than 50 percent.

As for Spain, the available yield data for Portugal start before fiscal centralization and limited government occurred. Structural breaks tests for both political transformations can thus be performed. The 1848 break coincided with the Third Civil War (1846–7) and the establishment of a stable centralized and limited regime in 1851. During the 1850s, yield spreads fell by more than 200 basis points. The 1863 break coincided with fiscal centralization in 1859. Thereafter, spreads decreased steadily,

---

[6] Recall from Chapter 4 that 14 observations for Spain with yields of 20% or more were excluded from the regression analysis. To ensure continuous data, however, these observations are included for the breaks tests.

although they were punctuated with spikes due to political instability at the end of the 1860s and financial crisis at the start of the 1890s.

The available yield data for Prussia do not start until nearly one decade after fiscal centralization took place in 1806. The Prussian breaks analysis thus runs from the end of the Napoleonic Wars (1803–15) onward. The 1830 break coincided with the establishment of the first *Zollverein* Customs Union in 1834 and led to a significant reduction in spreads of 53 percent over the following decade. The 1897 break coincided with the resignation of Chancellor Bismarck in 1890 and the adoption of an aggressive foreign policy known as *Weltpolitik* by the new emperor, Wilhelm II. Spreads rose over the 1890s but fell significantly by the start of the 1900s (see Figure 5.11). Although the establishment of limited government in 1848 did not coincide with a major turning point for the combination of the best two breaks with at least 15 observations per segment, several other sets of parameter values identified that year or ones nearby (see Table 6.1). Surprisingly, spreads did not decrease in the aftermath of constitutional reform. Chapter 5 examines the anomalous Prussian case.

In total, the results of this set of structural breaks tests provide statistical proof that political transformations reduced sovereign credit risk. Major turning points in the time series for yield spreads typically coincided with fiscal centralization and limited government. These findings thus serve as a rigorous counterpart to the descriptive and case-study evidence from Chapter 4. They also highlight the impacts of external and internal conflicts on public finances.

6.3. Two Mechanisms: Results

We now turn to the findings of the breaks tests for two mechanisms through which credit reductions occurred: increases in government revenues per head and improvements in fiscal prudence.

Tables 6.5 and 6.6 show the results of the structural breaks tests for per capita revenues and deficit ratios for Group 1 countries plus select Group 2 ones (Denmark, Portugal, and Sweden). For time series that were continuous from the seventeenth or eighteenth century onward, they display the combination of the best four breaks with 25 minimum observations per segment. For time series that did not become continuous until after 1815, they display the combination of the best two breaks with at least 15 observations per segment. Both sets of parameter values are representative of the general patterns that the breaks tests identify (see Tables 6.2

TABLE 6.5. *Major Breaks in Time Series for Per Capita Revenues*

Year	Percent Change	Event
Panel A: England, 1650–1913		
1797	+58%***	Start of War of the Second Coalition
	(7.18)	(1798–1801)
1822	−18%***	End of Napoleonic Wars (1803–15)
	(5.05)	
1853	+15%***	Start of Crimean War (1853–6)
	(7.24)	
1888	+10%***	Start of South African War (1899–1902)
	(4.08)	
Panel B: France, 1650–1913		
1795	+37%	French Revolution (1789–99) / fiscal
	(1.68)	centralization (1790)
1820	−15%**	End of Napoleonic Wars (1803–15) /
	(2.77)	Monarchy restored (1814–15)
1852	+32%***	Coup by Napoleon III (1851) / start of
	(3.83)	Crimean War (1853–6)
1877	+26%***	**Limited government (1870)** /
	(2.93)	Franco-Prussian War (1870–1)
Panel C: Portugal, 1762–1913		
1798	+41%***	French Revolutionary Wars (1792–1801)
	(5.73)	
1830	−8%	Second Civil War (1832–4)
	(0.87)	
1855	+20%***	**Limited government (1851)** / fiscal
	(5.58)	centralization (1859)
1888	+63%***	Financial crisis (1891)
	(5.63)	
Panel D: Prussia, 1688–1913		
1713	+94%***	Entrance into Great Northern War
	(5.88)	(1700–21)
1740	−22%***	Start of War of Austrian Succession
	(5.20)	(1740–8)
1771	−28%***	End of Seven Years' War (1756–63)
	(4.11)	
1820	+88%***	End of Napoleonic Wars (1803–15)
	(5.47)	
Panel E: Spain, 1703–1913		
1804	−42%***	Start of Napoleonic Wars (1803–15)
	(4.50)	
1838	+51%***	First Carlist War (1833–9) / fiscal
	(5.53)	centralization (1845)

(continued)

TABLE 6.5 *(continued)*

Year	Percent Change	Event
1863	+39%** (4.00)	Start of Naval War with Peru (1865–6)
1888	+0% (0.02)	Unidentified event
Panel F: Sweden, 1740–1913		
1787	+57%*** (2.93)	Russo-Swedish War of 1788–90
1812	−13% (0.69)	End of Russo-Swedish War of 1808–9 / constitutional adoption (1809)
1863	+16% (1.65)	**Fiscal centralization (1861) / limited government (1866)**
1888	+22%** (4.62)	Railway nationalization (1896)
Panel G: Austria, 1818–1910		
1832	0% (0.14)	Unidentified event
1847	+22%** (2.66)	**Fiscal centralization (1848)** / start of First Italian War of Independence (1848–9)
Panel H: Denmark, 1864–1913		
1879	+19%*** (7.25)	Railway nationalizations (1878–82)
1894	+12%*** (5.07)	**Fiscal centralization (1903)**
Panel I: Netherlands, 1816–1913		
1830	+8%** (2.65)	Start of Belgian War of Independence (1830–3)
1865	+14%*** (5.64)	Liberal economic reforms (1850s, 1860s)

Note: Per capita revenues are tax revenues collected by national governments. The first column shows the years for the four (two, panels G to I) best structural breaks with 25 (15, panels G to I) minimum observations according to the algorithm described in the text. The second column shows the percent change in average per capita revenues for the decades before and after each break. *T*-statistics in absolute values are in parentheses. The final column offers brief explanations for the turning points, which the text elaborates upon. Breaks are counted for fiscal centralization or limited government (in boldface) if they coincide by 10 years or less.

*Significant at 10%; **Significant at 5%; ***Significant at 1%.

Source: See text.

TABLE 6.6. *Major Breaks in Time Series for Deficit Ratios*

Year	Percent Change	Event
Panel A: Austria, 1781–1913		
1810	−57% (1.28)	End of Napoleonic Wars (1803–15)
1838	−34% (1.52)	**Fiscal centralization (1848)** / First Italian War of Independence (1848–9)
1863	−22% (0.73)	Second Schleswig-Holstein War (1864) / **limited government** (1867)
1888	−62%*** (3.77)	Railway nationalizations (1880s)
Panel B: England, 1692–1913		
1716	−98%*** (3.46)	End of War of Spanish Succession (1701–14)
1741	+814%*** (5.72)	Start of War of Austrian Succession (1740–8)
1766	−107%*** (5.92)	End of Seven Years' War (1756–63)
1797	+143%* (1.84)	Start of War of the Second Coalition (1798–1801)
Panel C: Sweden, 1740–1913		
1785	+3,528%* (1.80)	Russo-Swedish War of 1788–90
1810	−118% (0.96)	End of Russo-Swedish War of 1808–9 / constitutional adoption (1809)
1853	+8,831%*** (3.20)	First Schleswig-Holstein War (1848–9) / **fiscal centralization (1861)**
1879	−52% (1.34)	Unidentified event
Panel D: Denmark, 1864–1913		
1878	−141%** (2.73)	Railway nationalizations (1878–82)
1895	+56% (0.49)	**Fiscal centralization (1903)**
Panel E: France, 1816–1913		
1839	+629%** (2.41)	End of constitutional regime (1830–47) / First Italian War of Independence (1848–9)

(continued)

TABLE 6.6 *(continued)*

Year	Percent Change	Event
1856	−33% (0.64)	End of Crimean War (1853–6)
Panel F: Netherlands, 1816–1913		
1833	−25%*** (3.92)	End of Belgian War of Independence (1830–3)
1848	**−43%*** (4.17)	**Limited government (1848)**
Panel G: Spain, 1849–1913		
1873	**−165%*** (2.04)	**Limited government (1876)** / end of Third Carlist War (1872–6)
1888	+324% (0.98)	Unidentified event

Note: Deficit ratios are ratios of budget deficits to tax revenues for national governments. The first column shows the years for the four (two, panels D to G) best structural breaks with 25 (15, panels D to G) minimum observations according to the algorithm described in the text. The second column shows the percent change in average deficit ratios for the decades before and after each break. *T*-statistics in absolute values are in parentheses. The final column offers brief explanations for the turning points, which the text elaborates upon. Breaks are counted for fiscal centralization or limited government (in boldface) if they coincide by 10 years or less.
*Significant at 10%; **Significant at 5%; ***Significant at 1%.
Source: See text.

and 6.3). Portugal and Sweden were included because the available budgetary data span both political transformations, and Denmark because they span fiscal centralization.

England, which had a centralized and limited regime from 1688 onward, pursued a successful tax-smoothing policy over the eighteenth century and beyond (see Chapter 5). The major turning points identified by the structural breaks tests highlight this fiscal strategy. Breaks coincided with the onset of the War of the Austrian Succession (1740–8, deficit ratios), the War of the Second Coalition (1798–1801, revenues and deficit ratios), the Crimean War (1853–6, revenues), and the South African War (1899–1902, revenues). In each case, the start of external conflicts led to significant increases in the relevant fiscal indicator. The remaining breaks coincided with the end of the War of the Spanish Succession (1701–14, deficit ratios), the Seven Years' War (1756–63, deficit ratios), and the Napoleonic Wars (1803–15, revenues). In those cases, the end of external conflicts led to significant decreases in the fiscal variables of interest.

A data gap for expenditures during the Glorious Revolution of 1688 precluded structural breaks tests for deficit ratios near the establishment of limited government in England. Although breaks tests for revenues can be performed from 1650 onward, limited government did not coincide with a major turning point for the combination of the best four breaks with at least 25 observations per segment. However, Figure 5.1 indicates that there was a significant increase in revenues of 91 percent over the 1690s. The combination of the best five breaks with at least 25 observations per segment, moreover, identified 1688 as a major turning point (see Table 6.2).

For France, the 1793 break in the time series for revenues coincided with fiscal centralization and the French Revolution (1789–99). Although domestic political turmoil offset some of the positive effects of fiscal change in the short term, Figure 5.3 indicates that French revenues grew rapidly over the next two decades. The 1877 break coincided with the establishment of a stable centralized and limited regime and the Franco-Prussian War (1870–1). During the 1870s, there was a significant increase in revenues of 26 percent. The other best breaks in the French revenue series coincided with the end of the Napoleonic Wars (1803–15) and the restoration of the Bourbon monarchy (1814–15), and with the coup by Napoleon III (1851) and the start of the Crimean War (1853–6). Whereas the former set of events led to a significant decrease in revenues, the latter led to a significant increase.

As for French yield spreads, a data gap for French expenditures during the Revolution (1789–99) precluded structural breaks tests in the time series for deficit ratios near the year of fiscal centralization in France. The breaks analysis for French deficit ratios thus runs from the end of the revolutionary and Napoleonic era (1789–1815) onward. The 1839 break was within 10 years of the end of the July regime in 1848, the same year as the start of the First Italian War of Independence (1848–9). This set of events led to a significant increase in deficit ratios of more than 600 percent. The 1856 break coincided with the end of the Crimean War (1853–6) and led to an insignificant decrease in deficit ratios. Although the establishment of limited government in 1870 did not coincide with a major turning point for the combination of the best two breaks with at least 15 observations per segment, several other sets of parameter values identified that year or ones nearby (see Table 6.3). Furthermore, Figure 5.4 indicates that deficit ratios decreased by 165 percent over the 1870s.

For the Netherlands, gaps in the budgetary data during the Napoleonic Wars (1803–15) precluded structural breaks tests near the time of fiscal centralization. The breaks analysis for revenues and deficit ratios thus runs from 1816 onward. The 1848 break for deficit ratios coincided with the establishment of a centralized and limited regime, and the 1833 break coincided with the end of the Belgian War of Independence (1830–3). Both events led to significant decreases in deficit ratios over the decades that followed.

The 1830 break for Dutch revenues, by contrast, coincided with the Belgian Revolt (1830) and the start of the War of Independence (1830–3), and led to a significant rise in revenues. The 1865 break coincided with the liberal era of economic reforms during the 1850s and 1860s.[7] Although the establishment of limited government in 1848 did not coincide with a major turning point in the time series for revenues for the combination of the best four breaks with at least 25 observations per segment, Figure 5.5 indicates that, after a lag, Dutch revenues grew steadily over the 1860s and 1870s. Moreover, the combination of the best three breaks with at least 10 observations per segment identified 1841, the year after the constitutional reform of 1840, as a major turning point (see Table 6.2).

As for yield spreads, the lack of budgetary data before 1864 precluded structural breaks tests near the time of the establishment of limited government in Denmark. The breaks analysis for Danish revenues and deficit ratios thus runs from that year onward. The 1894 break for revenues and the 1895 break for deficit ratios each came within 10 years of fiscal centralization. Over the following decade, there were significant increases in both fiscal indicators. The 1879 break for revenues and the 1878 break for deficit ratios coincided with railway nationalizations, which led to a significant increase in the former variable and a significant decrease in the latter.

For Spain, the 1838 break in the time series for revenues coincided with the end of the First Carlist War (1833–9) and fiscal centralization in 1845. This set of events led to a significant increase in revenues of 51 percent over the following decade. Although the establishment of limited government in 1876 did not coincide with a major turning point for the combination of the best four breaks with at least 25 observations per segment, several other sets of parameter values identified nearby years (see Table 6.2). Furthermore, Figure 5.7 indicates that there was a significant increase in revenues of 35 percent over the late 1870s and early 1880s. The other best breaks in the revenue series coincided with the start of the Napoleonic Wars (1803–15) and the Naval War with Peru

[7] See van Zanden and van Riel (2010, pp. 65–79).

(1865–6), and with an unidentified event in 1888. Surprisingly, the onset of the Napoleonic Wars led to a significant decrease in revenues.

Since the lack of continuous expenditure data for Spain before 1849 precluded structural breaks tests for deficit ratios near the time of fiscal centralization, the breaks analysis runs from that year onward. The 1873 break coincided with the end of the Third Carlist War (1872–6) and the establishment of a stable centralized and limited regime in 1876. This set of events led to a significant decrease in deficit ratios of 165 percent. The second break coincided with an unidentified event in 1888.

Recall from the preceding section that structural breaks tests for yield spreads for Austria were not performed because the available data did not begin until after the establishment of a centralized and limited regime. Since the available budgetary data span both political transformations, however, breaks tests can be performed for Austrian revenues and deficit ratios. The 1838 break in the time series for deficit ratios came within 10 years of fiscal centralization and the First Italian War of Independence (1848–9), and the 1863 break coincided with the establishment of a stable centralized and limited regime and the Second Schleswig-Holstein War (1864). Both political transformations (along with external conflicts, which may have had offsetting effects) led to small decreases in deficit ratios over the decades that followed. The other best breaks coincided with the end of the Napoleonic Wars (1803–15) and the railway nationalizations during the 1880s. Each set of events led to decreases in deficit ratios.

Though budgetary figures exist for Austria from the late 1700s, the population data were not available until 1818 (see Chapter 5). The breaks analysis for Austrian revenues thus runs from 1816 onward. As for deficit ratios, the 1847 break in the time series for revenues coincided with fiscal centralization and the First Italian War of Independence (1848–9). This set of events led to a significant increase in revenues of 22 percent. The other best break in the revenue series coincided with an unidentified event in 1832 and had an insignificant effect. Although the establishment of limited government in 1867 did not coincide with a major turning point for the combination of the best two breaks with at least 15 observations per segment, Figure 5.9 indicates that there was a significant increase in revenues of 55 percent over the late 1860s and early 1870s. Moreover, the combination of the best three breaks with at least 15 observations per segment identified 1862 as a major turning point (see Table 6.2).

For Sweden, the 1863 break in the time series for revenues occurred between fiscal centralization in 1861 and the establishment of limited government in 1866. This set of political transformations led to a small increase in revenues over the following decade. The 1853 break in the time series for deficit ratios coincided with the start of the Crimean War (1853–6) and came within 10 years of fiscal centralization. This set of events, coupled with a new expansionary fiscal policy, led to a significant increase in deficit ratios.[8] Although the establishment of limited government did not coincide with a break for the time series for deficit ratios, they fell by 40 percent over the late 1860s and early 1870s. Furthermore, the 1810 break for deficit ratios (and the 1812 break for revenues) coincided with the constitutional change of 1809 and the end of the Russo-Swedish War of 1808–9. After this political reform, the executive kept absolute veto authority, and parliament met only once every five years (see Chapter 3). Although this set of events led to a decrease in deficit ratios of 118 percent over the 1810s, it had a negligible effect on revenues. Other best breaks coincided with the start of the Russo-Swedish War of 1788–90 (revenues and deficit ratios) and the railway nationalization of 1896 (revenues). Both events led to significant increases in the relevant fiscal indicators. The remaining break for deficit ratios coincided with an unidentified event in 1879 and had an insignificant impact.

Large gaps in the pre-1851 expenditure data for Portugal precluded structural breaks tests for deficit ratios. The breaks analysis thus centers on Portuguese revenues. The 1855 break fell between fiscal centralization in 1851 and the establishment of limited government in 1859. This set of political transformations led to a significant increase in revenues of 20 percent over the following decade. Other best breaks coincided with the French revolutionary wars (1792–1801), the Second Civil War (1832–4), and the financial crisis of 1891. Whereas the first and third events led to significant increases in revenues, the second had an insignificant effect.

As for Portugal, large gaps in the post-1806 expenditure data for Prussia precluded structural breaks tests for deficit ratios. The breaks analysis thus centers on Prussian revenues. The 1713 break coincided with Prussia's entrance into the Great Northern War (1700–21) and led to a significant increase in revenues. By contrast, the 1771 break coincided with the end of the Seven Years' War (1756–63), and led to a significant decrease. The other two best breaks coincided with the start of the War of Austrian Succession (1740–8) and the end of the Napoleonic Wars (1803–15). Surprisingly, the former turning point led to a significant decrease in revenues, but the latter one led to a significant increase. Recall from Chapter 5 that Prussian

---

[8] Though Sweden did not participate in the Crimean War, the conflict stimulated new demands for its exports. See Schön (2010, pp. 174–8).

revenues rose through the end of the Napoleonic Wars in 1815 but were not notably higher over the next three decades than during much of the eighteenth century. It is thus not surprising that fiscal centralization in 1806 did not coincide with a major turning point. Although the establishment of limited government in 1848 did not coincide with a major turning point for the combination of the best four breaks with at least 25 observations per segment, other parameter values identified nearby years (see Table 6.2). Furthermore, Figure 5.12 indicates that there was a notable increase in revenues over the 1850s and early 1860s.

In summary, the findings of this set of structural breaks tests offer statistical proof that increases in government revenues and improvements in fiscal prudence were two channels through which political transformations enhanced public finances. As for yield spreads, major turning points in the time series for revenues and deficit ratios generally coincided with fiscal centralization and limited government. These results thus bolster the descriptive and case-study evidence from Chapter 5. They also underscore the links between public finances and wars and political turmoil. Finally, the findings show the fiscal effects of major economic interventions like railway nationalizations.

To rigorously characterize the fiscal effects of political transformations, this chapter has reported the results of structural breaks tests, which assumed no a priori knowledge of major turning points in the fiscal series, but let the data speak for themselves. The results of the breaks tests, which typically identified fiscal centralization and limited government as key turning points, provide a statistical counterpart to the descriptive and case-study evidence from previous chapters. We can thus be even more confident that political transformations led to fiscal improvements. The findings also indicate the important effects of external and internal conflicts and other historical factors on public finances. To explicitly control for the fiscal effects of political and economic variables beyond political regimes, the next chapter uses econometric methods.

7

Estimating the Fiscal Effects of Political Regimes

When the data speak for themselves through the structural breaks analysis, they typically identify political transformations as major turning points in the time series for the various fiscal indicators. These breaks generally led to significant increases in government revenues and improvements in fiscal prudence, coupled with significant reductions in sovereign credit risk. The breaks tests thus provide rigorous proof that political transformations led to large improvements in public finances.

Like the case studies before them, however, the breaks tests also reveal the impact of historical factors besides political regimes on public finances. To account for the effects of external and internal conflicts, income growth, fiscal and monetary policies, country- and time-specific effects, and other elements, econometric techniques that exploit the panel nature of the data are now employed. Estimations of panel data increase informative content by combining variations across time and country. The key strength of this approach is the ability to systematically disentangle the role of political regimes from other potentially relevant factors through the use of control variables. By explicitly accounting for historical features beyond political regimes, the econometric analysis can either ratify or reject the findings of the case studies and structural breaks tests.

This chapter first describes the regression setup, including the panel specification, the control variables, and the issue of reverse causation. It then reports the results of the regressions for sovereign credit risk, followed by those for government revenues and fiscal prudence.

7.1. Econometric Basics

7.1.1. *Panel Specification*

The econometric method follows Beck and Katz (1995) and uses ordinary least squares with panel-corrected standard errors (PCSE). This technique, which is standard for panel datasets, corrects for any instances of contemporaneously correlated errors or panel heteroskedasticity and includes a common AR1 term to control for the possibility of serial correlation.[1]

Beck and Katz (1995) show that PCSE is superior to another technique, feasible generalized least squares (FGLS), which typically generates poor estimates of standard errors. The fact that ordinary least squares is less efficient than FGLS implies that the regression results will be stronger if the fiscal indicators still display significant coefficients. Beck and Katz (1995) also demonstrate that the use of a common AR1 term is superior to the use of country-specific ones. The inclusion of a lagged dependent variable is another way to control for serial correlation (see Beck and Katz, 1996). This approach delivers results that are similar to those reported later.[2]

The basic econometric specification is

$$F_{it} = \alpha + \beta_1 CA_{it} + \beta_2 FL_{it} + \beta_3 CL_{it} + \gamma' X_{it} + \beta_4 \mu_i + \beta_5 \tau + \varepsilon_{it}. \qquad (2)$$

Here F_{it} is the fiscal indicator for country i in year t. Depending on the specification, it represents yield spreads (against British consols, in basis points), per capita revenues (natural logarithms, in gold grams), or budget deficit-to-revenue ratios.[3] X_{it} is a vector of control variables, μ_i are country-specific fixed effects, τ is a binary variable for the Old Regime (to be described later) and ε_{it} is the disturbance term.

The binary variable CA_{it} (FL_{it}, CL_{it}) takes the value of 1 for each sample year that a country had a centralized and absolutist (fragmented

---

[1] Contemporaneously correlated errors, panel heteroskedasticity, and serial correlation are three econometric modeling concerns particular to panel data. Contemporaneously correlated errors occur if the standard errors for one country are associated with those for another country. Panel heteroskedasticity occurs if the variances of the standard errors differ by country. Finally, serial correlation occurs if the standard errors are temporally dependent. Also see Beck and Katz (1995, p. 636).

[2] A third method is first-differencing. However, Wooldridge (2003, chs. 13, 14) argues that this approach significantly reduces the variation in the independent variables, and discourages the use of first differences for time series that are very long.

[3] Wooldridge (2003, p. 189) provides rules of thumb for taking natural logarithms. The use of natural logs of average annual yields as the dependent variable in the regressions for sovereign credit risk generated results that were similar to those presented later.

and limited, centralized and limited) regime.[4] These dummies represent a clear, concise, and intuitive way to measure the fiscal impacts of political arrangements. Recall from Chapter 2 that, although fragmentation levels varied across pre-centralized states, all pre-centralized regimes were classified as entirely fragmented. Since fiscal divisions in some pre-centralized states were relatively small, this choice implies that some regimes counted as fully fragmented will encompass data associated with better fiscal outcomes like higher per capita revenues (see Chapters 2 and 5). Average improvements after fiscal centralization will therefore be smaller than otherwise. Systematic underestimation of the fiscal effects of centralization biases the data against the hypothesis that fiscal centralization improved public finances. The results of the regression analysis will thus be stronger than otherwise if they still indicate that fiscally centralized regimes had significant positive impacts on the fiscal variables of interest.

Similarly, recall from Chapter 3 that early years were always selected to date limited government. Since public finances in Europe have typically improved over time, this choice implies that some regimes classified as limited will encompass data associated with poorer fiscal outcomes. Average improvements after parliamentary reforms will therefore be smaller than otherwise. Systematic underestimation of the fiscal impacts of limited government biases the data against the hypothesis that constitutional change improved public finances. Any findings that still indicate that limited government had significant positive effects on the various fiscal indicators will thus be stronger than otherwise. At the same time, a robustness check also allows for uncertainty among investors and taxpayers about how long newly established parliamentary regimes would last by lagging the start dates by five years.

7.1.2. *Accounting for Conflict, Growth, and Other Factors*

Both the case-study evidence in Chapters 4 and 5 and the breaks tests in Chapter 6 indicate that external conflicts had important effects on public finances. Indeed, Hoffman and Rosenthal (1997) argue that the one true goal of absolutist monarchs was to wage war for personal glory and for homeland defense. In the short run, warfare had negative fiscal impacts due to the destruction of human and physical capital. Over the long term, however, Tilly (1990), Hoffman and Norberg (1994a), Hoffman and Rosenthal (2000), O'Brien (2001, 2005) Hoffman (2009), Karaman and

---

[4] The benchmark case of the fragmented and absolutist regime, FA_{it}, is omitted from the regression analysis.

Pamuk (2010), and Rosenthal and Wong (2011) argue that military competition fostered fiscal innovations that improved public finances.

External conflicts differed by characteristics such as magnitude and enemy strength. To evaluate the impact of wars on public finances, a new dataset based on Clodfelter (2002) was assembled. It includes all external conflicts fought in Western and Eastern Europe from 1650 to 1913 that involved at least one sample country. To calculate the scope of war, average military deaths per conflict year sustained by participant countries were computed. At times, sample countries simultaneously fought multiple wars. Non-overlapping average military deaths were summed in these cases. Appendix A.3 lists the concise details of all the control variables.

Since one of the core purposes of monarchs was to fight, rulers nearly always wished to go to battle. Indeed, military spending was by far the largest component of national budgets through the 1800s.[5] Financial conditions, however, were also relevant. One factor that influenced the decision to enter combat was an opponent's fiscal might. To proxy for enemy strength, coalition populations were calculated as sums of (available) total populations for coalition countries in the years that conflicts began. Non-overlapping coalition populations were summed if sample countries simultaneously fought multiple conflicts.

Financial factors also influenced the composition of military coalitions. Tilly (1990) argues that England, the Dutch Republic (i.e., the Netherlands before 1795), and France were the major European powers over the seventeenth to nineteenth centuries. Other states were available for hire as mercenaries. A binary variable that takes the value of 1 for each year that a country fought as part of an alliance with England, the Dutch Republic, or France accounts for this effect.

Financial conditions affected postwar outcomes as well. Data limitations preclude the use of figures for debt levels or currency debasements. However, systematic information is available for defaults, an extreme reaction to fiscal crisis that caused widespread damage to the financial sector and to the economy as a whole. Hoffman and Rosenthal (1997) argue that monarchs resorted to default as a way to handle large debt burdens accumulated during wars. A binary variable that takes the value of 1 for each episode of default on external debt according to Reinhart et al. (2003, table 2) measures this effect.[6]

---

[5] See Hoffman and Rosenthal (1997), Rosenthal (1998), and Lindert (2004, ch. 2). Also see Chapter 8.
[6] This source was supplemented with others. See Appendix 3.

Table 7.1 lists combatants, coalitions, and deaths for external conflicts in Europe from 1650 to 1913. On average, warfare led to more than 50,000 military deaths per conflict year and involved coalition populations of more than 25 million.[7] The least deadly conflict was the Spanish War (1727–9), with a yearly average of 269 military deaths. The deadliest year took place in 1809, when 600,000 soldiers died on the peninsular and Austrian fronts of the Napoleonic Wars (1803–15). The populations of Bosnia and Herzegovina made up the smallest coalition, at slightly more than 1 million inhabitants, during the Austrian conquest (1878). The largest coalition was Austria, France, and Spain, at 88 million inhabitants, during the First Italian War of Independence (1848–9). On average, countries formed military alliances with England, the Dutch Republic, or France in 10 percent of the years from 1650 to 1913. Spain fought most often (11 times) as an ally of one of the major European powers. The average government defaulted in 1 percent of the years from 1650 to 1913. France and Spain tied for the most default episodes over this period (7 times each). Nearly all French and Spanish defaults were related to armed conflicts.

We must also consider the fiscal impact of internal conflicts, which disrupted tax flows. A binary variable that takes the value of 1 for each year of civil war, coup, or revolution according to Clodfelter (2002) and the *Encyclopedia Britannica* (2010) accounts for this factor. Table 7.2 lists internal conflicts in Europe from 1650 to 1913. On average, states experienced domestic turmoil in 3 percent of the years from 1650 to 1913. Not surprisingly, England had the fewest internal conflicts over this period (2 events), while Portugal and Spain had the most (11 and 10 events, respectively).

Mokyr (1998, 1999) characterizes the Industrial Revolution as having had two phases. The first took place in Britain from around 1750 to 1825, and the second in continental Europe and North America from around 1870 to 1913.[8] As described in Chapter 5, systematic data for export earnings, wages, or measures of national production are not available, and modern reconstructions of pre-1815 GDP data tend toward educated guesses at best. Hohenberg and Lees (1985), Bairoch (1988), and Acemoglu et al. (2005), however, argue that there was a close relationship between urbanization rates and economic performance. A variable that calculated urban populations as fractions of total populations from

---

[7] Table 7.3 displays the descriptive statistics for the conflict-related controls.
[8] Old Regime economies were relatively stagnant. See Rosenthal (1992), Hoffman and Norberg (1994a), and Hoffman and Rosenthal (1997).

TABLE 7.1. *External Conflicts in Europe, 1650–1913*

Conflict	Years	Combatants and Coalitions	Deaths/Year
Franco-Spanish War	1648–59	Fra vs. Spa	0.007
First Anglo-Dutch War	1652–4	Eng vs. Fra, Net	0.017
First Northern War	1655–60	Aus, Den, Pol, Rus vs. Swe	NA
Anglo-Spanish War	1655–9	Eng vs. Spa	NA
Portuguese-Spanish War	1661–8	Por vs. Spa	NA
Habsburg-Ottoman War	1663–4	Aus vs. Tur	0.085
Second Anglo-Dutch War	1665–7	Eng vs. Den, Fra, Net	0.049
War of Devolution	1667–8	Eng, Net, Spa, Swe vs. Fra	0.020
Third Anglo-Dutch War	1672–4	Eng, Fra vs. Net	0.023
Franco-Dutch War	1672–9	Eng, Fra, Swe vs. Den, Net, Spa	0.045
Habsburg-Ottoman War	1683–9	Aus, Pol vs. Tur	0.125
French conquest of Luxembourg	1684	Fra, Net vs. Spa	0.020
War of Grand Alliance	1688–97	Aus, Eng, Net, Por, Spa vs. Fra	0.081
Great Northern War	1700–21	Den, Pru, Pol, Rus vs. Swe	0.318
War of Spanish Succession	1701–14	Aus, Eng, Net, Por, Pru vs. Fra, Spa	0.162
Venetian-Austrian-Turkish War	1714–18	Aus vs. Tur	0.280
War of Quadruple Alliance	1718–20	Aus, Eng, Fra, Net vs. Spa	0.150
Spanish War	1727–9	Eng, Fra vs. Spa	0.003
War of Polish Succession	1733–5	Aus, Rus vs. Fra, Pru, Spa	0.313
Austro-Russian-Turkish War	1735–9	Aus, Rus vs. Tur	0.240
War of Austrian Succession	1740–8	Aus, Eng, Net, Rus vs. Fra, Pru, Spa	0.289
Russo-Swedish War	1741–3	Rus vs. Swe	0.019
Seven Years' War	1756–63	Aus, Fra, Rus, Spa, Swe vs. Eng, Por, Pru	0.858
Corsican War	1768–9	Cor vs. Fra	0.050
War of Bavarian Succession	1778–89	Aus vs. Pru	0.016
Russo-Swedish War	1788–90	Rus vs. Swe	0.033
War of the First Coalition	1792–7	Aus, Eng, Net, Por, Pru, Spa vs. Fra	0.325
War of the Second Coalition	1798–1801	Aus, Eng, Pru, Rus, Tur vs. Fra, Net	0.386

(continued)

TABLE 7.1 *(continued)*

Conflict	Years	Combatants and Coalitions	Deaths/Year
Napoleonic Wars	1803–15		
War of the Third Coalition	1805–7	Aus, Eng, Pru, Rus, Swe vs. Fra, Net, Pol	2.333
Peninsular War	1807–14	Eng, Por, Spa vs. Fra, Net	3.000
Austrian War	1809	Aus vs. Fra, Net	3.000
Russian Campaign	1812	Aus, Den, Rus vs. Fra, Net, Pol	1.500
Leipzig Campaign	1813	Eng, Pru, Rus, Swe vs. Fra, Net	Included in Russian Campaign total.
Campaign in France	1814	Eng, Net, Rus, Pru, Swe vs. Fra	Included in Russian Campaign total.
Austrian Campaign	1815	Aus vs. Fra	0.600
Waterloo Campaign	1815	Aus, Eng, Net, Por, Pru, Spa vs. Fra	Included in Austrian Campaign total.
Russo-Swedish War	1808–9	Rus vs. Swe	0.031
Riego Rebellion	1823	Fra vs. Spa	0.065
Belgian War of Independence	1830–3	Bel. Eng, Fra vs. Net	0.007
Austro-Sardo War	1848–9	Aus vs. Sar	0.100
First Italian War of Independence	1848–9	Aus, Fra, Spa vs. Ita	0.055
First Schleswig-Holstein War	1848–9	Den, Swe vs. Pru	0.030
Crimean War	1853–6	Eng, Fra, Tur vs. Rus	1.538
Franco-Austrian War	1859	Aus vs. Fra	0.196
Second Italian War of Independence	1859–61	Aus vs. Ita	0.010
Second Schleswig-Holstein War	1864	Aus, Pru vs. Den	0.042
Austro-Prussian War	1866	Aus vs. Ita, Pru	0.164
Battle of Mentana	1867	Fra vs. Ita	0.013
Franco-Prussian War	1870–1	Fra vs. Pru	0.918
Austrian conquest of Bosnia	1878	Aus vs. Bos	0.035

Note: Average war deaths per year of conflict are in hundreds of thousands. Country abbreviations are Austria (Aus), Belgium (Bel), Bosnia (Bos), Corsica (Cor), Denmark (Den), England (Eng), France (Fra), Italy (Ita), the Netherlands (Net), Poland (Pol), Portugal (Por), Prussia (Pru), Russia (Rus), Sardinia (Sar), Spain (Spa), Sweden (Swe), and Turkey (Tur). For further details, see text and Appendix A.3.
Source: Clodfelter (2002).

TABLE 7.2. *Internal Conflicts in Europe, 1650–1913*

	Years	Event
Austria	1848	Year of Revolutions
Belgium	1789–90	Brabant Revolution
	1830	Belgian Revolution
Denmark	1848	Year of Revolutions
England	1649–51	Third English Civil War
	1688	Glorious Revolution
France	1789–99	French Revolution
	1799	Coup by Napoleon I
	1815	Bourbon Restoration
	1830	July Revolution
	1848	Year of Revolutions
	1851	Coup by Napoleon III
	1870	Fall of Second Empire
	1871	Paris Commune
Italy		No internal conflicts from 1861 to 1913
Netherlands	1785	Batavian Revolution
	1814–15	Establishment of Dutch Kingdom
	1830	Belgian Revolution
	1848	Year of Revolutions
Portugal	1808	Revolution of 1808
	1820	Revolution of 1820
	1820–3	First Civil War of Portuguese Revolution
	1823	Coup of 1823
	1827–8	Miguelite Insurrection
	1832–4	Second Civil War of Portuguese Revolution
	1836	Coup of 1836
	1846–7	Third Civil War of Portuguese Revolution
	1849	Costa Cabral coup
	1851	Saldanha coup
	1910	Establishment of First Portuguese Republic
Prussia	1848	Year of Revolutions
Spain	1820	Coup of 1820
	1823	Restoration of 1823
	1833–9	First Carlist War
	1843	Moderate coup
	1847–9	Matiners' (Second Carlist) War
	1854	Rebellion of 1854
	1863	Government collapse of 1863

(*continued*)

TABLE 7.2 *(continued)*

	Years	Event
	1868–70	Glorious Revolution
	1872–6	Third Carlist War (including Restoration of 1874)
	1909	La Semana Trágica
Sweden	1772	Coup of 1772
	1792	Assassination of Gustav III
	1809	Coup against Gustav IV

Note: All internal conflicts listed as civil wars, coups, or revolutions are included.
Source: See Appendix A.3.

De Vries (1984) proxies for income growth. This variable also captures country-specific rates of technological innovation and adoption. In addition, to further diminish the impact of the Second Industrial Revolution in continental Europe, regressions were performed for the period before 1870.

Beck (2008) argues that well-specified models often do not require fixed effects by unit or time. Rather than conclude that public finances were poor in Old Regime France simply because it was Old Regime France, for instance, or that 1789 was a volatile year simply because it was 1789, one wishes to explain fiscal effects in terms of substantive variables. The econometric framework spans four centuries of politics, external and internal conflicts, income growth, fiscal and monetary policies, and other elements. To round out this analysis, country fixed effects were introduced to capture constant but unmeasured features of states (e.g., culture, geography) that remained.

The database typically has observations for several centuries for Group 1 (and certain Group 2) countries. Greene (2000) and Wooldridge (2003) argue that fixed effects impose large costs in terms of lost degrees of freedom when time spans are long. Furthermore, Wooldridge claims that time dummies work best when the ratio of annual observations per country is small relative to the total number of countries. Since these ratios are very large here, the fixed-effects approach is problematic.

Focusing on the inclusion of substantive variables is thus the best econometric strategy in this context. Old Regime economies were typically agricultural and subsistence based. Persson (1999), Jacks (2005), and Keller and Shiue (2007) argue that market integration at both the national and international levels was poor. Warfare was by far the most salient type of widespread shock during a given year. The regression setup includes four war-related variables: battle deaths, coalition populations, mercenary status, and defaults. A binary variable for the Old Regime that captures the basic environmental differences between the period before the French Revolution and the nineteenth century supplements these and other substantive controls. This variable, which took the value of 1 for each year through 1788, not only conserved the maximum degrees of freedom, but divided the sample into two parts with roughly equal amounts of observations between them. As described in Chapter 3, Hoffman and Rosenthal (2000) argue that a fundamental shift in the nature of warfare took place around 1800, and there were fewer wars during the nineteenth century than before. Furthermore, Persson (1999), Jacks (2005), and Keller and Shiue (2007) claim that there were dramatic improvements in market integration over the 1800s. The Second Industrial Revolution also occurred during the latter part of the nineteenth century.[9] Thus, 1789 represents a natural cutoff year.

Some controls apply to only certain fiscal outcome variables. Bordo and Rockoff (1996) and Obstfeld and Taylor (2003) argue that adherence to the classic gold standard was a valuable signal of fiscal prudence. A binary variable that takes the value of 1 for each year that a country was on gold in the regressions for yield spreads and deficit ratios controls for this effect. Since states like Spain shadowed the gold standard but never made an official commitment to it, the coding for this variable is subjective. The present analysis uses the years in which currencies became de facto and de jure convertible into gold according to Meissner (2005, table 1). Bordo and Rockoff (1996) and Obstfeld and Taylor (2003) also control for "global" interest rate shocks that affected yield spreads in European asset markets in a given year. To account for systematic risk, an average yield spread was computed using the available data for all sample countries over the "safe" British consol in the regressions for yield spreads.

Another control is particular to the regressions for per capita revenues. The conversion of currency units into gold grams reduced inflation effects. Although the world gold stock was relatively stable through the early 1800s, large discoveries of gold in California and Australia around 1850 led to a dramatic increase. A variable from Velde and Weber (2000) that calculates the yearly change in the cumulative world gold stock measures this impact.

---

[9] As noted earlier, the data are also restricted to the period before 1870 to reduce the effects of this event.

TABLE 7.3. *Descriptive Statistics for Control Variables*

	Obs	Mean	Std Dev	Min	Max
War deaths	2,574	0.51	0.89	0.003	6
Enemy coalition size	2,574	2.64	1.64	00.12	8.76
Mercenary dummy	2,574	0.10	0.30	0	1
Default dummy	2,574	0.01	0.10	0	1
Internal war dummy	2,574	0.03	0.16	0	1
Urbanization rate	2,574	0.14	0.10	0.02	0.46
Old Regime dummy	2,574	0.49	0.50	0	1
Gold standard dummy	2,574	0.17	0.38	0	1
Average credit risk	1,674	227	183	−101	948
Change in gold stock	2,565	2.96	4.88	0.23	22.67
Railway nationalization dummy	2,574	0.01	0.11	0	1

Note: See text and Appendix A.3 for details about the control variables.
Source: See Appendix A.3.

A final control pertains to the regressions for deficit ratios. As already noted, military spending dominated national budgets through at least 1815. One of the key types of non-military public goods that nineteenth-century governments began to provide was transportation infrastructure, and above all railway networks.[10] The state operation of railways was typically a major undertaking, with notable implications for government budgets. A binary variable that takes the value of 1 for each year that a nationalization occurred according to Bogart (2009, table 1) accounts for this effect.

Table 7.3 displays the descriptive statistics for the controls. Mean urban populations constituted 14 percent of total populations. The lowest urbanization rates were 2 percent for Austria in the 1650s, while the highest were more than 40 percent for England from the 1870s onward. The average country was on the gold standard for 17 percent of sample years. England adhered to gold for the longest time, from 1774 to 1797 and from 1821 onward. Mean systematic risk was 227 basis points. Driven by the Dutch Republic, the lowest "global" spreads were during the 1780s and were negative (−101 basis points). The highest (948 basis points) took place during the Napoleonic Wars in 1811. The average

---

[10] Chapter 8 returns to this theme.

yearly increase in the cumulative world gold stock was nearly 3 million troy ounces. The smallest annual change (230,000 troy ounces) occurred from 1650 to 1651, and the largest (22.67 million troy ounces) from 1911 to 1912. On average, railway nationalizations took place in 1 percent of sample years. Austria, Belgium, and Germany tied for the most nationalization events over this period (six times each).

The econometric framework assumes that is possible to systematically disentangle the fiscal effects of political transformations from external and internal conflicts, economic growth, fiscal and monetary policies, country- and time-specific effects, and other elements. Since political regimes influenced each of these factors, coefficients on the controls rather than on the regime variables themselves may capture some of the positive effects of institutional change. In turn, the regime coefficients are likely to be underestimates of the total impact of political transformations. The results of the regression analysis will thus be stronger than otherwise if they still indicate that political transformations had significant positive effects on the fiscal variables of interest.

7.1.3. *Reverse Causation?*

Before describing the results of the econometric analysis, it is useful to consider the possibility of reverse causation from fiscal outcomes back to political transformations.[11] For instance, did high yield spreads affect government decisions to implement centralized tax institutions or limited government?

Endogeneity poses an econometric problem that is notoriously difficult to resolve. Political transformations, however, were largely exogenous to the various fiscal indicators. As described in Chapter 2, the establishment of uniform tax systems was often the result of radical, externally imposed reform. In the German territories, in the Low Countries, and on the Italian (and to a lesser extent, the Iberian) peninsula, fiscal centralization was the result of French conquest from 1792 onward.[12] Indeed, Acemoglu et al. (2009a) study this case as a quasi-natural experiment to test the long-term economic effects of the French Revolution.

Elsewhere, fiscal centralization often took place in the midst of large-scale administrative reforms that established new state bureaucracies.

---

[11] Reverse causation is one instance of simultaneity problems, which also include selection bias and measurement error. For an overview, see Persson and Tabellini (2003, chs. 5, 8).

[12] A similar argument holds for the establishment of uniform institutions in England after the Norman Conquest of 1066. See Brewer (1989, pp. 3–7).

Major institutional changes, moreover, typically occurred during times of economic, political, and social upheaval. The establishment of a uniform tax system in France itself during the Revolution (1789–99) illustrates the conflux of such factors, as does the case of Prussia during the Napoleonic Wars (1803–15), Austria during the Year of Revolutions (1848), and Portugal and Spain near times of civil wars.

A similar claim can be made with respect to the establishment of limited government. Berger and Spoerer (2001) examine the causes of the 1848 Year of Revolutions across 27 European countries. They argue that short-term grain shocks, and not the lack of representative institutions (or by extension, poor fiscal policies), were the key source of upheaval. More generally, Acemoglu et al. (2009b) find that economic development does not cause transitions to democracy. Rather, important historical junctures, such as the French Revolution or the Revolutions of 1848, set countries on divergent politico-economic paths.[13]

The last point relates to the exact timing of institutional change. The historical evidence suggests that states did not undertake political transformations in response to fiscal indicators, but that reforms were the result of exogenous shocks or the confluence of particular economic, geographical, political, and social factors. Even if political reforms did occur due to the state of public finances, however, the precise date of institutional change was unpredictable and subject to chance.

The Glorious Revolution of 1688 in England illustrates this argument.[14] Upon the death of Charles II in 1685, James II became king. Protestant elites were greatly troubled by the fact that James II was a devout Catholic with strong ties to France. The year 1688 was also the start of the War of the Grand Alliance, fought between France and a European-wide coalition including William III of Orange (who was crowned king of England alongside Queen Mary in 1689, after James II was deposed). One can argue that the coming together of particular events at a certain point in time (or, in a nutshell, chance) brought about limited government in England in 1688, but not before. Several previous attempts at institutional change failed, including the 1685 rebellion led by the duke of Monmouth. By this logic, one can also make the case that constitutional reform in England could have occurred on any number of occasions from 1640 to 1700, or not at all. Indeed, Pincus (2009) claims that

---

[13] Also see Moore (1966).
[14] Holmes (1993) and Smith (1997) provide general descriptions of English political events over the sixteenth and seventeenth centuries. Also see the citations listed in Chapter 3. Thanks to Daniel Bogart for insights on this topic.

the Glorious Revolution was contingent and not pre-ordained.[15] Similar arguments apply to France in 1789, the Year of Revolutions in 1848, and other critical junctures (see the earlier discussion). Highlighting the key role that chance plays in the particular timing of institutional change thus strengthens the argument that political transformations were largely exogenous to public finances.

7.2. Sovereign Credit Risk: Results

Sovereign credit functions as a concise statistic of a country's fiscal health. To assess the broad ways in which political regimes affected public finances, this section discusses the findings for the regressions that use yield spreads on government bonds as the dependent variable.[16]

Table 7.4 displays the results of this analysis. Column (1) includes the standard set of control variables. The findings indicate that political transformations had significant positive effects on credit risk for Group 1 countries. The move from the fragmented and absolutist regime to the centralized and absolutist one decreased yield spreads by more than 180 basis points, the move to the fragmented and limited one by nearly 370 basis points, and the move to the centralized and limited one by more than 200 basis points. Each coefficient is significant at the 1 percent level.

How about the controls? Enemy coalition size had a significant negative impact on credit risk. This finding suggests that spreads rose when states faced larger opponents, as the likelihood of defeat was higher. Facing the largest coalition (87.6 million) versus the smallest (1.2 million) increased spreads by almost 80 basis points. Surprisingly, war deaths had a significant positive effect on credit risk.[17] Due to their destructive impact, internal conflicts had a significant negative effect, increasing spreads by more than 90 basis points relative to periods of internal peace. Common shocks to European asset markets also led to significant increases in credit risk. Although adherence to the gold standard was associated with a large significant decrease in spreads, this result was not robust across specifications. Finally, mercenary status, defaults, and urbanization rates typically had negligible impacts on credit risk.

---

[15] Also see Mokyr (2010).

[16] The do-file for the regressions in this chapter is available at the website http://sites.google.com/site/mdincecco/.

[17] However, the use of a binary variable that does not distinguish between coalition populations and military deaths but simply takes the value of 1 for years of external conflicts had a significant negative effect on credit risk. See Dincecco (2009b).

TABLE 7.4. *Regression Results for Political Regimes and Sovereign Credit Risk*

	(1)	(2)	(3)	(4)	(5)	(6)
Centralized and absolutist regimes	-184*** (62.22)	-172** (78.02)	-170*** (68.80)	-190*** (55.90)	-56 (62.48)	-165** (79.74)
Fragmented and limited regimes	-369*** (64.78)	-275*** (63.05)	-306*** (56.89)	-293*** (46.29)	-55 (52.08)	-269*** (65.91)
Centralized and limited regimes	-203*** (64.35)	-214** (88.53)	-361*** (80.03)	-185*** (59.12)	-58 (66.47)	-196** (88.89)
War deaths	-22*** (3.65)	-18*** (3.26)	-19*** (3.41)	-14*** (3.71)	-27*** (2.84)	-20*** (3.12)
Enemy coalition size	9*** (2.24)	11*** (2.04)	12*** (2.06)	11*** (1.90)	14*** (1.88)	12*** (1.86)
Mercenary dummy	18 (47.55)	19 (45.32)	14 (39.72)	25 (32.63)	0.61 (36.45)	12 (38.41)
Default dummy	54 (47.44)	51 (45.96)	48 (40.15)	126*** (30.85)	20 (33.27)	48 (45.56)
Internal war dummy	91*** (28.40)	71*** (27.80)	59*** (23.28)	70*** (20.36)	28 (22.45)	68*** (27.60)
Urbanization rate	-33 (110.00)	-567* (340.33)	86 (311.55)	-564* (330.17)	-654* (344.60)	-373 (275.78)
Gold standard dummy	-82*** (25.94)	43 (28.08)	85*** (26.56)		3 (20.10)	-12 (15.38)
Average credit risk	0.25*** (0.02)	0.28*** (0.02)	0.26*** (0.02)	0.21*** (0.02)	0.30*** (0.02)	0.28*** (0.02)

(continued)

Old Regime dummy	-87*	-80**	-114***	-45*	-80*
	(45.19)	(39.53)	(33.13)	(27.11)	(26.50)
Country fixed effects	No	Yes	Yes	Yes	Yes	Yes
Groups	1	1	1	1	1 and 2	1 and 2, excluding Denmark, Portugal
Years	1750–1913	1750–1913	1750–1913	1750–1869	1750–1913	1750–1913
Regimes	Standard	Standard	Five-year lag	Standard	Standard	Standard
Observations	506	506	506	294	863	686
R-squared	0.24	0.40	0.43	0.52	0.23	0.38

Note: The dependent variable is the yearly yield spread against the British consol in basis points. The estimation technique is ordinary least squares with panel-corrected standard errors. A common AR1 term corrects for serial correlation. Standard errors are in parentheses. Group 1: Austria, France, the Netherlands, Prussia, and Spain. Group 2: Belgium, Denmark, Italy, Portugal, and Sweden. For further details, see text.
*Significant at 10%; **Significant at 5%; ***Significant at 1%.
Source: See text.

Column (2) adds the fixed effects by country and the dummy variable for the Old Regime. The impacts of the moves to the centralized and absolutist regime and the centralized and limited one on credit risk are similar in magnitude and significance to those shown in Column (1). Although the effect of the move to the fragmented and limited one falls by nearly 100 basis points, it remains highly significant. Surprisingly, the Old Regime is associated with a significant reduction in yield spreads. The Dutch Republic, which received loans at very low rates of interest, drives this result (see Chapter 4).

To allow for uncertainty among investors and taxpayers over whether new constitutions would last, Column (3) lags the start years of limited regimes by five years. The effects of the moves to the centralized and absolutist regime and the fragmented and limited one on credit risk remain similar in magnitude and significance to those shown in Column (2). The move to the centralized and limited regime now leads to a reduction in yield spreads of more than 360 basis points.

Recall from Section 7.1.2 that urbanization rates control for income effects. The impact of this variable on yield spreads is not robust across specifications. To further mitigate the impact of the Second Industrial Revolution, Column (4) restricts the data to the period before 1870. The effects of political transformations on credit risk are again similar in magnitude and significance to those shown in Column (2). Notably, defaults had a significant negative effect for the pre-1870 period, increasing spreads by nearly 130 basis points.

Column (5) adds Group 2 countries in the full specification that includes the standard set of controls plus the country fixed effects and the Old Regime dummy. Although the effects of political regimes on credit risk are positive, they are insignificant. This finding suggests that political transformations had larger fiscal impacts for core states, but weaker effects for the periphery. However, recall the anomalous nature of Danish and Portuguese yield spreads, which did not decrease by much over political regimes (see Table 4.2). Column (6) excludes the Danish and Portuguese data. This change restores the results from Columns (1) to (4). Once more, political transformations have significant positive effects, decreasing yield spreads by 165 to 270 basis points.

In total, this set of econometric tests provides further statistical proof that political transformations led to significant reductions in sovereign credit risk. The positive impact on yield spreads is typically large and robust to the specification. By explicitly controlling for historical factors beyond political regimes, the regression results bolster those of the case studies and structural breaks tests. Likewise, the findings verify the effects of external and internal conflicts and other elements on credit risk.

7.3. Two Mechanisms: Results

We now turn to the results of the econometric tests for two mechanisms through which credit reductions occurred: increases in government revenues per head and improvements in fiscal prudence.

7.3.1. Government Revenues

Table 7.5 displays the results for the regressions that use per capita revenues as the dependent variable. Column (1) includes the standard set of control variables. The findings indicate that political transformations had significant positive effects on revenues for Group 1 and 2 countries. The move from the fragmented and absolutist regime to the centralized and absolutist one increased revenues per head by 10 percent, the move to the fragmented and limited one by more than 30 percent, and the move to the centralized and limited one by 40 percent. Each coefficient is highly significant.

How about the controls? Enemy coalition size had a significant positive effect on per capita revenues. This finding suggests that states responded to opponent strength. Facing the largest coalition (87.6 million) versus the smallest (1.2 million) increased revenues by almost 20 percent. Income growth also had a significant positive impact. Moving from the smallest urbanization rate (0.02) to the largest (0.49) increased revenues by nearly 190 percent. Changes in the world gold stock led to significant increases in revenues as well. By contrast, internal conflicts had a significant negative impact, decreasing revenues by 6 percent. Finally, war deaths and mercenary status had negligible impacts on revenues.[18]

Column (2) adds the fixed effects by country and the dummy variable for the Old Regime. The effects of political transformations on per capita revenues are similar in magnitude and significance to those shown in Column (1). Not surprisingly, the Old Regime had a significant negative impact, decreasing revenues by 18 percent relative to the nineteenth century. Column (3) lags the start years of limited regimes by five years to allow for uncertainty among investors and taxpayers over whether new constitutions would last. The revenue effects of political transformations remain similar in magnitude and significance to those shown in Columns (1) and (2).

---

[18] Since defaults could be endogenous to revenue levels, they were omitted as a control from this set of regressions.

TABLE 7.5. *Regression Results for Political Regimes and Per Capita Revenues*

	(1)	(2)	(3)	(4)	(5)	(6)	(7)
Centralized and absolutist regimes	0.10** (0.05)	0.11*** (0.04)	0.13*** (0.04)	0.04 (0.06)	0.15** (0.07)	0.06 (0.06)	0.23*** (0.06)
Fragmented and limited regimes	0.33*** (0.06)	0.36*** (0.06)	0.35*** (0.06)	0.19*** (0.06)	0.34*** (0.06)	0.48*** (0.10)	0.75*** (0.09)
Centralized and limited regimes	0.40*** (0.06)	0.44*** (0.05)	0.41*** (0.05)	0.18** (0.08)	0.35*** (0.09)	0.40*** (0.07)	0.65*** (0.07)
War deaths	-0.01 (0.01)	-0.01 (0.01)	-0.01 (0.01)	-0.01 (0.01)	-0.01 (0.01)	-0.01 (0.01)	-0.02* (0.01)
Enemy coalition size	0.02*** (0.00)	0.01*** (0.00)	0.01*** (0.00)	0.01*** (0.00)	0.02*** (0.00)	0.01*** (0.00)	0.02*** (0.00)
Mercenary dummy	-0.03 (0.02)	-0.03 (0.02)	-0.03 (0.02)	-0.03 (0.03)	-0.03 (0.04)	-0.03 (0.03)	-0.03 (0.04)
Internal war dummy	-0.06*** (0.02)	-0.06*** (0.02)	-0.04** (0.02)	-0.07*** (0.02)	-0.08*** (0.02)	-0.06*** (0.02)	-0.07*** (0.02)
Urbanization rate	4.27*** (0.28)	3.42*** (0.31)	3.40*** (0.31)	4.47*** (0.48)	4.77*** (0.49)	3.70*** (0.37)	3.44*** (0.32)
Change in gold stock	0.03*** (0.00)	0.03*** (0.00)	0.03*** (0.00)	0.04*** (0.01)	0.02* (0.01)	0.02*** (0.01)	0.01*** (0.00)
Old Regime dummy	-0.18*** (0.04)	-0.18*** (0.04)	-0.18*** (0.04)	-0.21*** (0.03)	-0.29*** (0.03)	-0.15*** (0.04)	-0.27*** (0.05)

(continued)

Country fixed effects	No	Yes	Yes	Yes	Yes	Yes	Yes
Groups	1 and 2	1 and 2	1 and 2	1 and 2	1 and 2, excluding Prussia	1	1, excluding Prussia
Years	1650–1913	1650–1913	1650–1913	1650–1869	1650–1869	1650–1913	1650–1913
Regimes	Standard	Standard	Five-year lag	Standard	Standard	Standard	Standard
Observations	1,737	1,737	1,737	1,257	1,075	1,243	1,017
R-squared	0.13	0.44	0.45	0.50	0.62	0.31	0.48

Note: The dependent variable is the natural logarithm of yearly per capita revenues in gold grams. The estimation technique is ordinary least squares with panel-corrected standard errors. A common AR1 term corrects for serial correlation. Standard errors are in parentheses. Group 1: Austria, England, France, the Netherlands, Prussia, and Spain. Group 2: Belgium, Denmark, Italy, Portugal, and Sweden. For further details, see text.
*Significant at 10%; **Significant at 5%; ***Significant at 1%.
Source: See text.

As already described, income growth as captured by urbanization rates had a significant positive impact on per capita revenues. To further diminish the impact of the Second Industrial Revolution, Column (4) limits the data to the period before 1870. The revenue effects of the moves to the fragmented and limited regime and the centralized and limited one fall by 16 to 23 percentage points relative to those shown in Column (3) but remain highly significant. Although the impact of the move to the centralized and absolutist regime is positive, it becomes insignificant. Given the anomalous nature of public finances in Prussia (see Chapter 5), Column (5) excludes the Prussian revenue data for the regression on the pre-1870 panel. This change restores the significance (at the 5 percent level) of the impact of the move to the centralized and absolutist regime. The magnitudes of the effects of political transformations on per capita revenues are similar to those shown in the first three columns.

Column (6) restricts the sample to Group 1 countries in the full specification that includes the standard set of controls plus the country fixed effects and the Old Regime dummy. The revenue effects of the moves to the fragmented and limited regime and the centralized and limited one remain similar in magnitude and significance to those shown in Columns (1) to (3). Although the impact of the move to the centralized and absolutist regime remains positive, it becomes insignificant. Recall that Prussian public finances were anomalous (see earlier discussion and Chapter 5). Column (7) excludes the Prussian revenue data from the Group 1 sample. This change restores the significance (at the 1 percent level) of the revenue effect of the move to the centralized and absolutist regime. Indeed, political transformations have the strongest impacts yet. Now the shift from the fragmented and absolutist regime to the centralized and absolutist one leads to an increase in revenues per head of more than 20 percent, the shift to the fragmented and limited one by 75 percent, and the shift to the centralized and limited one by 65 percent.

Overall, this set of regressions offers additional statistical proof that increases in government funds were one channel through which political transformations improved public finances. The positive effect on per capita revenues is generally large and robust to the specification. By explicitly accounting for historical factors beyond political regimes, the econometric findings reinforce those of the case studies and structural breaks tests. Similarly, the results confirm the impacts of external and internal conflicts and income growth on government revenues.

7.3.2. *Deficit Ratios*

Table 7.6. displays the results for the regressions that use deficit ratios as the dependent variable.[19] Column (1) includes the standard set of control variables. The findings indicate that political transformations had significant positive effects on deficit ratios for Group 1 countries. The move from the fragmented and absolutist regime to the fragmented and limited one decreased deficit ratios by 0.21, and the move to the centralized and limited one by 0.07, both significant at the 1 percent level.

Although the move to the centralized and absolutist regime also has a positive effect on deficit ratios, it is insignificant. This result captures the tension between the pro and con impacts of fiscal centralization. Recall from Chapter 5 that larger revenues should have made it easier to pursue sound fiscal policies (e.g., France under Napoleon), but the consolidation of fiscal powers by executives may have had an adverse fiscal effect through wasted spending (e.g., the Netherlands under William I). Column (2) excludes the anomalous Prussian deficit data from the Group 1 sample (see the preceding section and Chapter 5). The impact of the move to the centralized and absolutist regime on deficit ratios is now significant at the 10 percent level. Furthermore, the fiscal effects of the moves to the fragmented and limited regime and the centralized and limited one are similar in magnitude and significance to those shown in Column (1).

How about the controls? Enemy coalition size had a significant negative impact on deficit ratios. This finding, like that for per capita revenues, suggests that states responded to opponent strength. Facing the largest coalition (87.6 million) versus the smallest (1.2 million) increased deficit ratios by 0.52. The result for war deaths is again surprising. As for sovereign credit risk, they had a significant positive effect on deficit ratios. Mercenary status also had a significant positive effect on deficit ratios, but only for the specifications that excluded the Prussian data. Internal conflicts had a significant negative impact, increasing deficit ratios by more than 0.10. By contrast, adherence to the gold standard led to a significant decrease in deficit ratios of 0.20 or more. Although urbanization rates were associated with a significant increase in deficit ratios, this result was not robust across specifications. Finally, defaults and railway nationalizations had negligible impacts on deficit ratios.

Column (3) adds the fixed effects by country and the dummy variable for the Old Regime. The positive impact of the move to the centralized

---

[19] Since serial correlation is not a major concern here, the AR1 term is omitted from this set of regressions. Also see Dincecco (2010a).

TABLE 7.6. Regression Results for Political Regimes and Deficit Ratios

	(1)	(2)	(3)	(4)	(5)	(6)	(7)	(8)	(9)	(10)
Centralized and absolutist regimes	0.00 (0.03)	-0.05* (0.03)	-0.03 (0.03)	-0.06* (0.03)	-0.04 (0.03)	-0.07*** (0.03)	-0.03 (0.04)	-0.07* (0.04)	0.03 (0.02)	-0.00 (0.03)
Fragmented and limited regimes	-0.21*** (0.05)	-0.23*** (0.05)	-0.44*** (0.05)	-0.44*** (0.04)	-0.43*** (0.05)	-0.44*** (0.05)	-0.53*** (0.06)	-0.54*** (0.06)	-0.24*** (0.03)	-0.27*** (0.04)
Centralized and limited regimes	-0.07*** (0.03)	-0.11*** (0.03)	-0.08*** (0.03)	-0.10*** (0.03)	-0.07* (0.03)	-0.09** (0.03)	-0.03 (0.05)	-0.11** (0.05)	-0.02 (0.02)	-0.06** (0.03)
War deaths	-0.06*** (0.01)	-0.09*** (0.01)	-0.05*** (0.01)	-0.07*** (0.01)	-0.05*** (0.01)	-0.07*** (0.01)	-0.06*** (0.02)	-0.07*** (0.02)	-0.06*** (0.01)	-0.06*** (0.01)
Enemy coalition size	0.06*** (0.01)	0.06*** (0.01)	0.06*** (0.01)	0.06*** (0.01)	0.05*** (0.01)	0.06*** (0.01)	0.06*** (0.01)	0.06*** (0.01)	0.06*** (0.00)	0.05*** (0.00)
Mercenary dummy	-0.01 (0.04)	-0.31*** (0.07)	0.01 (0.04)	0.15*** (0.06)	0.01 (0.04)	0.16*** (0.06)	-0.02 (0.05)	-0.09 (0.07)	-0.01 (0.03)	-0.02 (0.03)
Default dummy	-0.05 (0.09)	-0.12 (0.08)	-0.09 (0.08)	-0.10 (0.07)	-0.09 (0.08)	-0.10 (0.07)	-0.11 (0.10)	-0.12 (0.09)	-0.04 (0.06)	-0.05 (0.06)
Internal war dummy	0.15*** (0.06)	0.11* (0.05)	0.26*** (0.05)	0.24*** (0.04)	0.26*** (0.05)	0.25*** (0.05)	0.34*** (0.07)	0.33*** (0.07)	0.26*** (0.04)	0.23*** (0.04)
Urbanization rate	0.99*** (0.13)	0.71*** (0.13)	-0.13 (0.13)	-0.16 (0.14)	-0.16 (0.14)	-0.19 (0.14)	-1.16*** (0.28)	-1.37*** (0.30)	-0.60*** (0.12)	-0.58*** (0.13)
Gold standard dummy	-0.23*** (0.03)	-0.20*** (0.03)	-0.09*** (0.03)	-0.10*** (0.03)	-0.09*** (0.03)	-0.11*** (0.03)	0.10*** (0.04)	0.12*** (0.04)	-0.01 (0.02)	-0.02 (0.02)
RR nationalization dummy	0.03 (0.10)	0.02 (0.10)	-0.04 (0.08)	-0.06 (0.09)	-0.05 (0.08)	-0.07 (0.09)			-0.01 (0.04)	-0.00 (0.04)
Old Regime dummy	0.03 (0.02)		0.03 (0.02)	0.01 (0.03)	0.03 (0.03)	0.01 (0.03)	-0.03 (0.03)	-0.00 (0.04)	-0.03 (0.02)	-0.03 (0.02)

(continued)

Country fixed effects	No	No	Yes	Yes	Yes	Yes	Yes	Yes	Yes	Yes
Groups	1	1, excluding Prussia	1	1, excluding Prussia	1	1, excluding Prussia	1	1, excluding Prussia	1 and 2	1 and 2, excluding Sweden
Years	1650–1913	1650–1913	1650–1913	1650–1913	1650–1913	1650–1913	1650–1869	1650–1869	1650–1913	1650–1913
Regimes	Standard	Standard	Standard	Standard	Five-year lag	Five-year lag	Standard	Standard	Standard	Standard
Observations	1,017	875	1,017	875	1,017	875	788	655	1,470	1,296
R-squared	0.09	0.12	0.22	0.22	0.22	0.22	0.22	0.21	0.19	0.19

Notes: The dependent variable is the yearly budget deficit-to-revenue ratio. The estimation technique is ordinary least squares with panel-corrected standard errors. Standard errors are in parentheses. Group 1: Austria, England, France, the Netherlands, Prussia, and Spain. Group 2: Belgium, Denmark, Italy, Portugal, and Sweden. For further details, see text.

*Significant at 10%; **Significant at 5%; ***Significant at 1%.

Source: See text.

and limited regime on deficit ratios remains similar as before, while the positive effect of the move to the fragmented and limited one doubles in magnitude. Column (4) excludes the anomalous Prussia deficit data from this specification, and the negative coefficient on the centralized and absolutist regime from Column (3) becomes significant at the 10 percent level. The Old Regime had a negligible impact on deficit ratios.

Column (5) lags the start years of limited regimes by five years to allow for uncertainty among investors and taxpayers over whether new constitutions would last. The effects of the moves to the fragmented and limited regime and the centralized and limited one on deficit ratios are similar to those shown in Columns (3) and (4). Furthermore, the negative coefficient on the centralized and absolutist regime gains significance at the 1 percent level once the Prussia data are excluded (see Column (6)).

Recall from Section 7.1.2 that urbanization rates proxy for income effects. This variable does not display a consistent impact on deficit ratios. To further reduce the impact of the second Industrial Revolution, Column (7) restricts the data to the period before 1870. The effect of the move to the fragmented and limited regime on deficit ratios is greater than those shown in Columns (4) and (5). Although the impact of the move to the centralized and absolutist regime on deficit ratios is positive, it is again insignificant. For the first time, the positive effect of the move to the centralized and limited regimes on deficit ratios also loses significance. Column (8) excludes the anomalous Prussian deficit data, which restores the previous significant results. Now the move from the fragmented and absolutist regime to the fragmented and limited one leads to a decrease in deficit ratios of 0.54 (significant at the 1 percent level), the move to the centralized and limited one by 0.11 (significant at the 5 percent level), and the move to the centralized and absolutist one by 0.07 (significant at the 10 percent level).

Column (9) adds Group 2 countries in the full specification that includes the standard set of controls plus the country fixed effects and the Old Regime dummy. Although the impact of the move to the fragmented and limited regime on deficit ratios remains highly significant, the effects of the moves to the centralized and absolutist regime and the centralized and limited one are insignificant. This finding, which resembles that for sovereign credit risk, reinforces the argument that political transformations had larger fiscal impacts for core states, but weaker effects for the periphery. However, recall the anomalous nature of Swedish deficit ratios, which actually increased from the fragmented and absolutist regime to the centralized and limited one (see Table 5.3). Column (10) excludes the Swedish data. This change helps restore the previous set of results. The move to the centralized and limited regime again has a significant positive effect on deficit ratios. Although the effect of the move to the centralized and absolutist regime on deficit ratios remains insignificant, it regains the negative sign.

In summary, this set of econometric tests provides further statistical proof that improvements in fiscal prudence were another channel by which political transformations enhanced public finances. The positive impact on deficit ratios is typically large and robust to the specification. By explicitly accounting for historical factors beyond political regimes, the regression results bolster those of the case studies and structural breaks tests. One caveat concerns fiscal centralization. Although the econometric analysis indicates that the positive effect of new funds generally outweighed the negative effect of the executive consolidation of fiscal powers (see Chapter 5), this finding is stronger for core Group 1 countries. Finally, the regression results highlight the impacts of external and internal conflicts, economic growth, and gold standard adherence on deficit ratios.

The econometric analysis performed in this chapter offers rigorous statistical proof that political transformations led to significant improvements in public finances, even after controlling for the effects of external and internal conflicts, economic growth, fiscal and monetary policies, country- and time-specific effects, and other elements. The first set of regressions shows that levels of sovereign credit risk under fragmented and absolutist regimes were significantly higher than those under regimes that were centralized or limited. How so? The second and third sets indicate that fragmented and absolutist regimes collected lower revenues and pursued less prudent fiscal policies than other regime types. By explicitly accounting for historical features beyond political regimes, the regression analysis serves as a statistical "seal of approval" that ratifies the results of the cases studies and structural breaks tests.

Taken in combination, the descriptive, case-study, structural breaks, and econometric evidence provides powerful support for the argument that fiscal centralization and limited government had major positive effects on public finances. The final chapter assesses the book's key findings in light of the previous literature. It also examines how political transformations changed the ways in which states spent public funds and draws historical lessons for today's emerging and advanced economies.

8

The Institutional Balance of Modern Fiscal States

The qualitative and quantitative investigation performed in this book strongly indicates that political transformations had profound fiscal effects. The main findings are now assessed in light of the previous literature. The analysis then concludes by examining how political transformations changed the ways in which states spent public funds and by drawing historical lessons for today's emerging and advanced economies.

8.1. Assessment of Findings

Chapters 2 and 3 characterized the two fundamental political transformations that European states experienced in the past. Most Old Regime states were fiscally fragmented, or weak, in 1650. Local tax free-riding reduced the ability of national governments to gather revenues. Fiscal centralization, which generally took place after the fall of the Old Regime at the end of the eighteenth century, was the first fundamental political transformation that states underwent. However, the consolidation of fiscal powers may have exacerbated problems of executive control. Since strong rulers could still use government funds as they pleased, spending constraints were necessary. The establishment of parliamentary limits, which typically occurred during the nineteenth century, was the second fundamental political transformation that states experienced. By the eve of World War I in 1913, European states could gather large tax revenues, and rulers faced parliamentary spending constraints. The end result was a set of balanced fiscal and political institutions of the sort that characterizes modern systems of public finance in wealthy countries.

Most previous studies examine either the Old Regime (before 1789), French revolutionary and Napoleonic times (1789–1815), or the post-1815 period in isolation.[1] This parcelization overlooks the critical factors that link these different eras. The present analysis took a broad periodization that spanned the mid–seventeenth to the early twentieth centuries. This new perspective allowed the fusion of arguments for fiscal centralization and parliamentary reforms into an integrated analysis of long-run institutional change, a process that culminated in the resolution of weak- and strong-state problems alike, and not just one or the other.

The use of systematic methods of analysis was another distinguishing factor of the present investigation. Most previous works focus on particular polities or periods. This approach may overemphasize institutional features that could in reality be idiosyncratic or inconsequential. The present inquiry applied the same set of analytic tools to a new database that covered nearly a dozen sample countries. It was thus able to systematically test for the impacts of fiscal centralization and limited government both within and across European states over time.

Chapter 4 examined sovereign credit, a summary statistic of a nation's fiscal health. The descriptive and case-study evidence indicated that political transformations typically led to notable improvements in yield levels on government bonds. But how? Most previous studies analyze sovereign credit risk alone. This focus tends to neglect the direct effect of institutional changes on public finances. Chapter 5 identified two key mechanisms by which political transformations reduced credit risk: increases in government revenues per head and improvements in fiscal prudence. The inquiry was thus able to pinpoint the precise ways in which fiscal centralization and limited government affected public finances.

Case studies are by and large the dominant mode of analysis in European fiscal history. The comparative investigations that do exist are typically qualitatively oriented. This approach tends to disregard the powerful statistical tools that are available to social scientists. In Chapters 6 and 7 the data were subjected to a standard battery of rigorous tests. Structural breaks tests assumed no a priori knowledge of major turning points in the fiscal series, but let the data speak for themselves. The breaks tests provided statistical proof that political transformations were key turning points that led to significant improvements in public finances.

Generally speaking, the comparative literature does not rigorously disentangle the role of political regimes from other potential factors that

---

[1] See the citations listed in Chapter 1.

could affect fiscal outcomes. To systematically control for the effects of external and internal conflicts, income growth, fiscal and monetary policies, country- and time-specific effects, and other elements, regressions that exploited the panel nature of the data were performed. The results of the econometric analysis confirmed that, even after other important factors were accounted for, political transformations led to significant improvements in sovereign credit risk, government revenues, and fiscal prudence.

In total, the book's findings powerfully support the argument that fiscal centralization and limited government had major positive impacts on public finances. The final part of the analysis examines how political transformations changed the ways in which states spent public funds. It also draws historical lessons for today's emerging and advanced economies.

8.2. The Changing Role of Government

Advanced modern economies with balanced fiscal systems are able to gather large revenues and can channel funds toward public services with positive economic benefits. By the second half of the nineteenth century, most European states had undergone both political transformations. How did the composition of public expenditures change with the establishment of fiscally centralized and politically limited regimes? To answer, this section examines the evolution of central government spending from 1816 to 1913 for three Group 1 countries: France, the Netherlands, and Spain.[2]

Military expenditures were by far the largest component of national budgets through much of the 1800s (see Chapter 7). Spending by central governments on public services such as poor relief, unemployment compensation, health, housing, and education remained low through the start of World War I. Lindert (1994, 2004, ch. 2) attributes much of the growth in social spending to major suffrage reforms, which typically took place near the start or end of World War I (1914–18) and World War II (1939–45).[3] Although most of the regimes classified here as limited were elite democracies, parliamentary power of the purse had clear implications

---

[2] Cardoso and Lains (2010a) provide an overview of nineteenth-century trends in expenditure patterns in Europe.

[3] Also see Aidt et al. (2006) and Aidt and Jensen (2008) for Europe, and Husted and Kenny (1997) and Kenny and Lott (1999) for the United States. Ticchi and Vindingi (2009) claim that there is a fundamental relationship between war and suffrage.

for the composition of public expenditures.[4] Relative to absolutist regimes, limited governments should have spent smaller shares on foreign military adventures and royal consumption and greater amounts on public goods that would most benefit society. The present focus is on two non-military public services for which data are available: education and public works (e.g., transportation infrastructure).

Figure 8.1 plots the share of French government funds spent on education and public works from 1816 to 1913.[5] This share doubled from 5 to 10 percent under the short-lived centralized and limited July regime (1830–48). Napoleon III, who was first elected president in 1848, established an authoritarian regime in 1851 (see Chapters 3, 4, and 5). True to form, the share of military spending rose, peaking at 42 percent during the Crimean War (1853–6), while the share of expenditures on education and public works fell to 6 percent. Although non-military spending made a small comeback at the start of the 1860s, it fell to its lowest point (4 percent) with the onset of the Franco-Prussian War (1870–1), the second major conflict that Napoleon III fought. In the aftermath of this war, which France lost, Napoleon III was deposed and a stable centralized and limited regime was established. There was a rapid jump in the share of expenditures on education and public works, which reached 9 percent of total spending by the start of the 1880s. This share continued to increase, though at a slower rate, through 1913.

The Dutch case is similar to the French one. Figure 8.2 plots the share of government expenditures on education and public works in the Netherlands from 1816 to 1913.[6] Like Napoleon III, the absolutist ruler William I had a penchant for warfare (also see Chapters 3, 4, and 5). Although the king spent 10 percent of government funds on education and public works over the 1820s, this share was halved to 5 percent with the start of the Belgian War of Independence (1830–3). Military expenditures peaked at 46 percent during this conflict. William I also spent relatively large sums on the monarchy itself, amounting to nearly 3 percent of total yearly expenditures through 1830. When his fiscal troubles became public in 1839, William I was soon forced to abdicate. A stable

---

[4] Also see Chapters 3, 4, and 5. Carstairs (1980) and Flora (1983) provide time lines of franchise reforms in Europe over the nineteenth and twentieth centuries.

[5] Fontvieille (1976) provides disaggregated French data for expenditures on defense, education, public works, and other categories. Also see Figure 8.1.

[6] Van Zanden (1996) provides disaggregated Dutch data for expenditures on defense, education, public works, the monarchy, and other categories from 1816 to 1850, and van Zanden and van Riel (2010) do so from 1850 to 1913. Also see Figure 8.2.

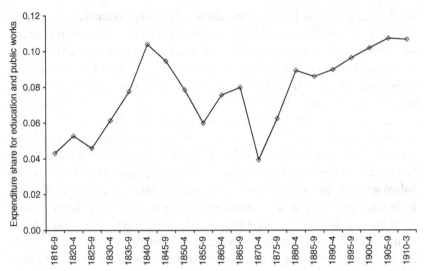

FIGURE 8.1. Expenditure share for education and public works, France, 1816–1913. Fontvieille (1976, tables 116–35) provides yearly data for total expenditures (*dépenses fonctionnelles de l'Etat*) and expenditures on education and on public works (*travaux publics*) for 1816–1913. Four-year averages for 1816–19 and 1910–13 and five-year averages for 1820–4, 1825–9, and so on through 1905–9 are computed.
Source: Fontvieille (1976).

centralized and limited regime was established in 1848, and there was a large rise in non-military spending during the liberal era of economic reforms of the 1850s and 1860s. By 1870, the share of expenditures on education and public works was nearly 20 percent of total spending. This share averaged 18 percent from 1880 to the start of World War I.

The trends in the Spanish data resemble those for France and the Netherlands. Figure 8.3 plots the share of government funds spent on education and public works in Spain from 1816 to 1913.[7] Military expenditures were very high (56 percent) at the start of the period. After peaking at more than 70 percent at the end of the 1820s, military spending fell steadily through the middle of the century. This share averaged 23 percent from the 1850s to the start of World War I. The share of expenditures on education and public works, by contrast, was very low at 3 percent or less through the end of the First Carlist War (1833–9). Major reforms in public finance, including fiscal centralization, were important markers of

---

[7] Carreras and Tafunell (2006) provide disaggregated Spanish data for expenditures on defense (Ministerio de Guerra plus Ministerio de Marina), education, public works, and other categories. Also see Figure 8.3.

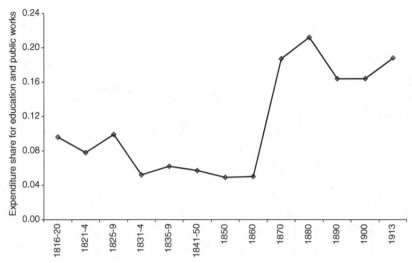

FIGURE 8.2. Expenditure share for education and public works, Netherlands, 1816–1913. Expenditure shares for 1816–50 are from van Zanden (1995, table 4), who provides four- or five-year averages for 1816–20, 1821–4, 1825–9, 1831–4, 1835–9, and 1841–50. The category for home affairs, which includes education and public works, is used. Expenditure shares for 1850–1913 are from van Zanden and van Riel (2010, table 2.3), who provide yearly shares for 1850, 1860, 1870, 1880, 1890, 1900, and 1913. The (explicit) categories for education and for infrastructure are used.

Sources: van Zanden (1996), van Zanden and van Riel (2010).

the consolidation of the liberal state in the 1840s. Non-military spending rose dramatically, from 1 percent at the start of that decade to 11 percent by the start of the 1860s, though it then fell back to 5 percent. A stable centralized and limited regime was established in the aftermath of the Third Carlist War (1872–6), and the share of expenditures on education and public works began to increase once more. By 1913, this share amounted to 15 percent of total spending.

Overall, the evolution of nineteenth-century expenditures in France, the Netherlands, and Spain fits the theoretical predictions. The establishment of centralized and limited regimes coincided with a broad shift in the composition of government expenditures away from defense and toward public services like education and public works. This result is consistent with the modern evidence, which indicates that governments in rich states play important economic roles.

One of the major types of public works that nineteenth-century governments spent funds on was transportation infrastructure, and in

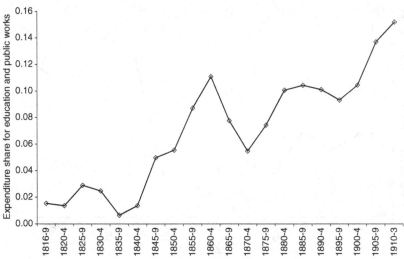

FIGURE 8.3. Expenditure share for education and public works, Spain, 1816–1913. Carreras and Tafunell (2006, table 12.8) provide yearly data, with some missing observations, for 1816–42. The category for home affairs (Ministerio de Estado), which includes education and public works, is used. Education expenditures (*gastos para instrucción pública*) are explicitly incorporated in 1842. Carreras and Tafunell (2006, table 12.13) provide yearly data for 1845 and 1849–99. The (new) category for the Ministerio de Fomento, which includes education and public works, is used. Carreras and Tafunell (2006, table 12.14) disaggregate the expenditures for the Ministerio de Fomento for 1900–13. The (explicit) categories for education (Ministerio de Educación y Ciencia) and public works (Ministerio de Obras Públicas), are used. Four-year averages for 1816–19 and 1910–13 and five-year averages for 1820–4, 1825–9, and so on through 1905–9 are computed. *Source*: Carreras and Tafunell (2006).

particular railway networks.[8] Fortunately, data for this outcome variable are readily available. Figure 8.4 plots cumulative railway kilometers per square kilometer of domestic territory from 1830 to 1913 for France, the Netherlands, and Spain. There was steady growth in railway networks in all three countries from the 1850s onward. By the start of World War I, the Netherlands was first, with 0.10 railway kilometer per square kilometer of territory, followed by France, with 0.07 railway kilometer per square kilometer of territory. Spain was relatively far behind, with 0.03 railway kilometer per square kilometer of territory. Again, the timing of transportation improvements broadly overlapped with the establishment of centralized and limited regimes.

[8] See O'Brien (1983), Bogart (2009), and Cardoso and Lains (2010a) for overviews.

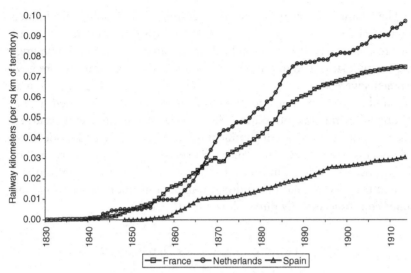

FIGURE 8.4. Cumulative railway kilometers, France, Netherlands, and Spain, 1830–1913. Mitchell (2003) provides the cumulative lengths in kilometers of open railway line for 1825–1913, which are scaled by total domestic areas in square kilometers from Dincecco (2010b).

Sources: Mitchell (2003), Dincecco (2010b).

The development of extensive railway networks is one way in which European states, equipped with new fiscal and political institutions designed to productively raise and use large tax funds, stimulated economic growth. An effective division of labor, mass production, and technological progress all required vast market access, which in turn called for efficient and expansive transportation networks.[9] We may view this argument as a nineteenth-century adaptation of Epstein's (2000) claim that early modern (i.e., pre-1800) growth was the result of reductions in jurisdictional fragmentation within polities, which created barriers to demand-side growth. For the post-1815 environment, one may argue that regular parliamentary control over budgets enabled states to guide tax funds – now large due to fiscal centralization – toward transportation infrastructure and other productive investments that further reduced transaction costs and generated greater development opportunities.

[9] In the words of Adam Smith, "The division of labor is limited by the extent of the market." This quotation is borrowed from Tortella (2000, p. 115), who provides a brief description of the links between transportation networks and Smithian growth in history. Also see O'Brien (1983). Bogart (2009), however, argues that nineteenth-century nationalizations reduced the development of railway networks.

The relationship between fiscally centralized and politically limited regimes and economic growth in European history is complex, and further research is required to establish clear causal links. Yet the findings suggest that sustained development was more likely in states where governments were able to solve two key political problems: fiscal fragmentation and absolutism. England possessed a centralized and limited regime before industrial takeoff during the middle of the eighteenth century. Likewise, most countries in continental Europe implemented modern fiscal systems before undergoing industrialization during the second half of the 1800s. The results thus point to the establishment of centralized and limited regimes as solid institutional foundations upon which European states could successfully pursue long-run growth.[10]

8.3. Historical Lessons for Development

The observation just made enables us to draw some simple lessons from history. Since diverse sets of economic, political, and social factors influence the particular nature of different eras, we must be cautious about the maps from historical to current environments. Yet the main point from the past bears upon the present, that fiscally centralized and politically limited regimes form part of a basic set of politico-economic institutions that underlie economic success over the long term. To illustrate, this section examines three modern cases that roughly correspond to the various historical regime types: North Korea (centralized and absolutist), Guatemala (fragmented and limited), and South Korea (centralized and limited).[11]

There are many recent instances of poor economic performance in states that loosely proxy for the notion of centralized and absolutist regimes. The example of North Korea under Kim Jong-Il (leader, 1994 to the present) provides concreteness.[12] North Korea is racially homogeneous,

---

[10] Similarly, Magnusson (2009) argues that nineteenth-century European states pursued large-scale investment policies that promoted industrialization.

[11] A modern proxy for the fragmented and absolutist regime could be a convex combination of the North Korean and Guatemalan cases, where class or ethnic divisions create internal fragmentation. Also see the later discussion in this chapter.

[12] The data for constraints on the executive for North Korea are taken from the Polity IV Database of Marshall and Jaggers (2008), the ethnic and GDP data from the World Factbook of the Central Intelligence Agency (2010), the military data from the World Factbook of the Central Intelligence Agency (2010), the U.S. Department of State (2010), and the Stockholm International Peace Research Institute (2010), and the personal data from Jin (2005).

and its political regime is authoritarian and highly centralized.[13] Per capita GDP was only US$1,900 in 2009, making North Korea one of the world's poorest countries. Like Napoleon III of France, William I of the Netherlands, and other powerful rulers from Europe's past, King Jong-Il spends large sums on the military. Defense expenditures constitute up to 25 percent of North Korean's GDP, and there are well over 1 million active duty military personnel. By contrast, defense spending in South Korea is less than 3 percent of GDP, and there are fewer than 700,000 active duty military personnel. Kim Jong-Il also engages in lavish spending beyond the military. According to one defector, he owns 17 personal residences. It is thus probable that parliamentary control over the budgetary process in North Korea would improve the allocation of state resources toward public services that would most benefit society.

Parliamentary power of the purse, however, is not always sufficient to ensure economic success. Weak fiscal states that are unable to raise enough in tax resources may underinvest in basic public services that promote growth (see Chapter 1). Guatemala is a rough proxy for the notion of fragmented and limited regimes.[14] Unlike North Korea, Guatemala is a constitutional democratic republic. Yet per capita GDP was only US$5,200 in 2009. Like traditional elites in Old Regime Europe, conservative oligarchs in present-day Guatemala oppose structural reforms to the tax system.[15] Between 2001 and 2003, the Supreme Court received more than 50 appeals from conservative interest groups to clarify, eliminate, or reduce taxes. As key taxes were overturned, the share of total taxes collected by the central government fell from the target of 12 percent of GDP.[16] Tax revenues, which rely heavily on indirect taxes, continue to sum to less than 10 percent of GDP.[17] By contrast, tax shares in rich countries are typically more than 20 percent of GDP, and in many cases more than 30 percent (see Figure 1.2). Underfunding contributes to the lack of public services in Guatemala such as transportation

[13] Myers (2010) provides an overview of the North Korean regime.
[14] The court and tax data for Guatemala are taken from the International Monetary Fund (2005) and the *Economist* (2006), the democracy and GDP data from the World Factbook of the Central Intelligence Agency (2010), and the road data from the World Development Indicators of the World Bank (2009).
[15] Ethnic rather than class divisions are another possible source of internal fragmentation. See Alesina et al. (2002).
[16] This target was established with the Peace Accords of 1996, which ended a long-standing guerrilla war.
[17] This trend is persistent. A 1952 study by Adler, Schlesinger, and Olson found that total taxation in Guatemala was too low and that the share of indirect taxes was too high.

infrastructure.[18] Only 35 percent of Guatemalan roads were paved in 2001, and there was only 0.13 road kilometer per square kilometer of territory, compared with 0.87 road kilometer per square kilometer of territory for (similarly sized) South Korea. It is thus likely that greater fiscal prowess by the central government in Guatemala would enable its parliament to implement new and better public services that would foster development.

South Korea is one recent example that roughly corresponds to the notion of centralized and limited regimes.[19] Unlike its counterpart in the North, it is a constitutional democratic republic, and unlike Guatemala, it is a powerful fiscal state. Furthermore, the evolution of fiscal institutions in South Korea loosely resembles the patterns that we observe in Europe's past, even if the timing of the Korean process was compressed. South Korea was exceptionally poor before the Korean War (1950–3). A highly centralized authoritarian regime was established in the aftermath of this conflict. Unlike the dictatorship in North Korea, which chose socialism, the one in South Korea chose a form of state capitalism. Large tax resources were used to promote industrialization in association with business conglomerates (*chaebol*), most notably by General Park Chung-Hee (leader, 1963–79). By 1980, when South Korea began to transform itself into a democracy, per capita GDP had reached nearly US$1,600, roughly twice that of the North. Democratic reform in South Korea roughly corresponds to the institutional shift from the centralized and absolutist regime to the centralized and limited one in European history. South Korea's fast economic development has continued to the present. It became a member of the Organisation for Economic Co-operation and Development (OECD) in 1996, and its economy is among the world's 20 largest. By 2009 per capita GPD was US$28,000. The education index for South Korea, which measures literacy and school enrollment from kindergarten to university, is also ranked among the world's top 10. Moreover, South Korea has an extensive transportation network of air, bus, ferry, highway, and rail routes. The evidence thus suggests that

---

[18] According to the *Economist* (2006), underfunding is also the key reason that the criminal justice system in Guatemala, which has long had one of the world's highest murder rates, functions so badly.

[19] The South Korean account is based on Glaeser et al. (2004) and Acemoglu (2005). Also see Wade (1990), Herbst (2000), and Kang (2002). The data for constraints on the executive are from the Polity IV Database of Marshall and Jaggers (2008), the economic and transportation data from the World Factbook of the Central Intelligence Agency (2010), and the education data from the Human Development Index of the United Nations (2010).

the centralized and limited regime in South Korea not only is able to gather large tax resources, but employs funds in productive ways that stimulate growth.

In sum, the results of the long-run historical analysis undertaken in this book lend new, rigorous credence to arguments that praise institutions like parliament that limit fiscal discretion by executives. Yet the findings also highlight what we may call the "opposite" problem. Fragmentation led to poor fiscal outcomes in Old Regime states, and parliamentary institutions did not become the principal mechanism by which to constrain rulers until after the establishment of national tax systems with uniform rates. Before then, local tax control by provincial elites restricted the fiscal authority of executives. This study indicates that fiscal centralization was just as important as limited government in developing modern systems of public finance. Indeed, it is the institutional balance between weak and strong fiscal elements that distinguishes the fiscal structures of today's advanced countries. To lay the proper institutional foundations for growth, emerging economies like Guatemala and North Korea must seek to overcome both types of fiscal problems, just as European states once did.

8.4. The Future of Entitlements

Most developed countries have long resolved the weak- and strong-state problems that many emerging economies still confront. Advanced economies, however, face daunting fiscal challenges of their own. A key fiscal problem concerns pay-as-you-go pension systems, whereby current workers pay for retired ones. The French case illustrates this phenomenon.[20] Like many advanced economies, France has an aging population and a long life expectancy. The French pension system, which accounts for 65 percent of all social spending, is very generous.[21] France's 5 million civil servants and public sector workers receive pensions based on salaries for their last six months of work, which are typically the highest of one's career. Furthermore, workers with very high seniority are often granted a final promotion, called the "tip of the hat" (*coup de chapeau*), to further increase pension income. Other perks abound. For instance, a mother of three who works in the public sector for 15 years can retire at nearly full

---

[20] This account is based on Hollinger (2010). Thanks to Jean-Laurent Rosenthal for insights on this topic.

[21] Social spending includes aid for the poor and unemployed, retirement pensions, expenditures on health and education, and housing subsidies. See Lindert (2004, p. 6).

pay in her mid-40s or early 50s. These factors all make for an untenable fiscal situation: in the absence of significant reforms, even optimistic forecasts indicate that there will be a funding shortfall of 72 to 115 billion euros by 2050.

Pension troubles are not unique to France. A 2008 report by the OECD estimates that, due to major demographic changes, most developed nations must make quick, dramatic reforms to strengthen their pay-as-you-go systems. British Prime Minister David Cameron recently proposed an austerity budget that would implement across-the-board cuts of 25 percent to reduce social spending and other government costs.[22] Similarly, U.S. Federal Reserve Chairman Ben Bernanke has argued that the overhaul of major entitlement programs, including Social Security, is vital to addressing long-term fiscal problems.[23] Pension reform has also become a priority for emerging countries in Asia, Eastern Europe, and Latin America.[24]

The pension debate not only is contentious, but will be with us for a long time. To paraphrase Lindert (2004, p. 4), although new information will not end this debate, it can enrich the level of discourse. This investigation establishes two key facts in this regard. First, modern fiscal systems strike an institutional balance that enables states to gather large tax amounts and employ funds in productive ways. Second, this outcome is the result of a deep process of institutional transformation that involved centuries of political reforms, wars, revolutions, defaults, technological change, and economic growth. The parallels between past and present are never absolute. Now the high costs of welfare, and not just warfare alone, drive policy debates. Yet the state's fundamental problem of how to best achieve fiscal objectives remains. To cope with new challenges, political regimes will have to undergo further institutional change. A proper understanding of the ways in which advanced economies first achieved modern systems of public finance allows us to chart a brighter fiscal future.

---

[22] See Burns (2010). In the words of Prime Minister Cameron (2010): "I have spent much of [my time in office] discussing ... the most urgent issue facing Britain today: our massive deficit and growing debt. How we deal with these things will affect our economy, our society – indeed our whole way of life.... And the effects of those decisions will stay with us for years, perhaps decades to come." For clarity, the words in brackets were simplified.

[23] See Bernanke (2006).

[24] See Queisser (1999).

Appendices

These data can be downloaded from the website http://sites.google.com/site/mdincecco/.

A.1. Database of Fiscal Indicators, 1650–1913

A.1.1. *Group 1*

Country	Year	Yield	Revenue	Expenditure	Population	Spread w/Consol	Rev/Pop	Def/Rev
Austria	1781		55930696	55083261				−0.02
Austria	1782		63557609	68642217				0.08
Austria	1783		54235826	60167870				0.11
Austria	1784		57559359	65067102				0.13
Austria	1785		64232908	70072264				0.09
Austria	1786		61730327	67569683				0.09
Austria	1787		61035257	65853830				0.08
Austria	1788		69869307	89946695				0.29
Austria	1789		67460021	96371458				0.43
Austria	1790		69066212	10440241				−0.85
Austria	1791		71475498	89946695				0.26
Austria	1792		69869307	73081689				0.05
Austria	1793		69066212	93159077				0.35
Austria	1794		74687880	121267419				0.62
Austria	1795		54610493	109220986				1.00
Austria	1796		51718612	123811223				1.39
Austria	1797		55678836	103515582				0.86
Austria	1798		56893081	103654518				0.82
Austria	1799		57879949	111418902				0.93
Austria	1800		58609768	113811991				0.94
Austria	1801		65188496	102929204				0.58
Austria	1802		56878349	78042385				0.37
Austria	1803		61553044	70085149				0.14
Austria	1804		64101539	67662736				0.06

Austria	1805	64639037	84261602			0.30
Austria	1806	39786692	74542883			0.87
Austria	1807	53200091	78660134			0.48
Austria	1808	54222549	63594347			0.17
Austria	1809	24690000	68092421			1.76
Austria	1810	21602704	55754038			1.58
Austria	1811	25097248	41710919			0.66
Austria	1812	32532278	35897687			0.10
Austria	1813	47895798	52121898			0.09
Austria	1814	26013375	38335500			0.47
Austria	1815	21333225	3777759			−0.82
Austria	1816	29762207	31190793			0.05
Austria	1817	29261421	29963695			0.02
Austria	1818	38721390	38721390	26451783	1.46	0.00
Austria	1819	39422880	50868232	26859193	1.47	0.29
Austria	1820	95060712	168909530	27266603	3.49	0.78
Austria	1821	99541117	144645686	27674014	3.60	0.45
Austria	1822	108232522	122248244	28072091	3.86	0.13
Austria	1823	100978797	145686966	28470168	3.55	0.44
Austria	1824	99101781	116909132	28868244	3.43	0.18
Austria	1825	95633411	111699824	29285321	3.27	0.17
Austria	1826	91886143	110870883	29702398	3.09	0.21
Austria	1827	97772722	112400137	30119475	3.25	0.15
Austria	1828	92573142	107109421	30484885	3.04	0.16
Austria	1829	93571409	111978899	30850296	3.03	0.20
Austria	1830	96760199	105975456	31215706	3.10	0.10
Austria	1831	94633934	143874355	31460283	3.01	0.52
Austria	1832	103560614	125362849	31704860	3.27	0.21

(continued)

A.1.1 (continued)

Country	Year	Yield	Revenue	Expenditure	Population	Spread w/Consol	Rev/Pop	Def/Rev
Austria	1833		102327750	124980458	31965099		3.20	0.22
Austria	1834		102131344	125700115	32122283		3.18	0.23
Austria	1835		103626326	127779830	32603625		3.18	0.23
Austria	1836		108324272	120704189	32950321		3.29	0.11
Austria	1837		110999593	117937068	33259452		3.34	0.06
Austria	1838		109252184	121562289	33678847		3.24	0.11
Austria	1839		111560329	124639816	34093563		3.27	0.12
Austria	1840		114099969	128071394	34506298		3.31	0.12
Austria	1841		112554011	127404888	34928755		3.22	0.13
Austria	1842		115887665	124618928	35351212		3.28	0.08
Austria	1843		117468080	129214888	35791607		3.28	0.10
Austria	1844		119360705	131066734	36237702		3.29	0.10
Austria	1845		120523698	133828262	36695741		3.28	0.11
Austria	1846		121306319	138523990	37153780		3.26	0.14
Austria	1847		116962346	155949795	36847771		3.17	0.33
Austria	1848		72071447	129871320	22645932		3.18	0.80
Austria	1849		67593060	170655744	22616994		2.99	1.52
Austria	1850		127140864	173608591	35780055		3.55	0.37
Austria	1851		138553238	182274481	35916403		3.86	0.32
Austria	1852		146274439	197152505	36238634		4.04	0.35
Austria	1853		165065116	222629841	36558615		4.52	0.35
Austria	1854		151766404	247075705	36896509		4.11	0.63
Austria	1855		181486614	282811295	37176795		4.88	0.56
Austria	1856		215313451	275452726	37457080		5.75	0.28
Austria	1857		237612842	278089478	37737366		6.30	0.17
Austria	1858		229408594	267279219	38000366		6.04	0.17

Austria	Year							
Austria	1859		191955976	398621223	35441160		5.42	1.08
Austria	1860		222125781	381619375	35704160		6.22	0.72
Austria	1861		219694269	360154540	35967160		6.11	0.64
Austria	1862		220421675	272083005	36230160		6.08	0.23
Austria	1863		241332826	294880839	36493160		6.61	0.22
Austria	1864		240220769	294718615	36756160		6.54	0.23
Austria	1865		311740698	430997207	37019160		8.42	0.38
Austria	1866		344421448	685924070	34941000		9.86	0.99
Austria	1867		332412403	681445426	35204000		9.44	1.05
Austria	1868		351349492	364125838	35467000		9.91	0.04
Austria	1869		347800508	406003858	35730000		9.73	0.17
Austria	1870		376179823	434162427	35925727		10.47	0.15
Austria	1871		362103121	461250405	36121455		10.02	0.27
Austria	1872		373833048	471758722	36317182		10.29	0.26
Austria	1873		394938351	511096690	36512909		10.82	0.29
Austria	1874	590	384959853	495729829	36708636	266	10.49	0.29
Austria	1875	594	382903656	635499785	36904364	274	10.38	0.66
Austria	1876	698	367277213	605196809	37100091	382	9.90	0.65
Austria	1877	737	388895541	727245173	37295818	422	10.43	0.87
Austria	1878	725	389785868	729844390	37491545	410	10.40	0.87
Austria	1879	717	395554561	750718507	37687273	409	10.50	0.90
Austria	1880	542	407805943	589218752	37883000	237	10.76	0.44
Austria	1881	506	446750244	789286189	38223300	205	11.69	0.77
Austria	1882	509	463810527	723494626	38563600	211	12.03	0.56
Austria	1883	488	473585054	706120368	38903900	191	12.17	0.49
Austria	1884	475	481969857	740435134	39244200	178	12.28	0.54
Austria	1885	465	492247494	727402827	39584500	162	12.44	0.48
Austria	1886	438	480915927	705822896	39924800	141	12.05	0.47

(continued)

A.1.1 (*continued*)

Country	Year	Yield	Revenue	Expenditure	Population	Spread w/Consol	Rev/Pop	Def/Rev
Austria	1887	455	487141263	763505733	40265100	161	12.10	0.57
Austria	1888	456	492544972	722544936	40605400	158	12.13	0.47
Austria	1889	435	546483141	964388927	40945700	146	13.35	0.76
Austria	1890	429	592354902	744464954	41286000	144	14.35	0.26
Austria	1891	426	628579916	738813636	41675100	139	15.08	0.18
Austria	1892	423	633314218	624813356	42064200	139	15.06	-0.01
Austria	1893	420	659063030	672526522	42453300	140	15.52	0.02
Austria	1894	410	660202120	998148891	42842400	137	15.41	0.51
Austria	1895	396	698787741	741570664	43231500	137	16.16	0.06
Austria	1896	391	726459634	748100136	43620600	143	16.65	0.03
Austria	1897	388	755753557	791066323	44009700	144	17.17	0.05
Austria	1898	398	776605139	798307130	44398800	150	17.48	0.03
Austria	1899	405	780552448	811414983	44787900	148	17.43	0.04
Austria	1900	415	803890676	846530278	45177000	139	17.79	0.05
Austria	1901	407	821423750	897660070	45605100	116	18.01	0.09
Austria	1902	398	843754508	885458706	46033200	106	18.33	0.05
Austria	1903	398	841656385	1227579259	46461300	113	18.12	0.46
Austria	1904	402	899724099	977448164	46889400	114	19.19	0.09
Austria	1905	408	875061279	963866255	47317500	123	18.49	0.10
Austria	1906	408	1005384609	981325151	47745600	125	21.06	-0.02
Austria	1907	416	1085611253	1131157185	48173700	119	22.54	0.04
Austria	1908	414	1144156109	1258963451	48601800	123	23.54	0.10
Austria	1909	412	1282820894	1450421081	49029900	114	26.16	0.13
Austria	1910	413	1335306403	1516135413	49458000	105	27.00	0.14
Austria	1911	413	1440363684	1505670604		98		0.05
Austria	1912	427	1491276313	1698922382		99		0.14
Austria	1913	457	1591253390	1876931932		118		0.18

England	1650	19307789		5221000	3.70	
England	1651	19307789		5228000	3.69	
England	1652	19307789		5240000	3.68	
England	1653	19307789		5234000	3.69	
England	1654	15336092		5219000	2.94	
England	1655	11364394		5246000	2.17	
England	1656	12157065		5281000	2.30	
England	1657	11639743		5284000	2.20	
England	1658	9845804		5206000	1.89	
England	1659	10004338		5136000	1.95	
England	1660	8026834		5130000	1.56	
England	1661	5671247	8729770	5141000	1.10	0.54
England	1662	11131289	13652811	5116000	2.18	0.23
England	1663	11316208	11135072	5105000	2.22	−0.02
England	1664	10347565	10595838	5129000	2.02	0.02
England	1665	18988474	21424826	5110000	3.72	0.13
England	1666	15836541	15427305	5067000	3.13	−0.03
England	1667	12438604	11395768	5059000	2.46	−0.08
England	1668	8979165	15519257	5047000	1.78	0.73
England	1669	13991508	12041653	5037000	2.78	−0.14
England	1670	7426262	12601336	5022000	1.48	0.70
England	1671	9763305	16983507	4983000	1.96	0.74
England	1672	19219104	16373585	4973000	3.86	−0.15
England	1673	16935874	22392032	4993000	3.39	0.32
England	1674	19349794	15464967	5008000	3.86	−0.20

(continued)

A.I.I (*continued*)

Country	Year	Yield	Revenue	Expenditure	Population	Spread w/Consol	Rev/Pop	Def/Rev
England	1675		13453373	10211540	5009000		2.69	−0.24
England	1676		10232251	12628427	5003000		2.05	0.23
England	1677		14199074	16928679	5021000		2.83	0.19
England	1678		16951249	21839990	5056000		3.35	0.29
England	1679		16605306	16826840	5024000		3.31	0.01
England	1680		13099741	13757488	4949000		2.65	0.05
England	1681		11039453	9526379	4930000		2.24	−0.14
England	1682		9455799	8963644	4900000		1.93	−0.05
England	1683		9893995	9773745	4886000		2.02	−0.01
England	1684		9963183	11793526	4888000		2.04	0.18
England	1685		9701804	12788638	4871000		1.99	0.32
England	1686		14468141	16563946	4865000		2.97	0.14
England	1687		16028732	17119693	4879000		3.29	0.07
England	1688		15052402		4897000		3.07	
England	1689		22071219		4917000		4.49	
England	1690		22071219		4916000		4.49	
England	1691		22071219		4931000		4.48	
England	1692		31603894	32710915	5967941		5.30	0.04
England	1693		29082348	42866289	5996725		4.85	0.47
England	1694		30781317	43066168	5984510		5.14	0.40
England	1695		31780710	47817130	5986294		5.31	0.50
England	1696		33706809	55896135	5998078		5.62	0.66
England	1697		23048944	55316067	6014863		3.83	1.40
England	1698		31994562	28842629	6035647		5.30	−0.10
England	1699		36929276	33546715	6053431		6.10	−0.09
England	1700		31065216	22891288	6066216		5.12	−0.26

England	1701	26953223	24614750	6484636	4.16	−0.09
England	1702	34819645	35827977	6523463	5.34	0.03
England	1703	39768340	37994819	6570291	6.05	−0.04
England	1704	38574074	39525196	6598118	5.85	0.02
England	1705	37844642	41999543	6612946	5.72	0.11
England	1706	37787431	47856452	6632773	5.70	0.27
England	1707	39124723	62552359	6654601	5.88	0.60
England	1708	37243933	55365309	6675428	5.58	0.49
England	1709	37229631	65505842	6690256	5.56	0.76
England	1710	37529985	69882434	6708083	5.59	0.86
England	1711	37036546	108306330	6704911	5.52	1.92
England	1712	41105631	56237767	6697738	6.14	0.37
England	1713	41334473	45496525	6709566	6.16	0.10
England	1714	38338081	44230746	6731393	5.70	0.15
England	1715	39668221	58840838	6740221	5.89	0.48
England	1716	39918517	50602548	6775048	5.89	0.27
England	1717	47692660	43087397	6813875	7.00	−0.10
England	1718	43995122	45902300	6852703	6.42	0.04
England	1719	44044324	44965264	6891530	6.39	0.02
England	1720	45646541	43329201	6876358	6.64	−0.05
England	1721	43426220	42835436	6873185	6.32	−0.01
England	1722	44992943	51050529	6881013	6.54	0.13
England	1723	43761986	41410683	6903840	6.34	−0.05
England	1724	42224906	39774647	6925668	6.10	−0.06
England	1725	43613176	40364141	6948495	6.28	−0.07
England	1726	40416816	40599929	6997323	5.78	0.00

(continued)

A.1.1 (*continued*)

Country	Year	Yield	Revenue	Expenditure	Population	Spread w/Consol	Rev/Pop	Def/Rev
England	1727		44701672	42921809	7032150		6.36	-0.04
England	1728		48982500	47260374	6981978		7.02	-0.04
England	1729		45532310	41314748	6897805		6.60	-0.09
England	1730		45635082	40408252	6835633		6.68	-0.11
England	1731		44397276	39044776	6834460		6.50	-0.12
England	1732		42354682	36304013	6860287		6.17	-0.14
England	1733		40256493	33498476	6891115		5.84	-0.17
England	1734		39763624	46420089	6948942		5.72	0.17
England	1735		41088640	42542590	6999770		5.87	0.04
England	1736		42055433	42281694	7045597		5.97	0.01
England	1737		44333732	37417757	7081425		6.26	-0.16
England	1738		41749084	34510921	7109252		5.87	-0.17
England	1739		42568674	38107008	7147080		5.96	-0.10
England	1740		42039882	45084024	7179907		5.86	0.07
England	1741		45466729	53796956	7195735		6.32	0.18
England	1742		46642730	62032796	7140562		6.53	0.33
England	1743		47507258	64956246	7141390		6.65	0.37
England	1744		47450951	67813875	7182217		6.61	0.43
England	1745		46733310	64619613	7242045		6.45	0.38
England	1746		45727976	71742212	7278872		6.28	0.57
England	1747		50640257	83318901	7306699		6.93	0.65
England	1748		52543746	87169045	7322527		7.18	0.66
England	1749		54864266	91835782	7361354		7.45	0.67
England	1750	3.00	54563839	51151316	7402182		7.37	-0.06
England	1751	2.98	51933341	43905882	7440009		6.98	-0.15
England	1752	2.88	51092857	51151316	7486106		6.83	0.00
England	1753	2.87	53395367	43659336	7538203		7.08	-0.18
England	1754	2.90	49922337	43874912	7589301		6.58	-0.12

England	1755	313	50781784	51235585	7639398	6.65	0.01
England	1756	336	51279501	73193693	7700154	6.66	0.43
England	1757	334	58300612	80475182	7738911	7.53	0.38
England	1758	325	57523417	94110801	7767667	7.41	0.64
England	1759	363	58559340	107711845	7802424	7.51	0.84
England	1760	368	66636653	130276937	7852180	8.49	0.96
England	1761	392	68575822	150103425	7907937	8.67	1.19
England	1762	397	68033048	143848289	7944693	8.56	1.11
England	1763	336	69677946	142301533	7944449	8.77	1.04
England	1764	353	74583083	102158611	7988206	9.34	0.37
England	1765	337	79742093	80267480	8049962	9.91	0.01
England	1766	336	74114935	79336735	8091719	9.16	0.07
England	1767	337	70794648	71741638	8120475	8.72	0.01
England	1768	330	72883206	64746704	8150232	8.94	−0.11
England	1769	339	79064185	71037003	8104988	9.76	−0.10
England	1770	362	80993886	78337531	8262745	9.80	−0.03
England	1771	344	78496600	71444980	8316501	9.44	−0.09
England	1772	339	78861480	78625603	8378258	9.41	0.00
England	1773	316	76794372	73228161	8442014	9.10	−0.05
England	1774	340	77882091	73383672	8502771	9.16	−0.06
England	1775	338	81659546	73487713	8585527	9.51	−0.10
England	1776	356	77720605	102882798	8662284	8.97	0.32
England	1777	383	81608105	110023569	8741040	9.34	0.35
England	1778	472	84040548	132277883	8825797	9.52	0.57
England	1779	488	87187394	147114475	8903553	9.79	0.69
England	1780	490	92144878	169221670	6954310	13.25	0.84

(continued)

A.1.1 (continued)

Country	Year	Yield	Revenue	Expenditure	Population	Spread w/Consol	Rev/Pop	Def/Rev
England	1781	519	97707121	191294062	9045066		10.80	0.96
England	1782	515	101155836	213114367	9113454		11.10	1.11
England	1783	472	92743990	175582216	9141843		10.14	0.89
England	1784	529	96695388	131717647	9224231		10.48	0.36
England	1785	501	113942827	117413874	9306619		12.24	0.03
England	1786	407	112171895	125076887	9399007		11.93	0.12
England	1787	401	121052354	110361959	9500395		12.74	−0.09
England	1788	401	123450887	117719423	9591784		12.87	−0.05
England	1789	391	122641566	117719423	9707172		12.63	−0.04
England	1790	389	125179891	125076887	9809560		12.76	0.00
England	1791	358	136157227	132434351	9921948		13.72	−0.03
England	1792	333	136900331	125076887	10027336		13.65	−0.09
England	1793	396	133398178	147149278	10125725		13.17	0.10
England	1794	445	137820014	198651526	10212113		13.50	0.44
England	1795	452	140181760	279583629	10319501		13.58	0.99
England	1796	488	142668583	279583629	10416889		13.70	0.96
England	1797	591	157042513	337883798	10541277		14.90	1.15
England	1798	593	197367075	344253415	10653665		18.53	0.74
England	1799	509	233180302	344821892	10769054		21.65	0.48
England	1800	470	230369020	459498124	10837442		21.26	0.99
England	1801	490	283416787	471321986	10911830		25.97	0.66
England	1802	423	296783681	396499768	16060000		18.48	0.34
England	1803	514	304205162	379880157	16255000		18.71	0.25
England	1804	525	357792530	448968836	16477000		21.71	0.25
England	1805	507	392177841	505980752	16716000		23.46	0.29
England	1806	489	423145924	514107790	16952000		24.96	0.21

England	1807	477	451245760	508010741	17185000	26.26	0.13
England	1808	452	468865856	536444051	17410000	26.93	0.14
England	1809	438	470204809	557420765	17639000	26.66	0.19
England	1810	441	490663497	551156257	17867000	27.46	0.12
England	1811	467	425125144	520927994	18102000	23.48	0.23
England	1812	501	397552958	539536158	18367000	21.64	0.36
England	1813	511	404737116	599010932	18645000	21.71	0.48
England	1814	452	465336658	674141569	18923000	24.59	0.45
England	1815	504	492364729	617014028	19218000	25.62	0.25
England	1816	481	491840477	506096722	19520000	25.20	0.03
England	1817	399	416197508	423373327	19814000	21.01	0.02
England	1818	385	420744081	406719278	20105000	20.93	−0.03
England	1819	427	413715596	413715596	20389000	20.29	0.00
England	1820	438	439265537	424623352	20686000	21.23	−0.03
England	1821	400	453907721	424623352	21008000	21.61	−0.06
England	1822	376	440405948	411045551	21339000	20.64	−0.07
England	1823	375	434090371	397303052	21666000	20.04	−0.08
England	1824	318	441134752	404373522	21978000	20.07	−0.08
England	1825	338	425223951	395898161	22281000	19.08	−0.07
England	1826	377	404660516	412017980	22576000	17.92	0.02
England	1827	354	404660516	412017980	22872000	17.69	0.02
England	1828	348	418879962	389484877	23190000	18.06	−0.07
England	1829	337	403229609	395898161	23505000	17.16	−0.02
England	1830	337	395804855	381145416	23815000	16.62	−0.04
England	1831	368	373551578	373551578	24135000	15.48	0.00
England	1832	357	373903819	373903819	24373000	15.34	0.00

(continued)

A.1.1 (continued)

Country	Year	Yield	Revenue	Expenditure	Population	Spread w/Consol	Rev/Pop	Def/Rev
England	1833	3.39	366572372	359240924	24602000		14.90	−0.02
England	1834	3.30	366658807	359325631	24862000		14.75	−0.02
England	1835	3.28	366658807	351992455	25134000		14.59	−0.04
England	1836	3.31	388383600	366399623	25406000		15.29	−0.06
England	1837	3.29	366658807	373991983	25651000		14.29	0.02
England	1838	3.20	373903819	381235266	25904000		14.43	0.02
England	1839	3.25	380607202	387926571	26199000		14.53	0.02
England	1840	3.33	381145416	388475136	26488000		14.39	0.02
England	1841	3.36	381325159	395991511	26751000		14.25	0.04
England	1842	3.27	373991983	403324688	27004000		13.85	0.08
England	1843	3.15	417991040	403324688	27256000		15.34	−0.04
England	1844	3.02	425324216	403324688	27525000		15.45	−0.05
England	1845	3.05	417991040	395991511	27776000		15.05	−0.05
England	1846	3.14	425324216	403324688	28002000		15.19	−0.05
England	1847	3.43	410657864	432657392	27972000		14.68	0.05
England	1848	3.50	425324216	432657392	27820000		15.29	0.02
England	1849	3.23	417991040	403324688	27669000		15.11	−0.04
England	1850	3.11	417991040	403324688	27524000		15.19	−0.04
England	1851	3.09	410657864	395991511	27393000		14.99	−0.04
England	1852	3.02	417991040	403324688	27448000		15.23	−0.04
England	1853	3.07	432657392	410657864	27542000		15.71	−0.05
England	1854	3.27	454656921	608653619	27658000		16.44	0.34
England	1855	3.31	513322330	681985381	27822000		18.45	0.33
England	1856	3.22	527988682	557321386	28011000		18.85	0.06
England	1857	3.26	491322801	498655977	28187000		17.43	0.01
England	1858	3.10	469323273	476656449	28390000		16.53	0.02

England	1859	316	513322330	513322330	28591000	17.95	0.00
England	1860	319	513322330	535321858	28778000	17.84	0.04
England	1861	328	505989154	527988682	28976000	17.46	0.04
England	1862	323	505989154	513322330	29245000	17.30	0.01
England	1863	324	498655977	498655977	29471000	16.92	0.00
England	1864	333	505989154	491322801	29681000	17.05	−0.03
England	1865	335	483989625	483989625	29925000	16.17	0.00
England	1866	342	498655977	491322801	30148000	16.54	−0.01
England	1867	323	498655977	527988682	30409000	16.40	0.06
England	1868	320	520655506	549988210	30690000	16.96	0.06
England	1869	323	542655034	491322801	30978000	17.52	−0.09
England	1870	325	498655977	498655977	31257000	15.95	0.00
England	1871	323	535321858	513322330	31556000	16.96	−0.04
England	1872	324	549858557	505869873	31874000	17.25	−0.08
England	1873	324	549858557	549858557	32177000	17.09	0.00
England	1874	324	542655034	535321858	32501000	16.70	−0.01
England	1875	320	549858557	549858557	33199000	16.56	0.00
England	1876	316	564521452	557190005	33200000	17.00	−0.01
England	1877	315	571718124	586377563	33576000	17.03	0.03
England	1878	315	593707283	608366722	33943000	17.49	0.02
England	1879	308	535321858	601320443	34304000	15.61	0.12
England	1880	305	601178689	593847242	34623000	17.36	−0.01
England	1881	300	615696441	608366722	34935000	17.62	−0.01
England	1882	298	637685600	637685600	35206000	18.11	0.00
England	1883	296	630504479	621173032	35450000	17.79	−0.01
England	1884	297	645167374	652498821	35724000	18.06	0.01

(continued)

A.1.1 *(continued)*

Country	Year	Yield	Revenue	Expenditure	Population	Spread w/Consol	Rev/Pop	Def/Rev
England	1885	302	659830269	674493164	36015000		18.32	0.02
England	1886	297	667319029	659985852	36313000		18.38	-0.01
England	1887	294	659985852	637986324	36598000		18.03	-0.03
England	1888	297	659830269	637835926	36881000		17.89	-0.03
England	1889	289	696651733	667319029	37178000		18.74	-0.04
England	1890	285	710982795	681663917	37485000		18.97	-0.04
England	1891	287	724958794	702990346	37802000		19.18	-0.03
England	1892	284	717804993	703155911	38134000		18.82	-0.02
England	1893	280	717467043	717467043	38490000		18.64	0.00
England	1894	272	747807638	740476190	38859000		19.24	-0.01
England	1895	259	799316199	769983494	39221000		20.38	-0.04
England	1896	248	820348563	805699482	39599000		20.72	-0.02
England	1897	245	848647377	819383674	39987000		21.22	-0.03
England	1898	248	863888889	863888889	40381000		21.39	0.00
England	1899	257	953088166	1055728430	40774000		23.37	0.11
England	1900	276	1025677267	1413969376	41155000		24.92	0.38
England	1901	291	1120918728	1501884570	41540000		26.98	0.34
England	1902	291	1180084846	1421965590	41893000		28.17	0.20
England	1903	284	1106005652	1135303815	42247000		26.18	0.03
England	1904	289	1120918728	1098939929	42611000		26.31	-0.02
England	1905	278	1128776809	1077468772	42981000		26.26	-0.05
England	1906	283	1135571260	1054982332	43361000		26.19	-0.07
England	1907	297	1150223793	1047656066	43737000		26.30	-0.09
England	1908	290	1111330193	1062058408	44124000		25.23	-0.05
England	1909	298	967751061	1151037247	44520000		21.74	0.19
England	1910	308	1495967932	1231973591	44916000		33.31	-0.18

England	1911	315	135663758 5	1275972648	45268000	29.97	−0.06
England	1912	328	1385970290	1349304409	45436000	30.50	−0.03
England	1913	339	1451968875	1407969818	45648000	31.81	−0.03
France	1650		13694541	51577244	18500000	0.74	2.77
France	1651		20883827	77046448	18580000	1.12	2.69
France	1652		17123299	56195956	18660000	0.92	2.28
France	1653		20305692	52145970	18740000	1.08	1.57
France	1654		25843014	78206251	18820000	1.37	2.03
France	1655		31250324	74728747	18900000	1.65	1.39
France	1656		27213113	76680452	18980000	1.43	1.82
France	1657		30822997		19060000	1.62	
France	1658		34432881		19140000	1.80	
France	1659		38042765		19220000	1.98	
France	1660		41652649		19300000	2.16	
France	1661		45262533		19380000	2.34	
France	1662		47079548	35023088	19460000	2.42	−0.26
France	1663		47779805	25014601	19540000	2.45	−0.48
France	1664		47960915	33893838	19620000	2.44	−0.29
France	1665		47536892	44536393	19700000	2.41	−0.06
France	1666		51429486	31086243	19780000	2.60	−0.40
France	1667		51362243	38768630	19860000	2.59	−0.25
France	1668		54965102	37519618	19940000	2.76	−0.32
France	1669		51390188	40995186	20020000	2.57	−0.20
France	1670		51774443	41546707	20100000	2.58	−0.20
France	1671		54025155	45076428	20200000	2.67	−0.17
France	1672		61182506	47254499	20300000	3.01	−0.23

(continued)

A.1.1 *(continued)*

Country	Year	Yield	Revenue	Expenditure	Population	Spread w/Consol	Rev/Pop	Def/Rev
France	1673		71537503	52768002	20400000		3.51	-0.26
France	1674		61004621	57640128	20500000		2.98	-0.06
France	1675		64539765	60015953	20600000		3.13	-0.07
France	1676		59353131	59154527	20700000		2.87	0.00
France	1677		63269843	62189606	20800000		3.04	-0.02
France	1678		61609217	59078782	20900000		2.95	-0.04
France	1679		58451341	68916306	21000000		2.78	0.18
France	1680		58007433	51574985	21100000		2.75	-0.11
France	1681		59848632	75797665	21150000		2.83	0.27
France	1682		62564212	107282153	21200000		2.95	0.71
France	1683		60662285	61856165	21250000		2.85	0.02
France	1684		72886425	83110350	21300000		3.42	0.14
France	1685		66799614	54086022	21350000		3.13	-0.19
France	1686		67167746	49728160	21400000		3.14	-0.26
France	1687		63034991	49489996	21450000		2.94	-0.21
France	1688		63271993	56920791	21500000		2.94	-0.10
France	1689		73523267	69698775	21550000		3.41	-0.05
France	1690		68842335	66597192	21600000		3.19	-0.03
France	1691		74548428	71124526	21440000		3.48	-0.05
France	1692		73363797	77470162	21280000		3.45	0.06
France	1693		72111179	77856493	21120000		3.41	0.08
France	1694		65261375	61740005	20960000		3.11	-0.05
France	1695		70078395	72795931	20800000		3.37	0.04
France	1696		70161108	72638746	20640000		3.40	0.04
France	1697		70653809	83243737	20480000		3.45	0.18
France	1698		54706314	94353821	20320000		2.69	0.72

France	1699	57464007	184174677	20160000	2.85	2.21
France	1700	55966340	54513391	20000000	2.80	−0.03
France	1701	58749519	70916968	19840000	2.96	0.21
France	1702	54894821	76378601	19680000	2.79	0.39
France	1703	47402049	78794259	19520000	2.43	0.66
France	1704	55176079	74957299	19360000	2.85	0.36
France	1705	55646506	91434794	19200000	2.90	0.64
France	1706	64672761	99866456	19040000	3.40	0.54
France	1707	66154365	117319978	18880000	3.50	0.77
France	1708	54995339	93151812	18720000	2.94	0.69
France	1709	53691702	101639526	18560000	2.89	0.89
France	1710	43094016	101179582	18400000	2.34	1.35
France	1711	45746624	118277752	18570000	2.46	1.59
France	1712	50451968	107690216	18740000	2.69	1.13
France	1713	51522240	94840557	18910000	2.72	0.84
France	1714	53041408	95661274	19080000	2.78	0.80
France	1715	74178496	65776964	19250000	3.85	−0.11
France	1716	74178492		19365300	3.83	
France	1717	75891200		19480600	3.90	
France	1718	53855700		19595900	2.75	
France	1719	44205067		19711200	2.24	
France	1720	31409419		19826500	1.58	
France	1721	41851764		19941800	2.10	
France	1722	62605767		20057100	3.12	
France	1723	47649214		20172400	2.36	
France	1724	41061676		20287700	2.02	

(continued)

A.1.1 (continued)

Country	Year	Yield	Revenue	Expenditure	Population	Spread w/Consol	Rev/Pop	Def/Rev
France	1725		46701470		20403000		2.29	
France	1726		68392827		20647400		3.31	
France	1727		66234194	61156452	20891800		3.17	−0.08
France	1728		62529677	61635484	21136200		2.96	−0.01
France	1729		65627419	65340000	21380600		3.07	0.00
France	1730		62497742	63423871	21625000		2.89	0.01
France	1731		65467742	63934839	21620000		3.03	−0.02
France	1732		62465806	66042581	21615000		2.89	0.06
France	1733		69268065	72238065	21610000		3.21	0.04
France	1734		82744839	87822581	21605000		3.83	0.06
France	1735		82393548	87024194	21600000		3.81	0.06
France	1736		74090323	73611290	22200000		3.34	−0.01
France	1737		63775161	63711290	22800000		2.80	0.00
France	1738		66681290	64924839	23400000		2.85	−0.03
France	1739		68980645	69172258	24000000		2.87	0.00
France	1740		67351935	67415806	24600000		2.74	0.00
France	1741		81180000	83032258	24600000		3.30	0.02
France	1742		102449032	97690645	24600000		4.16	−0.05
France	1743		87982258	93347419	24600000		3.58	0.06
France	1744		106185484	107910000	24600000		4.32	0.02
France	1745		114712258	112380968	24600000		4.66	−0.02
France	1746		106951935	107654516	24580000		4.35	0.01
France	1747		118320968	119151290	24560000		4.82	0.01
France	1748		121035484	114392903	24540000		4.93	−0.05
France	1749		119374839	119470645	24520000	182	4.87	0.00
France	1750	482	91750645	91782581	24500000		3.74	0.00

France	1751	475	74824839	85938387	24600000	177	3.04	0.15
France	1752	459	74633226	87439355	24700000	171	3.02	0.17
France	1753	457	74250000		24800000	170	2.99	
France	1754	418	74345806		24900000	128	2.99	
France	1755	470	95338065		25000000	157	3.81	
France	1756	504	116330323		25140000	168	4.63	
France	1757	510	137322581		25280000	175	5.43	
France	1758	519	157186452		25420000	194	6.18	
France	1759	542	92133871		25560000	178	3.60	
France	1760	678	91510171		25700000	310	3.56	
France	1761	687	161689355		25780000	295	6.27	
France	1762	693	131909516		25860000	296	5.10	
France	1763	595	102129677		25940000	259	3.94	
France	1764	567	84756774	103694516	26020000	214	3.26	0.22
France	1765	593	86449355	107399032	26100000	256	3.31	0.24
France	1766	630	106440968		26200000	295	4.06	
France	1767	675	96892577	97725581	26300000	339	3.68	0.01
France	1768	636	94529032	112955806	26400000	306	3.58	0.19
France	1769	714	99594000		26500000	374	3.76	
France	1770	953	106315355		26600000	591	4.00	
France	1771	1012	113036710		26200000	668	4.31	
France	1772	912	119758065		26400000	573	4.54	
France	1773	759	97339355	75527419	26600000	443	3.66	-0.22
France	1774	675	103886129	82553226	26800000	335	3.88	-0.21
France	1775	569	119528129		27000000	231	4.43	
France	1776	568	120837484		26100000	212	4.63	

(continued)

A.1.1 (continued)

Country	Year	Yield	Revenue	Expenditure	Population	Spread w/Consol	Rev/Pop	Def/Rev
France	1777	586	122181968		26462500	203	4.62	
France	1778	515	127435355		26825000	144	4.75	
France	1779	515	129888000		27187500	127	4.78	
France	1780	594	160092581	199596774	27550000	104	5.81	0.25
France	1781	597	139526129	168172258	26600000	78	5.25	0.21
France	1782	590	147554710		26862500	75	5.49	
France	1783	582	144393097		27125000	111	5.32	
France	1784	582	145019032		27387500	54	5.30	
France	1785	554	146072903	271451613	27650000	53	5.28	0.86
France	1786	550	147181065		27100000	143	5.43	
France	1787	571	149183419		27350000	169	5.45	
France	1788	602	150863226	180499355	27600000	202	5.47	0.20
France	1789	647	95231613	159741290	27850000	256	3.42	0.68
France	1790	634	36828000	144906300	28100000	244	1.31	2.93
France	1791	514	65799871	209587790	27500000	156	2.39	2.19
France	1792	549	76929387		27650000	216	2.78	
France	1793	577	31467310		27800000	181	1.13	
France	1794		45597115		27950000		1.63	
France	1795		60352020		28100000		2.15	
France	1796		75730771		28100000		2.70	
France	1797		91734247		28132500		3.26	
France	1798		151040486		28455000		5.31	
France	1799		137631888		28777500		4.78	
France	1800		133837307		29100000		4.60	
France	1801	960	152547338	177496039	28800000	470	5.30	0.16
France	1802	914	167216059	161451488	28975000	492	5.77	−0.03

	Year							
France	1803	931	189618299	204190306	29150000	417	6.50	0.08
France	1804	881	196361028	259785616	29325000	356	6.70	0.32
France	1805	843	213957228	226060167	29500000	336	7.25	0.06
France	1806	766	313513157	291342626	29500000	278	10.63	−0.07
France	1807	628	245404458	236305758	29625000	152	8.28	−0.04
France	1808	599	261971439	249552483	29750000	147	8.81	−0.05
France	1809	626	276697644	254072320	29875000	188	9.26	−0.08
France	1810	619	277957122	253529849	30000000	178	9.27	−0.09
France	1811	618	341124792	322943095	30100000	151	11.33	−0.05
France	1812	615	377197535	324885275	30150000	114	12.51	−0.14
France	1813	730	408135484	315015811	30200000	219	13.51	−0.23
France	1814	794	334756354	196799786	30250000	342	11.07	−0.41
France	1815	794	282898152	300660022	30300000	291	9.34	0.06
France	1816	853	333600217	341027909	30600000	372	10.90	0.02
France	1817	779	410137731	383979340	30762500	380	13.33	−0.06
France	1818	712	456641537	463100399	30925000	327	14.77	0.01
France	1819	725	302371620	289357013	31087500	298	9.73	−0.04
France	1820	666	303178978	292909387	31250000	228	9.70	−0.03
France	1821	588	301984088	293232331	31600000	188	9.56	−0.03
France	1822	556	306634469	306472997	31787500	179	9.65	0.00
France	1823	577	336829648	361050381	31975000	202	10.53	0.07
France	1824	497	319487604	318421892	32162500	178	9.93	0.00
France	1825	472	325623523	317130120	32350000	135	10.07	−0.03
France	1826	451	326915295	315515404	32900000	74	9.94	−0.03
France	1827	427	315612287	318744835	33000000	73	9.56	0.01
France	1828	419	332146974	330693730	33100000	72	10.03	0.00

(continued)

Country	Year	Yield	Revenue	Expenditure	Population	Spread w/Consol	Rev/Pop	Def/Rev
France	1829	376	329886372	327787242	33200000	39	9.94	-0.01
France	1830	405	329401957	353622689	33300000	68	9.89	0.07
France	1831	505	421763682	393667633	33600000	136	12.55	-0.07
France	1832	441	343417688	379135194	33700000	84	10.19	0.10
France	1833	393	375259877	366217470	33800000	54	11.10	-0.02
France	1834	389	335602465	343611453	33900000	60	9.90	0.02
France	1835	377	345000109	338121421	34000000	48	10.15	-0.02
France	1836	374	346291881	344257340	34250000	43	10.11	-0.01
France	1837	378	351039145	348455600	34412500	49	10.20	-0.01
France	1838	373	359112722	366863356	34575000	53	10.39	0.02
France	1839	373	381492679	380749909	34737500	48	10.98	0.00
France	1840	376	398511780	440494382	34900000	43	11.42	0.11
France	1841	386	445984415	460193911	35000000	50	12.74	0.03
France	1842	376	429740377	465361000	35175000	49	12.22	0.08
France	1843	370	445015585	466652773	35350000	55	12.59	0.05
France	1844	363	447243893	461162740	35525000	61	12.59	0.03
France	1845	356	449892026	480862269	35700000	52	12.60	0.07
France	1846	360	451958862	506051830	36000000	46	12.55	0.12
France	1847	388	443271693	526397245	36087500	44	12.28	0.19
France	1848	627	570963393	571932222	36175000	276	15.78	0.00
France	1849	563	462454513	531564335	36262500	240	12.75	0.15
France	1850	526	462454513	475695179	36350000	215	12.72	0.03
France	1851	528	439299493	471819862	36550000	219	12.02	0.07
France	1852	409	480216383	488612903	36662500	107	13.10	0.02
France	1853	387	492165277	499915912	36775000	80	13.38	0.02
France	1854	427	581943458	642010874	36887500	100	15.78	0.10

	Year							
France	1855	447	901980065	745675607	37000000	116	24.38	−0.17
France	1856	427	618113084	709183037	36900000	105	16.75	0.15
France	1857	441	580974628	611331279	37000000	114	15.70	0.05
France	1858	426	604226531	600351214	37100000	116	16.29	−0.01
France	1859	445	703693005	713058354	37200000	130	18.92	0.01
France	1860	436	633614353	673013411	37300000	116	16.99	0.06
France	1861	439	647823849	701109460	37400000	112	17.32	0.08
France	1862	431	703370062	714673070	37533400	108	18.74	0.02
France	1863	438	731466111	738570859	37666800	114	19.42	0.01
France	1864	454	711766582	728882566	37800200	122	18.83	0.02
France	1865	443	729528452	693358826	37933600	107	19.23	−0.05
France	1866	442	708214208	711443639	38067000	101	18.60	0.00
France	1867	435	700140631	700786517	37739667	112	18.55	0.00
France	1868	429	624894889	614560710	37412333	109	16.70	−0.02
France	1869	420	633614353	614883653	37085000	97	17.09	−0.03
France	1870	465	1009197173	1024698441	36757667	140	27.46	0.02
France	1871	555	1039876767	984007611	36430333	232	28.54	−0.05
France	1872	547	988851758	879374049	36103000	223	27.39	−0.11
France	1873	532	869265930	928138456	36303750	208	23.94	0.07
France	1874	494	842267887	898427691	36504500	170	23.07	0.07
France	1875	463	926846684	948160928	36705250	143	25.25	0.02
France	1876	436	1029219645	978840522	36906000	121	27.89	−0.05
France	1877	427	935243204	977548750	37006000	112	25.27	−0.05
France	1878	401	1107048931	1081213483	37106000	86	29.83	−0.02
France	1879	375	1127394346	1072816963	37206000	67	30.30	−0.05
France	1880	355	1140312070	1086703516	37306000	50	30.57	−0.05

(continued)

A.1.1 (*continued*)

Country	Year	Yield	Revenue	Expenditure	Population	Spread w/Consol	Rev/Pop	Def/Rev
France	1881	353	1222339616	1167762233	37406000	52	32.68	-0.04
France	1882	365	1176804639	1190691192	37510800	67	31.37	0.01
France	1883	379	1179711127	1199733599	37615600	83	31.36	0.02
France	1884	386	1113830736	1142895614	37720400	89	29.53	0.03
France	1885	373	1072494020	1119643711	37825200	71	28.35	0.04
France	1886	364	1023406669	1063774556	37930000	67	26.98	0.04
France	1887	370	1047304458	1053117434	37970600	76	27.58	0.01
France	1888	363	1055378036	1040199710	38011200	66	27.76	-0.01
France	1889	350	1056346865	1048596231	38051800	61	27.76	-0.01
France	1890	328	1089932947	1060868068	38092400	43	28.61	-0.03
France	1891	315	1086380573	1052148605	38113000	28	28.49	-0.03
France	1892	306	1088318231	1091547662	38160200	22	28.52	0.00
France	1893	306	1087026459	1114476622	38187400	27	28.47	0.03
France	1894	298	1116737224	1123841972	38214600	25	29.22	0.01
France	1895	294	1103173614	1108986589	38241800	35	28.85	0.01
France	1896	294	1109633476	1112538963	38269000	45	29.00	0.00
France	1897	290	1139343240	1138051468	38305400	45	29.74	0.00
France	1898	292	1169054005	1139343240	38341800	44	30.49	-0.03
France	1899	296	1181002900	1159042769	38378200	39	30.77	-0.02
France	1900	298	1232027909	1210067778	38414600	22	32.07	-0.02
France	1901	296	1154844509	1212974266	38451000	5	30.03	0.05
France	1902	298	1156784167	1194566510	38529800	7	30.02	0.03
France	1903	305	1184555274	1161626314	38608600	21	30.68	-0.02
France	1904	308	1207484233	1175189924	38687400	19	31.21	-0.03
France	1905	302	1216203697	1197150054	38766200	23	31.37	-0.02
France	1906	307	1239132657	1243976803	38845000	24	31.90	0.00

Country	Year							
France	1907	328	1281438202	1253019210	38914400	32.93	31	−0.02
France	1908	312	1280792316	1298554186	38983800	32.85	21	0.01
France	1909	307	1337307358	1351839797	39053200	34.24	9	0.01
France	1910	306	1380258789	1395760058	39122600	35.28	−2	0.01
France	1911	313	1514280174	1468745198	39192000	38.64	−1	−0.03
France	1912	324	1568534614	1531719101	39152600	40.06	−4	−0.02
France	1913	345	1644426241	1636352664	39113200	42.04	6	0.00
Netherlands	1720		19977281	22885834	1900000	10.51		0.15
Netherlands	1721		20639390	23337968	1900000	10.86		0.13
Netherlands	1722		19512904	22541142	1900000	10.27		0.16
Netherlands	1723		19795403	21595891	1900000	10.42		0.09
Netherlands	1724		19977857	22730023	1900000	10.51		0.14
Netherlands	1725		20350270	23357455	1900000	10.71		0.15
Netherlands	1726		20783895	23121971	1900000	10.94		0.11
Netherlands	1727		21531422	23561603	1900000	11.33		0.09
Netherlands	1728		22086869	24012653	1900000	11.62		0.09
Netherlands	1729		22063798	24352119	1900000	11.61		0.10
Netherlands	1730		22032979	24470065	1900000	11.60		0.11
Netherlands	1731		21953172	23961468	1900000	11.55		0.09
Netherlands	1732		22138735	23763684	1900000	11.65		0.07
Netherlands	1733		21371815	23248235	1900000	11.25		0.09
Netherlands	1734		21405273	22943032	1900000	11.27		0.07
Netherlands	1735		21238532	22759456	1900000	11.18		0.07
Netherlands	1736		21390457	23451864	1900000	11.26		0.10
Netherlands	1737		21579696	23636897	1900000	11.36		0.10
Netherlands	1738		21604369	22920230	1900000	11.37		0.06

(continued)

A.1.1 (continued)

Country	Year	Yield	Spread w/Consol	Population	Expenditure	Revenue	Rev/Pop	Def/Rev
Netherlands	1739			1900000	22289210	21096331	11.10	0.06
Netherlands	1740			1900000	22719418	21234507	11.18	0.07
Netherlands	1741			1900000	23711322	21421473	11.27	0.11
Netherlands	1742			1900000	27417607	21694525	11.42	0.26
Netherlands	1743			1900000	26631130	21544545	11.34	0.24
Netherlands	1744			1900000	27859346	21847941	11.50	0.28
Netherlands	1745			1900000	32465024	21106346	11.11	0.54
Netherlands	1746			1900000	32445007	23820620	12.54	0.36
Netherlands	1747			1900000	36454324	28872428	15.20	0.26
Netherlands	1748			1900000	46327231	29052044	15.29	0.59
Netherlands	1749			1900000	30896127	20811318	10.95	0.48
Netherlands	1750			1900000	32225393	24733362	13.02	0.30
Netherlands	1751			1900000	29879226	25214420	13.27	0.19
Netherlands	1752			1908000	35052085	25846699	13.55	0.36
Netherlands	1753			1912000	32705929	25821481	13.50	0.27
Netherlands	1754			1916000	27723131	25248528	13.18	0.10
Netherlands	1755			1920000	26343567	25023182	13.03	0.05
Netherlands	1756			1924000	26809340	24557572	12.76	0.09
Netherlands	1757			1928000	29068249	25255010	13.10	0.15
Netherlands	1758			1932000	26892388	25760795	13.33	0.04
Netherlands	1759			1936000	27018772	25635500	13.24	0.05
Netherlands	1760			1940000	26860787	26387503	13.60	0.02
Netherlands	1761			1944000	26756710	25530025	13.13	0.05
Netherlands	1762			1948000	26976608	26135425	13.42	0.03
Netherlands	1763			1952000	28516124	25668041	13.15	0.11
Netherlands	1764			1956000	26770055	25243298	12.91	0.06

Netherlands	1765		25285204	33382337	1960000		12.90	0.32
Netherlands	1766		25623663	25951682	1964000		13.05	0.01
Netherlands	1767		25044252	26157920	1968000		12.73	0.04
Netherlands	1768		24805779	26588452	1972000		12.58	0.07
Netherlands	1769		24382262	26758215	1976000		12.34	0.10
Netherlands	1770		25033761	28403774	1980000		12.64	0.13
Netherlands	1771		24898318	26424278	1984000		12.55	0.06
Netherlands	1772		25022261	26645911	1988000		12.59	0.06
Netherlands	1773		24865207	25795030	1992000		12.48	0.04
Netherlands	1774		25148282	26087757	1996000		12.60	0.04
Netherlands	1775		25202809	26618466	2000000		12.60	0.06
Netherlands	1776		24361617	27426882	2004000		12.16	0.13
Netherlands	1777		24115359	30003061	2008000		12.01	0.24
Netherlands	1778		24679234	27516811	2012000		12.27	0.11
Netherlands	1779		24487626	26004614	2016000		12.15	0.06
Netherlands	1780	241	24933000	26996642	2020000	−249	12.34	0.08
Netherlands	1781	257	24615385	35187064	2024000	−262	12.16	0.43
Netherlands	1782	260	24722048	39188465	2028000	−256	12.19	0.59
Netherlands	1783	263	25153653	33519705	2032000	−208	12.38	0.33
Netherlands	1784	272	25008485	32896915	2036000	−256	12.28	0.32
Netherlands	1785	280	24445035	35714336	2040000	−221	11.98	0.46
Netherlands	1786	277	24583449	30097154	2044000	−131	12.03	0.22
Netherlands	1787	299	24611847	31175130	2048000	−102	12.02	0.27
Netherlands	1788	302	24032027	36763506	2052000	−98	11.71	0.53
Netherlands	1789	322	24782182	39497507	2056000	−69	12.05	0.59
Netherlands	1790	327	23875227	42272469	2060000	−62	11.59	0.77

(continued)

A.1.1 (continued)

Country	Year	Yield	Revenue	Expenditure	Population	Spread w/Consol	Rev/Pop	Def/Rev
Netherlands	1791	336	24736223	32248144	2064000	-22	11.98	0.30
Netherlands	1792	314	25476112	32867083	2068000	-19	12.32	0.29
Netherlands	1793	384	30130393	38970571	2072000	-13	14.54	0.29
Netherlands	1794	379	29760031	46602480	2076000	-66	14.34	0.57
Netherlands	1795	433	16144935		2080000	-20	7.76	
Netherlands	1796	447			2084000	-41		
Netherlands	1797	539			2088000	-52		
Netherlands	1798	612			2092000	19		
Netherlands	1799	592			2096000	83		
Netherlands	1800	598			2100000	127		
Netherlands	1801	586			2118000	96		
Netherlands	1802	574			2136000	152		
Netherlands	1803	634	21775693	45728956	2154000	120	10.11	1.10
Netherlands	1804	748	21767438	45338464	2172000	222	10.02	1.08
Netherlands	1805	730	21083792	43492852	2190000	223	9.63	1.06
Netherlands	1806	741	26646515	51171294	2208000	252	12.07	0.92
Netherlands	1807	703	29357964	49202940	2226000	226	13.19	0.68
Netherlands	1808	725	27028022	49141859	2244000	273	12.04	0.82
Netherlands	1809	760	28972936	41989762	2262000	322	12.81	0.45
Netherlands	1810	1393	26623177	46030727	2280000	952	11.68	0.73
Netherlands	1811		26530730	43085661	2298000		11.55	0.62
Netherlands	1812		26811991	40798201	2316000		11.58	0.52
Netherlands	1813		27098137	38528734	2334000		11.61	0.42
Netherlands	1814	666	27533703	36466860	2352000	214	11.71	0.32
Netherlands	1815	609	24715198	56610147	2100000	105	11.77	1.29
Netherlands	1816	574	24564915	38227947	2047000	93	12.00	0.56

Netherlands	1817	576	24892689	37176096	2090538	177	11.91	0.49
Netherlands	1818	580	25173637	35908758	2134077	195	11.80	0.43
Netherlands	1819	570	25396786	33111552	2177615	143	11.66	0.30
Netherlands	1820	552	25139766	37998578	2221154	114	11.32	0.51
Netherlands	1821	524	22613274	35040495	2264692	124	9.99	0.55
Netherlands	1822	525	23427897	38154003	2308231	149	10.15	0.63
Netherlands	1823	520	23668135	44826935	2351769	145	10.06	0.89
Netherlands	1824	440	24094905	46997966	2395308	122	10.06	0.95
Netherlands	1825	430	24175421	48253115	2438846	92	9.91	1.00
Netherlands	1826	490	22999416	51961643	2482385	113	9.27	1.26
Netherlands	1827	476	23271439	53933545	2525923	122	9.21	1.32
Netherlands	1828	437	23351698	51203464	2569462	89	9.09	1.19
Netherlands	1829	394	23405748	48565415	2613000	57	8.96	1.07
Netherlands	1830	622	23568942	44720557	2637800	285	8.94	0.90
Netherlands	1831	600	28381348	61828613	2662600	232	10.66	1.18
Netherlands	1832	590	28764609	61150706	2687400	233	10.70	1.13
Netherlands	1833	517	29203405	59737011	2712200	178	10.77	1.05
Netherlands	1834	485	29431917	53600771	2737000	155	10.75	0.82
Netherlands	1835	452	29852376	46458594	2761800	123	10.81	0.56
Netherlands	1836	453	30336560	48392588	2786600	122	10.89	0.60
Netherlands	1837	471	30459332	57317259	2811400	142	10.83	0.88
Netherlands	1838	464	30361848	61636376	2836200	144	10.71	1.03
Netherlands	1839	465	30345046	58744116	2861000	140	10.61	0.94
Netherlands	1840	478	30520998	54069262	2880600	145	10.60	0.77
Netherlands	1841	484	31146802	54531275	2900200	148	10.74	0.75
Netherlands	1842	478	31843375	54877196	2919800	151	10.91	0.72

(continued)

A.1.1 (*continued*)

Country	Year	Yield	Revenue	Expenditure	Population	Spread w/Consol	Rev/Pop	Def/Rev
Netherlands	1843	459	32547004	53171449	2939400	144	11.07	0.63
Netherlands	1844	413	33376796	53495485	2959000	110	11.28	0.60
Netherlands	1845	403	33899742	54057981	2978600	99	11.38	0.59
Netherlands	1846	418	33977078	52725144	2998200	104	11.33	0.55
Netherlands	1847	441	34226691	55312777	3017800	97	11.34	0.62
Netherlands	1848	560	33851778	55332271	3037400	210	11.14	0.63
Netherlands	1849	487	33720816	51868746	3057000	164	11.03	0.54
Netherlands	1850	440	35076276	43260740	3082200	129	11.38	0.23
Netherlands	1851	424	35562987	45982318	3107400	115	11.44	0.29
Netherlands	1852	399	35360898	42805298	3132600	97	11.29	0.21
Netherlands	1853	388	36193674	43120394	3157800	81	11.46	0.19
Netherlands	1854	421	37882136	51582842	3183000	94	11.90	0.36
Netherlands	1855	394	38115709	52987084	3208200	62	11.88	0.39
Netherlands	1856	388	35543029	57679477	3233400	66	10.99	0.62
Netherlands	1857	389	36214012	58067296	3258600	62	11.11	0.60
Netherlands	1858	379	37681815	53005753	3283800	69	11.48	0.41
Netherlands	1859	394	37229612	61586612	3309000	79	11.25	0.65
Netherlands	1860	384	37839133	53668504	3336100	65	11.34	0.42
Netherlands	1861	390	38030162	60349503	3363200	63	11.31	0.59
Netherlands	1862	386	38901229	57912635	3390300	63	11.47	0.49
Netherlands	1863	385	39573610	62249917	3417400	61	11.58	0.57
Netherlands	1864	395	40745198	62998345	3444500	63	11.83	0.55
Netherlands	1865	401	40546694	61942873	3471600	66	11.68	0.53
Netherlands	1866	432	43146573	66033017	3498700	91	12.33	0.53
Netherlands	1867	457	44913261	69833883	3525800	134	12.74	0.55
Netherlands	1868	445	44124044	59660680	3552900	125	12.42	0.35

Netherlands	1869	449	45630565	58240633	3580000	126	12.75	0.28
Netherlands	1870	460	46575172	61572378	3623300	136	12.85	0.32
Netherlands	1871	433	48483342	58677275	3666600	110	13.22	0.21
Netherlands	1872	466	50610411	67213095	3709900	142	13.64	0.33
Netherlands	1873	435	52316707	66411443	3753200	111	13.94	0.27
Netherlands	1874	401	55186611	61573376	3796500	77	14.54	0.12
Netherlands	1875	395	56269053	73551690	3839800	75	14.65	0.31
Netherlands	1876	401	58608059	68894994	3883100	85	15.09	0.18
Netherlands	1877	394	57984106	72144435	3926400	79	14.77	0.24
Netherlands	1878	397	58465286	70676005	3969700	82	14.73	0.21
Netherlands	1879	390	59683313	70097442	4013000	82	14.87	0.17
Netherlands	1880	384	62728380	68848965	4062800	79	15.44	0.10
Netherlands	1881	372	64535769	75190259	4112600	72	15.69	0.17
Netherlands	1882	379	63926941	79086758	4162400	81	15.36	0.24
Netherlands	1883	387	63318113	83774734	4212200	91	15.03	0.32
Netherlands	1884	379	63318113	81126332	4262000	81	14.86	0.28
Netherlands	1885	376	65144597	74337900	4311800	74	15.11	0.14
Netherlands	1886	343	66362253	75433790	4361600	46	15.22	0.14
Netherlands	1887	346	66971081	74581431	4411400	52	15.18	0.11
Netherlands	1888	334	68188737	77077626	4461200	36	15.28	0.13
Netherlands	1889	320	69406393	75525114	4511000	31	15.39	0.09
Netherlands	1890	312	69406393	76742770	4570300	28	15.19	0.11
Netherlands	1891	322	71841705	79208524	4629600	35	15.52	0.11
Netherlands	1892	320	73059361	80091324	4688900	35	15.58	0.10
Netherlands	1893	306	70015221	82130898	4748200	26	14.75	0.17
Netherlands	1894	282	71841705	80000000	4807500	10	14.94	0.11

(continued)

A.1.1 (continued)

Country	Year	Yield	Revenue	Expenditure	Population	Spread w/Consol	Rev/Pop	Def/Rev
Netherlands	1895	270	73668189	81187215	4866800	11	15.14	0.10
Netherlands	1896	278	74051593	80698027	4926100	29	15.03	0.09
Netherlands	1897	287	74658574	84036419	4985400	42	14.98	0.13
Netherlands	1898	293	75872534	91198786	5044700	45	15.04	0.20
Netherlands	1899	304	79514416	90773900	5104000	47	15.58	0.14
Netherlands	1900	324	83763278	93566009	5179400	48	16.17	0.12
Netherlands	1901	321	72376944	92599914	5254800	30	13.77	0.28
Netherlands	1902	310	76103501	99025875	5330200	19	14.28	0.30
Netherlands	1903	320	77929985	99512938	5405600	36	14.42	0.28
Netherlands	1904	321	79147641	106605784	5481000	33	14.44	0.35
Netherlands	1905	321	80365297	105814307	5556400	43	14.46	0.32
Netherlands	1906	326	84627093	108249619	5631800	43	15.03	0.28
Netherlands	1907	342	83922208	110740826	5707200	45	14.70	0.32
Netherlands	1908	337	84242424	117515152	5782600	47	14.57	0.39
Netherlands	1909	329	87878788	119575758	5858000	31	15.00	0.36
Netherlands	1910	340	91515152	123575758	5949545	32	15.38	0.35
Netherlands	1911	359	93333333	126303030	6041091	44	15.45	0.35
Netherlands	1912	379	95757576	131939394	6132636	51	15.61	0.38
Netherlands	1913	388	100606061	144666667	6224182	49	16.16	0.44
Prussia	1688		1106662	1250441	1214111		0.91	0.13
Prussia	1689		1128661	1831874	1235695		0.91	0.62
Prussia	1690		1301659	1999121	1257662		1.03	0.54
Prussia	1691		1665943	2951140	1280020		1.30	0.77
Prussia	1692		1363949	2509459	1302775		1.05	0.84
Prussia	1693		2982989	5107443	1325934		2.25	0.71
Prussia	1694		2473161	4240888	1349506		1.83	0.71

Prussia	1695	2386606	4099170	1373496	1.74	0.72
Prussia	1696	2414777	4539832	1397913	1.73	0.88
Prussia	1697	2595821	4765989	1422764	1.82	0.84
Prussia	1698	3283096	4264235	1448057	2.27	0.30
Prussia	1699	2888561	4568878	1473799	1.96	0.58
Prussia	1700	3297987	3707930	1499999	2.20	0.12
Prussia	1701	3155588	3722588	1510826	2.09	0.18
Prussia	1702	3432254	3904200	1521731	2.26	0.14
Prussia	1703	3471636	4308133	1532715	2.27	0.24
Prussia	1704	4004260	4914423	1543778	2.59	0.23
Prussia	1705	3952068	5139913	1554921	2.54	0.30
Prussia	1706	4193280	5681522	1566144	2.68	0.35
Prussia	1707	3941004	5498431	1577449	2.50	0.40
Prussia	1708	4205240	5619218	1588835	2.65	0.34
Prussia	1709	3872381	5897468	1600303	2.42	0.52
Prussia	1710	3662090	6075423	1611854	2.27	0.66
Prussia	1711	4050211	6385091	1623488	2.49	0.58
Prussia	1712	2891346	4417667	1635207	1.77	0.53
Prussia	1713	2462404	3116704	1647010	1.50	0.27
Prussia	1714	7281287	6439180	1658898	4.39	-0.12
Prussia	1715	7804747	6061120	1670872	4.67	-0.22
Prussia	1716	7901385	6235428	1682932	4.70	-0.21
Prussia	1717	8673225	7504068	1695080	5.12	-0.13
Prussia	1718	8556377	7950639	1707315	5.01	-0.07
Prussia	1719	9001158	8140786	1719638	5.23	-0.10
Prussia	1720	10153951	8284284	1732050	5.86	-0.18

(continued)

A.1.1 (*continued*)

Country	Year	Yield	Revenue	Expenditure	Population	Spread w/Consol	Rev/Pop	Def/Rev
Prussia	1721		8989599	8577196	1744552		5.15	-0.05
Prussia	1722		9242054	8036938	1757145		5.26	-0.13
Prussia	1723		10581749	9425619	1769827		5.98	-0.11
Prussia	1724		10091549	9190971	1782602		5.66	-0.09
Prussia	1725		10379885	9378785	1795469		5.78	-0.10
Prussia	1726		10474618	9588389	1808429		5.79	-0.08
Prussia	1727		11286343	11079788	1821482		6.20	-0.02
Prussia	1728		10072407	9111295	1834629		5.49	-0.10
Prussia	1729		10071332	9466685	1847872		5.45	-0.06
Prussia	1730		10480046	9624656	1861210		5.63	-0.08
Prussia	1731		10537373	9106786	1874644		5.62	-0.14
Prussia	1732		10880328	9536401	1888175		5.76	-0.12
Prussia	1733		10747533	9988883	1901804		5.65	-0.07
Prussia	1734		10908812	9945551	1915531		5.69	-0.09
Prussia	1735		10994583	9997380	1929357		5.70	-0.09
Prussia	1736		11281493	10001193	1943283		5.81	-0.11
Prussia	1737		11062970	10329751	1957310		5.65	-0.07
Prussia	1738		11535004	10371087	1971438		5.85	-0.10
Prussia	1739		11326643	10076126	1985667		5.70	-0.11
Prussia	1740		11491289	10094953	2000000		5.75	-0.12
Prussia	1741		11871166	10601508	3500000		3.39	-0.11
Prussia	1742		13001010	12276255	3526933		3.69	-0.06
Prussia	1743		12254263	15270712	3554073		3.45	0.25
Prussia	1744		17093711	15587340	3581423		4.77	-0.09
Prussia	1745		17812066	15794165	3608983		4.94	-0.11
Prussia	1746		17304592	15208350	3636755		4.76	-0.12

Prussia	1747	17264517	14988990	3664741	4.71	−0.13
Prussia	1748	17283793	15254031	3692943	4.68	−0.12
Prussia	1749	17303177	15258579	3721361	4.65	−0.12
Prussia	1750	16949352	14754133	3749998	4.52	−0.13
Prussia	1751	17649106	15381475	3761540	4.69	−0.13
Prussia	1752	17645254	15309773	3773118	4.68	−0.13
Prussia	1753	13314197	11563124	3784732	3.52	−0.13
Prussia	1754	13435334	11586586	3796381	3.54	−0.14
Prussia	1755	13437793	11708858	3808067	3.53	−0.13
Prussia	1756	13339218	11644861	3819788	3.49	−0.13
Prussia	1757	13848868	12104260	3831546	3.61	−0.13
Prussia	1758	22604094	18559107	3843339	5.88	−0.18
Prussia	1759	20804010	16424192	3855169	5.40	−0.21
Prussia	1760	18887690	15592284	3867035	4.88	−0.17
Prussia	1761	19330069	14303995	3878939	4.98	−0.26
Prussia	1762	22219465	15503886	3890878	5.71	−0.30
Prussia	1763	17439387	29749763	3902854	4.47	0.71
Prussia	1764	21573721	19622180	3914867	5.51	−0.09
Prussia	1765	14773560	12469927	3926917	3.76	−0.16
Prussia	1766	15491533	12542606	3939004	3.93	−0.19
Prussia	1767	15456246	12545904	3951129	3.91	−0.19
Prussia	1768	14689537	12371039	3963290	3.71	−0.16
Prussia	1769	16685185	12331361	3975489	4.20	−0.26
Prussia	1770	17303381	12537387	3987726	4.34	−0.28
Prussia	1771	17431194	12620385	4000000	4.36	−0.28
Prussia	1772	17098841	12402003	4337887	3.94	−0.27

(continued)

A.1.1 (continued)

Country	Year	Yield	Revenue	Expenditure	Population	Spread w/Consol	Rev/Pop	Def/Rev
Prussia	1773		17253914	12479258	4704315		3.67	−0.28
Prussia	1774		18697630	13514054	5101696		3.66	−0.28
Prussia	1775		16195984	14007567	5532645		2.93	−0.14
Prussia	1776		16248651	14050551	5999997		2.71	−0.14
Prussia	1777		16281663	14094965	6058083		2.69	−0.13
Prussia	1778		16279751	14092140	6116730		2.66	−0.13
Prussia	1779		16315427	14129580	6175946		2.64	−0.13
Prussia	1780		16292081	14162646	6235736		2.61	−0.13
Prussia	1781		16486596	14298291	6296104		2.62	−0.13
Prussia	1782		22464692	18816637	6357057		3.53	−0.16
Prussia	1783		22156160	18506671	6418600		3.45	−0.16
Prussia	1784		22187560	19011691	6480739		3.42	−0.14
Prussia	1785		22669433	19081226	6543479		3.46	−0.16
Prussia	1786		23106949	19558291	6606826		3.50	−0.15
Prussia	1787		22645562	19271690	6670787		3.39	−0.15
Prussia	1788		20981902	16556106	6735368		3.12	−0.21
Prussia	1789		20629173	19015705	6800573		3.03	−0.08
Prussia	1790		19675259	19611662	6866408		2.87	0.00
Prussia	1791		20589124	18723460	6932882		2.97	−0.09
Prussia	1792		20470236	17377464	6999999		2.92	−0.15
Prussia	1793		20926925	19325571	7348155		2.85	−0.08
Prussia	1794		21604236	17890957	7713625		2.80	−0.17
Prussia	1795		20778674	19886266	8097271		2.57	−0.04
Prussia	1796		19526438	17561899	8500001		2.30	−0.10
Prussia	1797		21147563	17072852	8622337		2.45	−0.19
Prussia	1798		20252948	19651007	8746434		2.32	−0.03

Prussia	1799		20554757	18424979	8872316		2.32	−0.10
Prussia	1800		20916044	18666285	9000010		2.32	−0.11
Prussia	1801		21251159	18599902	9113066		2.33	−0.12
Prussia	1802		21933305	18110020	9227541		2.38	−0.17
Prussia	1803		21106940	18394045	9343455		2.26	−0.13
Prussia	1804		20339428	17108149	9460825		2.15	−0.16
Prussia	1805		20326904	17499080	9579669		2.12	−0.14
Prussia	1806		16413396	14296362	9700006		1.69	−0.13
Prussia	1807		14543259		4899999		2.97	
Prussia	1808		13606782		4916526		2.77	
Prussia	1809		11184295		4933109		2.27	
Prussia	1810		7213886		4949747		1.46	
Prussia	1811		16895120		4966441		3.40	
Prussia	1812		18763031		4983193		3.77	
Prussia	1813		24679715		5000000		4.94	
Prussia	1814		18804805		6372052		2.95	
Prussia	1815	506	12737883		8120609	3	1.57	
Prussia	1816	513	14214883		10348991	32	1.37	
Prussia	1817	546	14533104		10528851	147	1.38	
Prussia	1818	586	19654666		10711838	201	1.83	
Prussia	1819	579	21251894		10897980	152	1.95	
Prussia	1820	572	54386082		11087382	134	4.91	
Prussia	1821	557	55686715	55686715	11280075	157	4.94	0.00
Prussia	1822	559	55868296		11476118	183	4.87	
Prussia	1823	596	55417001		11675568	222	4.75	
Prussia	1824	515	55771918		11878484	196	4.70	

(continued)

A.1.1 (continued)

Country	Year	Yield	Revenue	Expenditure	Population	Spread w/Consol	Rev/Pop	Def/Rev
Prussia	1825	505	55220711		12084898	167	4.57	
Prussia	1826	493	54919122		12294928	116	4.47	
Prussia	1827	454	55786332		12508609	100	4.46	
Prussia	1828	441	55547775		12726002	93	4.36	
Prussia	1829	412	55795851	55795851	12853429	75	4.34	0.00
Prussia	1830	409	56330399		12982131	72	4.34	
Prussia	1831	441	56901915		13112153	73	4.34	
Prussia	1832	427	58058723		13243446	70	4.38	
Prussia	1833	413	58716129		13376054	74	4.39	
Prussia	1834	403	59529690		13509989	73	4.41	
Prussia	1835	396	59510187		13704052	68	4.34	
Prussia	1836	394	59565976		13900903	63	4.29	
Prussia	1837	391	59808131		14100581	62	4.24	
Prussia	1838	390	60161342	94760925	14303127	70	4.21	0.58
Prussia	1839	386	60626975		14508583	61	4.18	
Prussia	1840	386	61633250		14716990	53	4.19	
Prussia	1841	384	62537842	62537842	14928391	48	4.19	0.00
Prussia	1842	383	65055327		15117083	56	4.30	
Prussia	1843	384	65710607		15308196	69	4.29	
Prussia	1844	345	66980859		15501688	43	4.32	
Prussia	1845	352	68719893		15704966	47	4.38	
Prussia	1846	366	70245476		15910946	52	4.41	
Prussia	1847	376	70105529	70105529	16119590	33	4.35	0.00
Prussia	1848	460	74740820		16250922	110	4.60	
Prussia	1849	413	78819982	90094367	16383323	90	4.81	0.14
Prussia	1850	410	84423162	84086670	16516803	99	5.11	0.00

Prussia	1851	399	84166037		16651371	90	5.05	
Prussia	1852	376	90657119		16787035	74	5.40	−0.01
Prussia	1853	402	102934626	102306829	16923805	95	6.08	
Prussia	1854	444	93661480		17054422	117	5.49	
Prussia	1855	417	102706266	98500380	17186008	86	5.98	−0.04
Prussia	1856	424	122903640	135041092	17319685	102	7.10	0.10
Prussia	1857	430	128113775		17454403	104	7.34	
Prussia	1858	423	134814461		17590169	113	7.66	
Prussia	1859	442	140299631		17726990	126	7.91	
Prussia	1860	424	143044573	136757396	17972976	105	7.96	−0.04
Prussia	1861	407	147407486		18222334	79	8.09	
Prussia	1862	400	146652504		18475194	77	7.94	
Prussia	1863	410	162189211		18736178	86	8.66	
Prussia	1864	419	164452505		19000805	86	8.66	
Prussia	1865	410	165681589		19269214	75	8.60	
Prussia	1866	462	179361141	196417227	21620276	120	8.30	0.10
Prussia	1867	442	183571053	166950416	23971337	119	7.66	−0.09
Prussia	1868	452	170518913	164026139	24170368	132	7.05	−0.04
Prussia	1869	454	175052172		24369399	131	7.18	
Prussia	1870	461	178904323	172526000	24568430	136	7.28	−0.04
Prussia	1871	444	199199968		24783861	120	8.04	
Prussia	1872	426	146133076		24999291	101	5.85	
Prussia	1873	430	155849587		25214722	106	6.18	
Prussia	1874	424	171154599	146145978	25430152	99	6.73	−0.15
Prussia	1875	425	163653344	144610505	25742404	105	6.36	−0.12
Prussia	1876	422	173742921		26049745	106	6.67	

(continued)

A.1.1 (continued)

Country	Year	Yield	Revenue	Expenditure	Population	Spread w/Consol	Rev/Pop	Def/Rev
Prussia	1877	423	189412551		26357087	108	7.19	
Prussia	1878	425	202469712		26664428	110	7.59	
Prussia	1879	418	209637010		26971770	110	7.77	
Prussia	1880	405	214950067	204524875	27279111	100	7.88	−0.05
Prussia	1881	397	238001268		27486983	97	8.66	
Prussia	1882	398	264258929		27694855	100	9.54	
Prussia	1883	396	286425426		27902726	99	10.27	
Prussia	1884	391	311083286		28110598	94	11.07	
Prussia	1885	387	336260947	325498374	28318470	85	11.87	−0.03
Prussia	1886	381	350929940		28645832	84	12.25	
Prussia	1887	379	365279711		28973194	85	12.61	
Prussia	1888	375	380975609		29300557	77	13.00	
Prussia	1889	375	394875859		29627919	86	13.33	
Prussia	1890	378	409027332	388238923	29955281	93	13.65	−0.05
Prussia	1891	380	435232656		30335249	93	14.35	
Prussia	1892	376	461733264		30715218	92	15.03	
Prussia	1893	375	486378660		31095186	96	15.64	
Prussia	1894	376	513787443		31475155	104	16.32	
Prussia	1895	381	539826996		31855123	122	16.95	
Prussia	1896	380	565807118		32378600	131	17.47	
Prussia	1897	386	591494258		32902077	141	17.98	
Prussia	1898	356	613574124		33425555	108	18.36	
Prussia	1899	341	641060752		33949032	84	18.88	
Prussia	1900	346	666529490	621724418	34472509	70	19.34	−0.07
Prussia	1901	337	682287998		35036672	46	19.47	
Prussia	1902	328	694080108		35600835	37	19.50	

Prussia	1903	331	707168013		36164998	46	19.55	
Prussia	1904	335	721539480		36729161	46	19.64	
Prussia	1905	336	731925645	678339784	37293324	58	19.63	−0.07
Prussia	1906	345	794811187		37867703	62	20.99	
Prussia	1907	360	858846293		38442082	63	22.34	
Prussia	1908	362	928958210		39016461	71	23.81	
Prussia	1909	352	994429579		39590840	54	25.12	
Prussia	1910	358	1059474565	1004172762	40165219	50	26.38	−0.05
Prussia	1911	361	1116609467		40709991	46	27.43	
Prussia	1912	377	1171084676		41254763	49	28.39	
Prussia	1913	395	1227707892		41799535	57	29.37	
Spain	1703		2458176		7517647		0.33	
Spain	1704		2681107		7523529		0.36	
Spain	1705		2904039		7529412		0.39	
Spain	1706		3126971		7535294		0.41	
Spain	1707		3349903		7541176		0.44	
Spain	1708		3572834		7547059		0.47	
Spain	1709		3795766		7552941		0.50	
Spain	1710		4018698		7558824		0.53	
Spain	1711		3976529		7564706		0.53	
Spain	1712		4185527		7570588		0.55	
Spain	1713		4320649		7576471		0.57	
Spain	1714		4300196		7582353		0.57	
Spain	1715		4448973		7588235		0.59	
Spain	1716		4490667		7594118		0.59	
Spain	1717		4387372		7600000		0.58	

(continued)

A.I.I (*continued*)

Country	Year	Yield	Revenue	Expenditure	Population	Spread w/Consol	Rev/Pop	Def/Rev
Spain	1718		4561941		7651515		0.60	
Spain	1719		4794566		7703030		0.62	
Spain	1720		4915983		7754545		0.63	
Spain	1721		5022365		7806061		0.64	
Spain	1722		5023094		7857576		0.64	
Spain	1723		4958577		7909091		0.63	
Spain	1724		4903874		7960606		0.62	
Spain	1725		5076259		8012121		0.63	
Spain	1726		5725123		8063636		0.71	
Spain	1727		5891364		8115152		0.73	
Spain	1728		5873726		8166667		0.72	
Spain	1729		6008685		8218182		0.73	
Spain	1730		6198205		8269697		0.75	
Spain	1731		6408930		8321212		0.77	
Spain	1732		6400533		8372727		0.76	
Spain	1733		6521543		8424242		0.77	
Spain	1734		6909345		8475758		0.82	
Spain	1735		6967212		8527273		0.82	
Spain	1736		6914096		8578788		0.81	
Spain	1737		6976897		8630303		0.81	
Spain	1738		7270431		8681818		0.84	
Spain	1739		7375739		8733333		0.84	
Spain	1740		7145914		8784848		0.81	
Spain	1741		7221192		8836364		0.82	
Spain	1742		7743667		8887879		0.87	

Spain	1743	7512734	8939394	0.84
Spain	1744	7378654	8990909	0.82
Spain	1745	7819675	9042424	0.86
Spain	1746	7524354	9093939	0.83
Spain	1747	7197564	9145455	0.79
Spain	1748	7366681	9196970	0.80
Spain	1749	7672812	9248485	0.83
Spain	1750	7734454	9300000	0.83
Spain	1751	7808228	8914444	0.88
Spain	1752	7733600	8928889	0.87
Spain	1753	7903719	8943333	0.88
Spain	1754	7291799	8957778	0.81
Spain	1755	6683463	8972222	0.74
Spain	1756	6969726	8986667	0.78
Spain	1757	5909843	9001111	0.66
Spain	1758	8123116	9015556	0.90
Spain	1759	7260617	9030000	0.80
Spain	1760	9941137	9044444	1.10
Spain	1761	8528025	9058889	0.94
Spain	1762	6588936	9073333	0.73
Spain	1763	8199513	9087778	0.90
Spain	1764	8426282	9102222	0.93
Spain	1765	9415378	9116667	1.03
Spain	1766	7755333	9131111	0.85
Spain	1767	8575051	9145556	0.94
Spain	1768	8099378	9160000	0.88

(continued)

Country	Year	Yield	Revenue	Expenditure	Population	Spread w/Consol	Rev/Pop	Def/Rev
Spain	1769		7032384		9256842		0.76	
Spain	1770		8846251		9353684		0.95	
Spain	1771		7595468		9450526		0.80	
Spain	1772		9529998		9547368		1.00	
Spain	1773		8254034		9644211		0.86	
Spain	1774		10487363		9741053		1.08	
Spain	1775		9413468		9837895		0.96	
Spain	1776		9586187		9934737		0.96	
Spain	1777		8500555		10031579		0.85	
Spain	1778		11988991		10128421		1.18	
Spain	1779		9481622		10225263		0.93	
Spain	1780		8983009		10322105		0.87	
Spain	1781		9160397		10418947		0.88	
Spain	1782		8616044		10515789		0.82	
Spain	1783		10544381		10612632		0.99	
Spain	1784		12529672		10709474		1.17	
Spain	1785		13400914		10806316		1.24	
Spain	1786		13047384		10903158		1.20	
Spain	1787		11683960		11000000		1.06	
Spain	1788		14309747		11050000		1.29	
Spain	1789		14926224		11100000		1.34	
Spain	1790		15419756		11150000		1.38	
Spain	1791		15325445		11200000		1.37	
Spain	1792		15182265		11250000		1.35	
Spain	1793		16817972		11300000		1.49	
Spain	1794		19485777		11350000		1.72	

Spain	1795	20410317		11400000	1.79	
Spain	1796	21248469		11450000	1.86	
Spain	1797	25049230		11500000	2.18	
Spain	1798	22321132		11566038	1.93	
Spain	1799	20286296		11632075	1.74	
Spain	1800	18518783		11698113	1.58	
Spain	1801	17069253	19441215	11764151	1.45	0.14
Spain	1802	24122713	25948091	11830189	2.04	0.08
Spain	1803	24953255	2675254	11896226	2.10	−0.89
Spain	1804	25721137		11962264	2.15	
Spain	1805	17354686	25214880	12028302	1.44	0.45
Spain	1806	15769948	25354677	12094340	1.30	0.61
Spain	1807	14529573	20058526	12160377	1.19	0.38
Spain	1808	12628188		12226415	1.03	
Spain	1809	11323400		12292453	0.92	
Spain	1810	10280031		12358491	0.83	
Spain	1811	8504854		12424528	0.68	
Spain	1812	7463021		12490566	0.60	
Spain	1813	5570008	11944711	12556604	0.44	1.14
Spain	1814	3562629	3485181	12622642	0.28	−0.02
Spain	1815	14650460	18910391	12688679	1.15	0.29
Spain	1816	10731038	12655224	12754717	0.84	0.18
Spain	1817	19901781	17350270	12820755	1.55	−0.13
Spain	1818	28610598		12886792	2.22	
Spain	1819	23148320	19430905	12952830	1.79	−0.16
Spain	1820	13406123	18085619	13018868	1.03	0.35

(continued)

A.1.1 (continued)

Country	Year	Yield	Revenue	Expenditure	Population	Spread w/Consol	Rev/Pop	Def/Rev
Spain	1821	1015	14593377	18449153	13084906	615	1.12	0.26
Spain	1822	797	16007322	16007322	13150943	421	1.22	0.00
Spain	1823	1565	13929587		13216981	1190	1.05	
Spain	1824		11989332		13283019		0.90	
Spain	1825		13087861		13349057		0.98	
Spain	1826		13646031		13415094		1.02	
Spain	1827		14602469	10687874	13481132		1.08	-0.27
Spain	1828		14571615	10990040	13547170		1.08	-0.25
Spain	1829		14901610		13613208		1.09	
Spain	1830		16360726	14502109	13679245		1.20	-0.11
Spain	1831		16739090	14242493	13745283		1.22	-0.15
Spain	1832		17411320		13811321		1.26	
Spain	1833		16687808	10234874	13877358		1.20	-0.39
Spain	1834	1207	14569537	15159875	13943396	877	1.04	0.04
Spain	1835	1003	14514764	21088821	14009434	674	1.04	0.45
Spain	1836	1275	14970144	21776918	14075472	944	1.06	0.45
Spain	1837	1401	14720403	31011658	14141509	1072	1.04	1.11
Spain	1838	1552	15517740	29271002	14207547	1232	1.09	0.89
Spain	1839	1379	29384387	48203600	14273585	1054	2.06	0.64
Spain	1840	1155	24577374		14339623	832	1.71	
Spain	1841	1309	19995165	26805639	14405660	973	1.39	0.34
Spain	1842	1298	21063889	29700563	14471698	971	1.46	0.41
Spain	1843	1057	23665115		14537736	743	1.63	
Spain	1844	861	26262433		14603774	559	1.80	
Spain	1845	759	29275302	28318593	14669811	455	2.00	-0.03
Spain	1846	806	30630870		14735849	492	2.08	

Spain	1847	928	26339461		14801887	584	1.78	−0.10
Spain	1848	1219	25545496		14867925	869	1.72	−0.01
Spain	1849	923	24528343	21953940	14933962	600	1.64	0.08
Spain	1850	797	23479445	23194846	15000000	486	1.57	0.03
Spain	1851	782	22975086	24883785	15065000	472	1.53	0.03
Spain	1852	632	23925803	24633667	15130000	330	1.58	0.04
Spain	1853	636	24738708	25441512	15195000	329	1.63	0.04
Spain	1854	800	25732504	26719504	15260000	473	1.69	−0.03
Spain	1855	800	26839460	25991898	15325000	468	1.75	0.00
Spain	1856	688	32696106	32767339	15390000	366	2.12	−0.01
Spain	1857	732	35849881	35417086	15455000	406	2.32	0.06
Spain	1858	666	33932712	35805856	15518333	356	2.19	−0.04
Spain	1859	686	38345110	36780003	15581667	371	2.46	0.06
Spain	1860	628	41213587	43487440	15645000	309	2.63	0.14
Spain	1861	601	41392967	47337316	15702471	273	2.64	0.24
Spain	1862	553	38367622	47690596	15759941	231	2.43	0.16
Spain	1863	550	42357610	49117568	15817412	226	2.68	−0.20
Spain	1864	589	64992312	52067705	15874882	256	4.09	0.18
Spain	1865	636	45544448	53865782	15932353	301	2.86	0.17
Spain	1866	779	44205679	51863952	15989824	438	2.76	−0.11
Spain	1867	835	56482949	50247347	16047294	512	3.52	−0.14
Spain	1868	828	57289586	49354942	16104765	508	3.56	0.18
Spain	1869	990	46270762	54637331	16162235	667	2.86	0.13
Spain	1870	1047	51253317	58120828	16219706	723	3.16	0.30
Spain	1871	933	39491415	51382078	16277176	609	2.43	0.38
Spain	1872	992	38958671	53614201	16334647	668	2.39	

(continued)

A.1.1 (continued)

Country	Year	Yield	Revenue	Expenditure	Population	Spread w/Consol	Rev/Pop	Def/Rev
Spain	1873	1478	49500006	58466325	16392118	1154	3.02	0.18
Spain	1874	1619	57470264	52306055	16449588	1295	3.49	-0.09
Spain	1875	1505	52090639	58788007	16507059	1185	3.16	0.13
Spain	1876		91366408	54239505	16564529		5.52	-0.41
Spain	1877		70227107	58585180	16622000		4.22	-0.17
Spain	1878		75591258	60999513	16714800		4.52	-0.19
Spain	1879		56124840	61833707	16807600		3.34	0.10
Spain	1880	1615	58171787	62497381	16900400	1310	3.44	0.07
Spain	1881	403	85589746	62073562	16993200	103	5.04	-0.27
Spain	1882	513	64890724	61996537	17086000	215	3.80	-0.04
Spain	1883	663	64286781	66257838	17178800	367	3.74	0.03
Spain	1884	566	64938686	66010787	17271600	369	3.76	0.02
Spain	1885	695	63108386	69296981	17364400	393	3.63	0.10
Spain	1886	665	67839705	68826188	17457200	368	3.89	0.01
Spain	1887	607	61809289	64403753	17550000	313	3.52	0.04
Spain	1888	565	58159834	65033971	17605900	258	3.30	0.12
Spain	1889	534	60664093	65120089	17661800	246	3.43	0.07
Spain	1890	534	62754517	66766954	17717700	249	3.54	0.06
Spain	1891	559	67216894	71876345	17773600	272	3.78	0.07
Spain	1892	634	66593506	68291864	17829500	350	3.74	0.03
Spain	1893	626	72146037	65490498	17885400	346	4.03	-0.09
Spain	1894	595	69413890	68897162	17941300	323	3.87	-0.01
Spain	1895	582	73132623	75477195	17997200	322	4.06	0.03
Spain	1896	644	78865192	75251667	18053100	396	4.37	-0.05
Spain	1897	650	81744517	87040098	18109000	405	4.51	0.06
Spain	1898	945	99353630	98411394	18270667	697	5.44	-0.01

Country	Year	Yield	Revenue	Expenditure	Population	Spread w/Consol	Rev/Pop	Def/Rev
Spain	1899	666	58575914	51157037	18432333	409	3.18	-0.13
Spain	1900	566	52369557	49593597	18594000	291	2.82	-0.05
Spain	1901	560	50947251	49100974	18727300	269	2.72	-0.04
Spain	1902	492	52011084	48404846	18860600	200	2.76	-0.07
Spain	1903	447	52846259	51674163	18993900	163	2.78	-0.02
Spain	1904	467	51741235	49046899	19127200	178	2.71	-0.05
Spain	1905	434	54698942	50866867	19260500	156	2.84	-0.07
Spain	1906	419	66429356	60237298	19393800	136	3.43	-0.09
Spain	1907	428	67641302	63633385	19527100	131	3.46	-0.06
Spain	1908	418	65734295	62322691	19660400	128	3.34	-0.05
Spain	1909	412	66524121	69709783	19793700	114	3.36	0.05
Spain	1910	425	74606474	72125952	19927000	117	3.74	-0.03
Spain	1911	420	74905495	74461892	20064600	105	3.73	-0.01
Spain	1912	426	76970596	81025067	20202200	98	3.81	0.05
Spain	1913	440	98427756	91984980	20339800	101	4.84	-0.07

Note: From left to right, the columns display countries, years, yields on long-term government bonds in basis points (Yield), gross government revenues and expenditures in gold grams (Revenue, Expenditure), populations, yield spreads against the British consol in basis points (Spread w/Consol), per capita government revenues in gold grams (Rev/Pop), and budget deficit-to-revenue ratios (Def/Rev).

Source: See Appendix 2.

A.1.2. *Group 2*

Country	Year	Yield	Revenue	Expenditure	Population	Spread w/Consol	Rev/Pop	Def/Rev
Belgium	1831		38753171	38430228	4090000		9.48	
Belgium	1832	600	51025009	52962668	4106467	243	12.43	0.04
Belgium	1833	494	30033708	31325480	4122933	156	7.28	0.04
Belgium	1834	455	32617253	32617253	4139400	125	7.88	0.00
Belgium	1835	445	30356651	29064879	4155867	116	7.30	−0.04
Belgium	1836	439	34231968	33265139	4172333	107	8.20	−0.03
Belgium	1837	441	33586082	34231968	4188800	112	8.02	0.02
Belgium	1838	438	40367887	39076115	4205267	118	9.60	−0.03
Belgium	1839	441	37461399	40044944	4221733	116	8.87	0.07
Belgium	1840	442	54577383	53608554	4238200	109	12.88	−0.02
Belgium	1841	443	32617253	37138456	4254667	107	7.67	0.14
Belgium	1842	436	33586082	41659659	4271133	109	7.86	0.24
Belgium	1843	431	33909025	38753171	4287600	116	7.91	0.14
Belgium	1844	432	35523740	62973904	4304067	130	8.25	0.77
Belgium	1845	451	36492570	43274375	4320533	146	8.45	0.19
Belgium	1846	461	36492570	39722001	4337000	147	8.41	0.09
Belgium	1847	482	36492570	41336716	4356300	139	8.38	0.13
Belgium	1848	580	35200797	43597318	4375600	230	8.04	0.24
Belgium	1849	545	36815513	36169627	4394900	222	8.38	−0.02
Belgium	1850	498	37784342	38430228	4414200	187	8.56	0.02
Belgium	1851	484	38107285	38430228	4433500	175	8.60	0.01
Belgium	1852	478	39722001	42628489	4452800	176	8.92	0.07
Belgium	1853	461	41336716	43597318	4472100	154	9.24	0.05
Belgium	1854	493	42628489	46180863	4491400	167	9.49	0.08

Belgium	1855	480	44889090	47472635	4510700	149	9.95	0.06
Belgium	1856	468	45857920	48441464	4530000	145	10.12	0.06
Belgium	1857	461	47149692	47149692	4559800	135	10.34	0.00
Belgium	1858	454	50056180	46826749	4589600	145	10.91	−0.06
Belgium	1859	452	50379123	49410294	4619400	137	10.91	−0.02
Belgium	1860	449	50056180	51347952	4649200	130	10.77	0.03
Belgium	1861	442	50379123	52639725	4679000	114	10.77	0.04
Belgium	1862	437	51993838	57160928	4708800	114	11.04	0.10
Belgium	1863	410	52639725	60390359	4738600	86	11.11	0.15
Belgium	1864	426	52962668	60067416	4768400	93	11.11	0.13
Belgium	1865	425	54577383	61036245	4798200	90	11.37	0.12
Belgium	1866	436	54577383	65557448	4828000	94	11.30	0.20
Belgium	1867	443	55869155	62005074	4877429	120	11.45	0.11
Belgium	1868	423	56837985	62005074	4926857	103	11.54	0.09
Belgium	1869	402	59744473	64588619	4976286	79	12.01	0.08
Belgium	1870	402	61682131	70078652	5025714	77	12.27	0.14
Belgium	1871	404	67172164	76860457	5075143	81	13.24	0.14
Belgium	1872	391	68786879	81381660	5124571	67	13.42	0.18
Belgium	1873	387	73308083	113353026	5174000	63	14.17	0.55
Belgium	1874	408	78475172	97528815	5223429	84	15.02	0.24
Belgium	1875	408	79444001	94299384	5272857	88	15.07	0.19
Belgium	1876	408	82350489	94945270	5322286	92	15.47	0.15
Belgium	1877	398	83319319	124656035	5371714	83	15.51	0.50
Belgium	1878	397	83965205	112707140	5421143	82	15.49	0.34
Belgium	1879	381	87194636	111092425	5470571	73	15.94	0.27
Belgium	1880	365	94299384	123687206	5520000	60	17.08	0.31
Belgium	1881	356	95914099	129823124	5574900	56	17.20	0.35
Belgium	1882	356	97205872	136604929	5629800	58	17.27	0.41

(continued)

A.1.2 (*continued*)

Country	Year	Yield	Revenue	Expenditure	Population	Spread w/Consol	Rev/Pop	Def/Rev
Belgium	1883	358	97851758	131114897	5684700	62	17.21	0.34
Belgium	1884	356	98820587	116905401	5739600	59	17.22	0.18
Belgium	1885	343	101081189	113353026	5794500	41	17.44	0.12
Belgium	1886	321	102050018	113030083	5849400	24	17.45	0.11
Belgium	1887	328	104633563	111738311	5904300	34	17.72	0.07
Belgium	1888	329	107540051	114967742	5959200	31	18.05	0.07
Belgium	1889	325	109154766	120457775	6014100	36	18.15	0.10
Belgium	1890	327	110123596	134990214	6069000	42	18.15	0.23
Belgium	1891	319	111738311	129823124	6131500	32	18.22	0.16
Belgium	1892	312	112061254	131114897	6194000	27	18.09	0.17
Belgium	1893	306	113675970	127562523	6256500	26	18.17	0.12
Belgium	1894	310	117228344	130146067	6319000	38	18.55	0.11
Belgium	1895	306	120457775	132406669	6381500	46	18.88	0.10
Belgium	1896	323	125624864	141449076	6444000	74	19.49	0.13
Belgium	1897	311	139188474	165023922	6506500	66	21.39	0.19
Belgium	1898	301	141772019	224122508	6569000	53	21.58	0.58
Belgium	1899	305	151460312	184077564	6631500	48	22.84	0.22
Belgium	1900	315	159533889	185369337	6694000	39	23.83	0.16
Belgium	1901	308	161794491	195057630	6767000	17	23.91	0.21
Belgium	1902	301	162763320	198610004	6840000	10	23.80	0.22
Belgium	1903	301	165992751	202808264	6913000	17	24.01	0.22
Belgium	1904	301	172128670	222184850	6986000	12	24.64	0.29
Belgium	1905	301	187629938	202162378	7059000	23	26.58	0.08
Belgium	1906	301	192797028	249312070	7132000	18	27.03	0.29
Belgium	1907	307	199578833	248020297	7205000	10	27.70	0.24
Belgium	1908	317	199255890	248666183	7278000	27	27.38	0.25

Country	Year							
Belgium	1909	315	208298296	253833273	7351000	17	28.34	0.22
Belgium	1910	320	220247191	267719826	7424000	12	29.67	0.22
Belgium	1911	334	224445451	261906850	7422200	19	30.24	0.17
Belgium	1912	362	243822037	289357013	7420400	33	32.86	0.19
Belgium	1913	391			7418600	52		
Denmark	1821	676				276		
Denmark	1822	564				187		
Denmark	1823	579				204		
Denmark	1824	497				178		
Denmark	1825	478				141		
Denmark	1826	530				153		
Denmark	1827	484				129		
Denmark	1828	485				137		
Denmark	1829	438				101		
Denmark	1830	435				98		
Denmark	1831	487				119		
Denmark	1832	437				80		
Denmark	1833	406				68		
Denmark	1834	398				69		
Denmark	1835	390				61		
Denmark	1836	394				63		
Denmark	1837	410				81		
Denmark	1838	400				80		
Denmark	1839	398				72		
Denmark	1840	384				51		
Denmark	1841	378				42		
Denmark	1842	362				36		
Denmark	1843	346				31		

(continued)

A.1.2 (*continued*)

Country	Year	Yield	Revenue	Expenditure	Population	Spread w/Consol	Rev/Pop	Def/Rev
Denmark	1844	339				37		
Denmark	1845	337				32		
Denmark	1846	340				26		
Denmark	1847	351				8		
Denmark	1848	406				56		
Denmark	1849	430				107		
Denmark	1850	409			2344000	97		
Denmark	1851	388			2370400	79		
Denmark	1852	440			2396800	138		
Denmark	1853	475			2423200	168		
Denmark	1854	510			2449600	183		
Denmark	1855	499			2476000	168		
Denmark	1856	430			2503200	158		
Denmark	1857	489			2530400	162		
Denmark	1858	489			2557600	180		
Denmark	1859				2584800			
Denmark	1860				2612000			
Denmark	1861				2631200			
Denmark	1862				2650400			
Denmark	1863				2669600			
Denmark	1864	449	15582892	15982454	2688800	117	5.80	0.03
Denmark	1865	442	11430345	18963982	1696500	106	6.74	0.66
Denmark	1866	458	15333281	13886745	1714200	116	8.94	−0.09
Denmark	1867	455	14507578	15099724	1731900	132	8.38	0.04
Denmark	1868	458	16868049	14250593	1749600	138	9.64	−0.16
Denmark	1869	475	13596059	17221674	1767300	152	7.69	0.27
Denmark	1870	482	13769842	15888279	1785000	157	7.71	0.15

Denmark	1871	473	15721470	16818317	1803400	149	8.72	0.07
Denmark	1872	448	15126918	15487082	1821800	123	8.30	0.02
Denmark	1873	436	15298389	16721495	1840200	112	8.31	0.09
Denmark	1874	432	16699123	17425172	1858600	107	8.98	0.04
Denmark	1875	433	16854111	22823275	1877000	113	8.98	0.35
Denmark	1876	435	16700284	17063334	1895400	119	8.81	0.02
Denmark	1877	445	17695501	19234240	1913800	131	9.25	0.09
Denmark	1878	450	17587536	17587536	1932200	135	9.10	0.00
Denmark	1879	430	18546307	16933585	1950600	122	9.51	-0.09
Denmark	1880	415	19730471	17717157	1969000	111	10.02	-0.10
Denmark	1881	406	20488640	19283426	1989300	106	10.30	-0.06
Denmark	1882	406	21046367	20236892	2009600	108	10.47	-0.04
Denmark	1883	405	21764607	20555462	2029900	109	10.72	-0.06
Denmark	1884	402	22180678	20164253	2050200	105	10.82	-0.09
Denmark	1885	400	20998167	19382923	2070500	97	10.14	-0.08
Denmark	1886	392	20606384	20202338	2090800	95	9.86	-0.02
Denmark	1887	357	20580087	23404805	2111100	62	9.75	0.14
Denmark	1888	356	21863587	24492874	2131400	59	10.26	0.11
Denmark	1889	354	22655720	24473986	2151700	65	10.53	0.07
Denmark	1890	359	22609466	25031909	2172000	74	10.41	0.11
Denmark	1891	370	22613107	26651161	2197273	83	10.29	0.18
Denmark	1892	374	22268418	26317221	2222545	89	10.02	0.18
Denmark	1893	371	23034737	25459446	2247818	91	10.25	0.11
Denmark	1894	359	23501188	25121960	2273091	87	10.34	0.07
Denmark	1895	343	25184923	24778714	2298364	84	10.96	-0.02
Denmark	1896	349	25898287	29944894	2323636	101	11.15	0.16
Denmark	1897	350	27497824	26689065	2348909	105	11.71	-0.03
Denmark	1898	350	28118910	54229327	2374182	102	11.84	0.93

(continued)

A.1.2 (*continued*)

Country	Year	Yield	Revenue	Expenditure	Population	Spread w/Consol	Rev/Pop	Def/Rev
Denmark	1899	362	27774680	30592402	2399455	105	11.58	0.10
Denmark	1900	378	26960000	31386269	2424727	102	11.12	0.16
Denmark	1901	363	26695642	31953874	2450000	71	10.90	0.20
Denmark	1902	354	29869247	31080162	2477800	63	12.05	0.04
Denmark	1903	353	31835484	31432503	2505600	68	12.71	-0.01
Denmark	1904	359	38754491	31891717	2533400	70	15.30	-0.18
Denmark	1905	355	35030402	39862182	2561200	77	13.68	0.14
Denmark	1906	356	40914102	34095085	2589000	73	15.80	-0.17
Denmark	1907	363	38366749	45560515	2586200	66	14.84	0.19
Denmark	1908	370	37439779	37842358	2583400	80	14.49	0.01
Denmark	1909	368	33031893	43505421	2580600	70	12.80	0.32
Denmark	1910	374	36669617	53594056	2577800	65	14.23	0.46
Denmark	1911	375	41100374	56009333	2575000	61	15.96	0.36
Denmark	1912	393	45804864	43394082	2644200	65	17.32	-0.05
Denmark	1913	419	49723247	42505356	2713400	80	18.33	-0.15
Italy	1862	739	155012686	302274737	25195400	417	6.15	0.95
Italy	1863	722	169222182	295815875	25373800	398	6.67	0.75
Italy	1864	770	186338166	313577746	25552200	437	7.29	0.68
Italy	1865	800	208944183	318744835	25730600	464	8.12	0.53
Italy	1866	944	199255890	442754984	25909000	602	7.69	1.22
Italy	1867	990	230904313	308733599	26087400	667	8.85	0.34
Italy	1868	954	241561435	364602755	26265800	634	9.20	0.51
Italy	1869	832	281283436	356852120	26444200	509	10.64	0.27
Italy	1870	835	279668721	385916999	26622600	510	10.50	0.38
Italy	1871	734	311963030	364925698	26801000	411	11.64	0.17
Italy	1872	607	326172526	382041682	26966900	283	12.10	0.17

Italy	1873	635	338121421	397865893	27132800	311	12.46	0.18
Italy	1874	635	347809714	379135194	27298700	310	12.74	0.09
Italy	1875	596	353945632	390761145	27464600	276	12.89	0.10
Italy	1876	593	362665096	410783617	27630500	278	13.13	0.13
Italy	1877	597	401418267	423701341	27796400	283	14.44	0.06
Italy	1878	568	384625227	406908300	27962300	253	13.76	0.06
Italy	1879	522	394959406	408523016	28128200	214	14.04	0.03
Italy	1880	492	394636462	407231243	28294100	187	13.95	0.03
Italy	1881	497	412721276	420794853	28460000	197	14.50	0.02
Italy	1882	503	419826024	651376223	28660750	205	14.65	0.55
Italy	1883	505	430483146	446307358	28861500	208	14.92	0.04
Italy	1884	467	438664371		29062250	170	15.09	
Italy	1885	461	446845596		29263000	159	15.27	
Italy	1886	446	455026821	473757521	29463750	149	15.44	0.04
Italy	1887	451	469236318	484091700	29664500	157	15.82	0.03
Italy	1888	457	484414643	518646611	29865250	160	16.22	0.07
Italy	1889	464	484737586	570963393	30066000	175	16.12	0.18
Italy	1890	465	504437115	540929685	30266750	180	16.67	0.07
Italy	1891	477	497332367	535116709	30467500	190	16.32	0.08
Italy	1892	471	493457050	520907213	30668250	187	16.09	0.06
Italy	1893	470	500884741	533824937	30869000	190	16.23	0.07
Italy	1894	505	489904676	562889815	31069750	233	15.77	0.15
Italy	1895	439	507020660	534470823	31270500	180	16.21	0.05
Italy	1896	439	527366075	557722726	31471250	191	16.76	0.06
Italy	1897	421	521553099	533501993	31672000	176	16.47	0.02
Italy	1898	411	526074302	532210221	31872750	163	16.51	0.01
Italy	1899	406	535439652	532856107	32073500	148	16.69	0.00
Italy	1900	409	539637912	535762595	32274250	133	16.72	−0.01

(continued)

A.1.2 (continued)

Country	Year	Yield	Revenue	Expenditure	Population	Spread w/Consol	Rev/Pop	Def/Rev
Italy	1901	403	55785067	546419717	32475000	111	17.11	−0.02
Italy	1902	396	56321 2758	584204059	32694600	105	17.23	0.04
Italy	1903	397	579682856	579036970	32914200	112	17.61	0.00
Italy	1904	396	577099311	57354 6937	33133800	107	17.42	−0.01
Italy	1905	388	598413556	587756433	33353400	110	17.94	−0.02
Italy	1906	380	628447264	779584632	33573000	97	18.72	0.24
Italy	1907	373	631030808	671398695	33792600	76	18.67	0.06
Italy	1908	370	628447264	703693005	34012200	80	18.48	0.12
Italy	1909	356	689160565	785074665	34231800	68	20.13	0.14
Italy	1910	366	722423704	790564697	34451400	57	20.97	0.09
Italy	1911	371	776032258	855799203	34671000	56	22.38	0.10
Italy	1912	364	799284161	917481334	34844500	36	22.94	0.15
Italy	1913	362	816723088	1013072490	35018000	23	23.32	0.24
Portugal	1762		977846	896903				−0.08
Portugal	1763		1506255	1184309				−0.21
Portugal	1764		1583591	1338973				−0.15
Portugal	1765		1505181	1409829				−0.06
Portugal	1766		1764966	1586206				−0.10
Portugal	1767		1484665	1343931				−0.09
Portugal	1768		1631709	1489663	2410000		0.68	−0.09
Portugal	1769		1498008	1356201	2425818		0.62	−0.09
Portugal	1770		1466322	1383680	2441636		0.60	−0.06
Portugal	1771		1334370	1271435	2457455		0.54	−0.05
Portugal	1772		1351419	1274349	2473273		0.55	−0.06
Portugal	1773		1397499	1319325	2489091		0.56	−0.06
Portugal	1774		1563760	1393675	2504909		0.62	−0.11

Portugal	1775	1592369	1464070	2520727	0.63	−0.08
Portugal	1776	1799677	1628164	2536545	0.71	−0.10
Portugal	1777	1795684		2552364	0.70	
Portugal	1778	1791690		2568182	0.70	
Portugal	1779	1787697		2584000	0.69	
Portugal	1780	1783703		2599818	0.69	
Portugal	1781	1779710		2615636	0.68	
Portugal	1782	1775716		2631455	0.67	
Portugal	1783	1771723		2647273	0.67	
Portugal	1784	1767730		2663091	0.66	
Portugal	1785	1763736		2678909	0.66	
Portugal	1786	1759743		2694727	0.65	
Portugal	1787	1755749		2710545	0.65	
Portugal	1788	1751756		2726364	0.64	
Portugal	1789	1747762		2742182	0.64	
Portugal	1790	1743769		2758000	0.63	
Portugal	1791	1739776		2773818	0.63	
Portugal	1792	1735782		2789636	0.62	
Portugal	1793	1731789		2805455	0.62	
Portugal	1794	1727795		2821273	0.61	
Portugal	1795	1723802		2837091	0.61	
Portugal	1796	1719808		2852909	0.60	
Portugal	1797	1715815		2868727	0.60	
Portugal	1798	1711509		2884545	0.59	
Portugal	1799	2038968		2900364	0.70	
Portugal	1800	3001910	3380432	2916182	1.03	0.13
Portugal	1801	2763025	3646386	2932000	0.94	0.32

(continued)

181

A.1.2 (*continued*)

Country	Year	Yield	Revenue	Expenditure	Population	Spread w/Consol	Rev/Pop	Def/Rev
Portugal	1802		2427102	2572815	2936700		0.83	0.06
Portugal	1803		2931532		2941400		1.00	
Portugal	1804		2873553		2946100		0.98	
Portugal	1805		2715466		2950800		0.92	
Portugal	1806		2557378		2955500		0.87	
Portugal	1807		2399291		2960200		0.81	
Portugal	1808		2241204		2964900		0.76	
Portugal	1809		2083116		2969600		0.70	
Portugal	1810		1925029		2974300		0.65	
Portugal	1811		1766941		2979000		0.59	
Portugal	1812		1608854	1588449	2983700		0.54	−0.01
Portugal	1813		1912139		2988400		0.64	
Portugal	1814		2215423		2993100		0.74	
Portugal	1815		2518708		2997800		0.84	
Portugal	1816		2821992		3002500		0.94	
Portugal	1817		3125277	3453797	3007200		1.04	0.11
Portugal	1818		2946975		3011900		0.98	
Portugal	1819		2768674		3016600		0.92	
Portugal	1820		2590372		3021300		0.86	
Portugal	1821		2412070	2489171	3026000		0.80	0.03
Portugal	1822		2408811		3028571		0.80	
Portugal	1823		2405552		3031143		0.79	
Portugal	1824	334	2402293		3033714	15	0.79	
Portugal	1825	351	2399033		3036286	13	0.79	
Portugal	1826	4C1	2395774		3038857	24	0.79	
Portugal	1827	414	2392515	3231692	3041429	59	0.79	0.35

Portugal	1828	503	4220617	5697259	3044000	156	1.39	0.35
Portugal	1829	642	3849257		3046571	305	1.26	
Portugal	1830	533	3477896		3049143	196	1.14	
Portugal	1831	637	3106536		3051714	268	1.02	
Portugal	1832	595	2735175		3054286	238	0.90	
Portugal	1833	487	2363815		3056857	148	0.77	
Portugal	1834	383	1992454	3395558	3059429	53	0.65	0.70
Portugal	1835	327	2529980	4417562	3062000	-1	0.83	0.75
Portugal	1836	414	2237068	3659139	3116000	83	0.72	0.64
Portugal	1837	752	2963099	3387069	3170000	423	0.93	0.14
Portugal	1838	933	2144966	2607902	3224000	613	0.67	0.22
Portugal	1839	915	2246313	2208235	3395000	589	0.66	-0.02
Portugal	1840	876	2311823	2519740	3566000	544	0.65	0.09
Portugal	1841	931	2270800	2808029	3737000	595	0.61	0.24
Portugal	1842	836	2875236	4700161	3745231	510	0.77	0.63
Portugal	1843	724	2592221	4640842	3753462	409	0.69	0.79
Portugal	1844	626	3195266	3888289	3761692	324	0.85	0.22
Portugal	1845	481	2920434	3635649	3769923	176	0.77	0.24
Portugal	1846	605	3023062		3778154	291	0.80	
Portugal	1847	1070	3125689	3592879	3786385	727	0.83	0.15
Portugal	1848	1457	3203726		3794615	1106	0.84	
Portugal	1849	1012	3281762		3802846	689	0.86	
Portugal	1850	883	3359799		3811077	572	0.88	
Portugal	1851	893	3437835		3819308	583	0.90	
Portugal	1852	809	3515872	3413568	3827538	507	0.92	-0.03
Portugal	1853	726	3554514	4173553	3835769	419	0.93	0.17
Portugal	1854	779	3437717	3579489	3844000	453	0.89	0.04
Portugal	1855	684	3599968	4439165	3863750	352	0.93	0.23

(continued)

A.1.2 (*continued*)

Country	Year	Yield	Revenue	Expenditure	Population	Spread w/Consol	Rev/Pop	Def/Rev
Portugal	1856	580	3613190	4289328	3883500	258	0.93	0.19
Portugal	1857	640	3792223	4789411	3903250	314	0.97	0.26
Portugal	1858	647	4186522	5894947	3923000	338	1.07	0.41
Portugal	1859	672	4118723	5791626	3960333	356	1.04	0.41
Portugal	1860	674	3967763	5091534	3997667	355	0.99	0.28
Portugal	1861	644	4213692	5061459	4035000	316	1.04	0.20
Portugal	1862	644	4467066	6724381	4086000	321	1.09	0.51
Portugal	1863	618	4650128	7040249	4137000	294	1.12	0.51
Portugal	1864	625	5023077	6817349	4188000	293	1.20	0.36
Portugal	1865	634	5819842	6801206	4213929	299	1.38	0.17
Portugal	1866	677	5070382	6861739	4239857	336	1.20	0.35
Portugal	1867	736	4848204	7390485	4265786	413	1.14	0.52
Portugal	1868	765	5331044	9715473	4291714	446	1.24	0.82
Portugal	1869	862	5333547	6896326	4317643	539	1.24	0.29
Portugal	1870	954	5545457	10619097	4343571	630	1.28	0.91
Portugal	1871	850	5555320	6848518	4369500	527	1.27	0.23
Portugal	1872	725	5952383	7993659	4395429	400	1.35	0.34
Portugal	1873	718	6638468	7757768	4421357	394	1.50	0.17
Portugal	1874	643	7614894	8914233	4447286	318	1.71	0.17
Portugal	1875	583	7798686	9577304	4473214	263	1.74	0.23
Portugal	1876	564	8533920	10450742	4499143	248	1.90	0.22
Portugal	1877	584	8684892	12117115	4525071	269	1.92	0.40
Portugal	1878	596	8562207	11416616	4551000	281	1.88	0.33
Portugal	1879	580	9223328	11546581	4593417	272	2.01	0.25
Portugal	1880	575	7770537	10456571	4635833	271	1.68	0.35
Portugal	1881	565	8570384	11288909	4678250	265	1.83	0.32

Portugal	1882	564	9691224	12151800	4720667	266	2.05	0.25
Portugal	1883	563	9220421	11272492	4763083	266	1.94	0.22
Portugal	1884	603	9712772	11497158	4805500	306	2.02	0.18
Portugal	1885	660	10275004	13104594	4847917	358	2.12	0.28
Portugal	1886	601	10321495	13465123	4890333	304	2.11	0.30
Portugal	1887	534	11152709	13505941	4932750	239	2.26	0.21
Portugal	1888	481	12252977	14519956	4975167	184	2.46	0.19
Portugal	1889	451	12558948	16527110	5017583	162	2.50	0.32
Portugal	1890	488	12738524	17393192	5060000	203	2.52	0.37
Portugal	1891	706	14255355	18335967	5096300	419	2.80	0.29
Portugal	1892	1179	16309789	22911763	5132600	895	3.18	0.40
Portugal	1893	1370	17015264	19283322	5168900	1090	3.29	0.13
Portugal	1894	1271	19068105	18869650	5205200	999	3.66	-0.01
Portugal	1895	1020	18649364	19170198	5241500	761	3.56	-0.03
Portugal	1896	377	22036752	21087189	5277800	129	4.18	-0.04
Portugal	1897	446	23137607	26744945	5314100	201	4.35	0.16
Portugal	1898	488	25132070	29035878	5350400	240	4.70	0.16
Portugal	1899	396	23141465	24823236	5386700	139	4.30	0.07
Portugal	1900	414	23577343	27073743	5423000	138	4.35	0.15
Portugal	1901	390	24545774	24097223	5471636	99	4.49	-0.02
Portugal	1902	336	21223035	22475539	5520273	45	3.84	0.06
Portugal	1903		21306374	22377819	5568909		3.83	0.05
Portugal	1904	498	21531996	22281484	5617545	209	3.83	0.03
Portugal	1905	433	20010270	19835762	5666182	155	3.53	-0.01
Portugal	1906	424	19554923	19700938	5714818	141	3.42	0.01
Portugal	1907	443	19339624	19731366	5763455	146	3.37	0.02
Portugal	1908	479	25630515	27029361	5812091	189	4.41	0.05
Portugal	1909	480	25446066	26335972	5860727	182	4.34	0.03

(continued)

A.1.2 (continued)

Country	Year	Yield	Revenue	Expenditure	Population	Spread w/Consol	Rev/Pop	Def/Rev
Portugal	1910	448	24923372	25186967	5909364	140	4.22	0.01
Portugal	1911	449	23545353	22704253	5958000	134	3.95	-0.04
Portugal	1912	457	22494361	23588240	5972333	129	3.77	0.05
Portugal	1913	471	30960407	29520941	5986667	132	5.17	-0.05
Sweden	1740		2762236	2223853				-0.19
Sweden	1741		3518053	3522058				0.00
Sweden	1742		3206324	3125126				-0.03
Sweden	1743		2816845	2851986				0.01
Sweden	1744		3060722	2595464				-0.15
Sweden	1745		2498944	2145173				-0.14
Sweden	1746		3040586	2674571				-0.12
Sweden	1747		2733309	3216751				0.18
Sweden	1748		3117034	2754706				-0.12
Sweden	1749		3370764	2686654				-0.20
Sweden	1750		4751489	3613233	1781000		2.67	-0.24
Sweden	1751		3459140	4028444	1795300		1.93	0.16
Sweden	1752		3788248	4302157	1809600		2.09	0.14
Sweden	1753		4157156	3871686	1823900		2.28	-0.07
Sweden	1754		4201455	3894985	1838200		2.29	-0.07
Sweden	1755		3738046	3752182	1852500		2.02	0.00
Sweden	1756		3819330	3664391	1866800		2.05	-0.04
Sweden	1757		3506768	4094929	1881100		1.86	0.17
Sweden	1758		3422517	4854030	1895400		1.81	0.42
Sweden	1759		3267354	3747680	1909700		1.71	0.15
Sweden	1760		3079434	3941902	1924000		1.60	0.28
Sweden	1761		3003844	3677949	1935900		1.55	0.22

Sweden	1762	1820077	2229394	1947800	0.93	0.22
Sweden	1763	2195312	3879294	1959700	1.12	0.77
Sweden	1764	2284744	2569173	1971600	1.16	0.12
Sweden	1765	2062139	2400309	1983500	1.04	0.16
Sweden	1766	3520117	2550528	1995400	1.76	-0.28
Sweden	1767	3967079	3653669	2007300	1.98	-0.08
Sweden	1768	4896196	4342762	2019200	2.42	-0.11
Sweden	1769	4423939	3759972	2031100	2.18	-0.15
Sweden	1770	2615568	2797478	2043000	1.28	0.07
Sweden	1771	3499388	3312634	2050500	1.71	-0.05
Sweden	1772	3767904	3484334	2058000	1.83	-0.08
Sweden	1773	2836819	3470312	2065500	1.37	0.22
Sweden	1774	3724864	3637038	2073000	1.80	-0.02
Sweden	1775	3796687	3420252	2080500	1.82	-0.10
Sweden	1776	3696129	4339301	2088000	1.77	0.17
Sweden	1777	3792571	4190469	2095500	1.81	0.10
Sweden	1778	5913092	4075350	2103000	2.81	-0.31
Sweden	1779	3978069	4281294	2110500	1.88	0.08
Sweden	1780	3724193	4238234	2118000	1.76	0.14
Sweden	1781	3811710	4077322	2124400	1.79	0.07
Sweden	1782	4182090	4347028	2130800	1.96	0.04
Sweden	1783	5129399	4613961	2137200	2.40	-0.10
Sweden	1784	4071557	4191309	2143600	1.90	0.03
Sweden	1785	4048430	4515802	2150000	1.88	0.12
Sweden	1786	3931782	4575647	2157600	1.82	0.16
Sweden	1787	4388845	4895474	2165200	2.03	0.12
Sweden	1788	4416470	4924259	2172800	2.03	0.11
Sweden	1789	4969278	16771670	2180400	2.28	2.38

(continued)

A.1.2 (continued)

Country	Year	Yield	Revenue	Expenditure	Population	Spread w/Consol	Rev/Pop	Def/Rev
Sweden	1790		12408291	13225762	2188000		5.67	0.07
Sweden	1791		9955223	10539227	2206600		4.51	0.06
Sweden	1792		7791998	15833940	2225200		3.50	1.03
Sweden	1793		5601810	6213677	2243800		2.50	0.11
Sweden	1794		5470034	6836142	2262400		2.42	0.25
Sweden	1795		7325816	7507339	2281000		3.21	0.02
Sweden	1796		7509368	9411862	2294200		3.27	0.25
Sweden	1797		5697480	6010619	2307400		2.47	0.05
Sweden	1798		6265049	6393383	2320600		2.70	0.02
Sweden	1799		7202240	8008156	2333800		3.09	0.11
Sweden	1800		7303488	8459029	2347000		3.11	0.16
Sweden	1801		6855618	7609176	2363000		2.90	0.11
Sweden	1802		10479476	8706992	2379000		4.40	-0.17
Sweden	1803		24121248	9795517	2395000		10.07	-0.59
Sweden	1804		10103138	10635202	2411000		4.19	0.05
Sweden	1805		11162362	10917388	2427000		4.60	-0.02
Sweden	1806		10243678	9799079	2420800		4.23	-0.04
Sweden	1807		9550781	9762355	2414600		3.96	0.02
Sweden	1808		16305087	24507227	2408400		6.77	0.50
Sweden	1809		7161454	18083591	2402200		2.98	1.53
Sweden	1810		7497813	10974779	2396000		3.13	0.46
Sweden	1811		6132363	6581754	2409800		2.54	0.07
Sweden	1812		11319787	6687007	2423600		4.67	-0.41
Sweden	1813		17756232	18270734	2437400		7.28	0.03
Sweden	1814		17632153	18300931	2451200		7.19	0.04
Sweden	1815		9810290	6771042	2465000		3.98	-0.31

Sweden	1816	6851063	6662404	2489000	2.75	-0.03
Sweden	1817	8084722	7584795	2513000	3.22	-0.06
Sweden	1818	8753754	8239587	2537000	3.45	-0.06
Sweden	1819	7712969	7597971	2561000	3.01	-0.01
Sweden	1820	6552622	6248789	2585000	2.53	-0.05
Sweden	1821	6800623	7373561	2622200	2.59	0.08
Sweden	1822	7138108	7168425	2659400	2.68	0.00
Sweden	1823	6918370	6487876	2696600	2.57	-0.06
Sweden	1824	6825025	7095141	2733800	2.50	0.04
Sweden	1825	7270957	7046723	2771000	2.62	-0.03
Sweden	1826	7997332	7527346	2794400	2.86	-0.06
Sweden	1827	7170121	7377742	2817800	2.54	0.03
Sweden	1828	7330416	7286348	2841200	2.58	-0.01
Sweden	1829	8875538	5335918	2864600	3.10	-0.40
Sweden	1830	8319721	8901124	2888000	2.88	0.07
Sweden	1831	8239298	8374684	2915400	2.83	0.02
Sweden	1832	7570683	7556901	2942800	2.57	0.00
Sweden	1833	7547093	7427887	2970200	2.54	-0.02
Sweden	1834	8088789	8260364	2997600	2.70	0.02
Sweden	1835	8769035	8650922	3025000	2.90	-0.01
Sweden	1836	9486402	9606750	3047800	3.11	0.01
Sweden	1837	9860986	10461479	3070600	3.21	0.06
Sweden	1838	9947941	9810895	3093400	3.22	-0.01
Sweden	1839	9861171	9871000	3116200	3.16	0.00
Sweden	1840	9674364	9695392	3139000	3.08	0.00
Sweden	1841	9786217	9677698	3174600	3.08	-0.01
Sweden	1842	9433355	9645554	3210200	2.94	0.02
Sweden	1843	9093597	9003771	3245800	2.80	-0.01

(continued)

A.1.2 (*continued*)

Country	Year	Yield	Revenue	Expenditure	Population	Spread w/Consol	Rev/Pop	Def/Rev
Sweden	1844		8462414	8446235	3281400		2.58	0.00
Sweden	1845		9528463	9458612	3317000		2.87	−0.01
Sweden	1846		10466239	10225306	3347800		3.13	−0.02
Sweden	1847		10322639	10169435	3378600		3.06	−0.01
Sweden	1848		10348299	10105034	3409400		3.04	−0.02
Sweden	1849		10757611	10580063	3440200		3.13	−0.02
Sweden	1850		11022209	11014021	3471000		3.18	0.00
Sweden	1851		11473264	11616675	3505000		3.27	0.01
Sweden	1852		11100804	11768003	3539000		3.14	0.06
Sweden	1853		11778365	11376882	3573000		3.30	−0.03
Sweden	1854		12760054	13261118	3607000		3.54	0.04
Sweden	1855		14071110	14344912	3641000		3.86	0.02
Sweden	1856		15856787	16180063	3684800		4.30	0.02
Sweden	1857		15108175	17283255	3728600		4.05	0.14
Sweden	1858		13630962	21150568	3772400		3.61	0.55
Sweden	1859		13903847	20751719	3816200		3.64	0.49
Sweden	1860		14901737	21629324	3860000		3.86	0.45
Sweden	1861		16165406	19907290	3890900		4.15	0.23
Sweden	1862		14467362	18551878	3921800		3.69	0.28
Sweden	1863		12288877	16137758	3952700		3.11	0.31
Sweden	1864		10102640	14619736	3983600		2.54	0.45
Sweden	1865		18784828	25958272	4014500		4.68	0.38
Sweden	1866		17378882	27876835	4045400		4.30	0.60
Sweden	1867		17112722	21336150	4076300		4.20	0.25
Sweden	1868	551	16415662	22250142	4107200	232	4.00	0.36
Sweden	1869	513	16673413	22253089	4138100	190	4.03	0.33

Sweden	1870	499	21781191	23436870	4169000	175	5.22	0.08
Sweden	1871	486	25184607	23858299	4208700	163	5.98	-0.05
Sweden	1872	479	26164846	26864316	4248400	155	6.16	0.03
Sweden	1873	479	29688893	29359618	4288100	155	6.92	-0.01
Sweden	1874	475	32935578	38975172	4327800	150	7.61	0.18
Sweden	1875	474	32431091	39471464	4367500	154	7.43	0.22
Sweden	1876	466	34595589	40923444	4407200	150	7.85	0.18
Sweden	1877	470	33947939	40926720	4446900	155	7.63	0.21
Sweden	1878	469	32792842	43548835	4486600	154	7.31	0.33
Sweden	1879	421	29445867	39070956	4526300	114	6.51	0.33
Sweden	1880	395	33457434	35974686	4566000	90	7.33	0.08
Sweden	1881	396	35618987	36568365	4587900	96	7.76	0.03
Sweden	1882	395	35443621	33463974	4609800	97	7.69	-0.06
Sweden	1883	397	36039032	35125174	4631700	101	7.78	-0.03
Sweden	1884	395	36368789	35044060	4653600	98	7.82	-0.04
Sweden	1885	390	36334162	36778118	4675500	87	7.77	0.01
Sweden	1886	381	34908798	40031144	4697400	84	7.43	0.15
Sweden	1887	382	32966939	40573631	4719300	88	6.99	0.23
Sweden	1888	380	38183850	38467862	4741200	83	8.05	0.01
Sweden	1889	380	40109392	39013897	4763100	92	8.42	-0.03
Sweden	1890	383	41885758	39933308	4785000	99	8.75	-0.05
Sweden	1891	388	40288037	43998120	4820200	101	8.36	0.09
Sweden	1892	383	39497995	43749109	4855400	98	8.13	0.11
Sweden	1893	378	41090665	44149179	4890600	99	8.40	0.07
Sweden	1894	371	47116197	44205671	4925800	99	9.57	-0.06
Sweden	1895	301	49360999	42776069	4961000	42	9.95	-0.13
Sweden	1896	295	50275591	54364634	4996200	47	10.06	0.08
Sweden	1897	294	56277614	48126215	5031400	50	11.19	-0.14

(continued)

A.1.2 (*continued*)

Country	Year	Yield	Revenue	Expenditure	Population	Spread w/Consol	Rev/Pop	Def/Rev
Sweden	1898	303	58759693	51378415	5066600	55	11.60	-0.13
Sweden	1899	318	62798568	57846673	5101800	61	12.31	-0.08
Sweden	1900	333	61785744	64661927	5137000	57	12.03	0.05
Sweden	1901	333	58142012	69940749	5175500	42	11.23	0.20
Sweden	1902	321	60637447	74497389	5214000	30	11.63	0.23
Sweden	1903	317	75263502	74544849	5252500	32	14.33	-0.01
Sweden	1904	327	76737932	82073138	5291000	38	14.50	0.07
Sweden	1905	340	80590375	83904265	5329500	62	15.12	0.04
Sweden	1906	343	78599340	85933611	5368000	60	14.64	0.09
Sweden	1907	352	86354641	94495827	5406500	55	15.97	0.09
Sweden	1908	360	81509997	108510667	5445000	70	14.97	0.33
Sweden	1909	350	86668670	111276701	5483500	52	15.81	0.28
Sweden	1910	359	98446586	108785888	5522000	50	17.83	0.11
Sweden	1911	365	97451268	108866834	5560200	51	17.53	0.12
Sweden	1912	382	100146499	102157473	5598400	54	17.89	0.02
Sweden	1913	406	104451398	104435273	5636600	67	18.89	-0.02

Note: From left to right, the columns display countries, years, yields on long-term government bonds in basis points (Yield), gross government revenues and expenditures in gold grams (Revenue, Expenditure), populations, yield spreads against the British consol in basis points (Spread w/Consol), per capita government revenues in gold grams (Rev/Pop), and budget deficit-to-revenue ratios (Def/Rev).

Source: See Appendix 2.

A.2. Fiscal Data Sources

The composite time series for revenues, populations, and expenditures are typically composed of hosts of shorter series. The sub-series for revenues are abbreviated as R1, R2, and so forth, those for populations as P1, P2, and so forth, and those for expenditures as E1, E2, and so forth. Similarly, British Historical Statistics (Mitchell, 1988) is abbreviated as BHS, the Global Financial Database as GFD, and International Historical Statistics (Mitchell, 2003) as IHS. For further details, see Chapters 4 and 5.

A.2.1. *Group 1*

Austria. Austrian data on 10-year government bonds are from the GFD. For 1874–9, the silver 5s bond is used; for 1880–1913, the gold 4s bond. For 1874–9, monthly data are used to compute yearly averages; for 1880–1913, weekly data. Yields are for bonds traded in London.

R1 is central government revenue in Austria, 1781–1913, from IHS. This series covers Austria-Hungary (i.e., Cisleithania plus Transleithania) through 1847 and for 1850–67 and Cisleithania only for 1848–9 and for 1868–1913. Lombardy is included through 1858 and Venetia through 1865. Total revenues are for fiscal receipts only through 1864 and for ordinary receipts for 1865–75. They include certain extraordinary receipts for 1876–1913. Since the IHS data include cash saldi and loan proceeds for 1875–90, updated figures without saldi or loan proceeds from Michael Pammer were used for those years.[1] R2 is central government revenue in Transleithania, 1868–1913, from IHS. The composite series for central government revenues is R1, 1781–1867, and R1 plus R2, 1868–1913.

P1 is the population of Austria for 1818, 1821, 1824, 1827, 1830, 1834, 1837, 1840, 1843, 1846, 1851, 1857, 1869, 1880, 1890, 1900, and 1910 from IHS. Data are for the civil population of Cisleithania only. P2 is the population of Lombardy for 1832–40, 1842–4, and 1846–54, from Michael Pammer. P3 is the population of Venetia for 1832–40, 1842–4, and 1846–54, also from Michael Pammer. For P2 and P3, the years 1841, 1845, and 1849–50 are interpolated. Due to lack of data, the 1832 figures are used for 1818–31, and the 1854 figures are used for 1855–8 for Lombardy and 1855–65 for Venetia. P4 is the population of Hungary for 1787, 1793, 1804, 1817, 1843, 1846, 1850, 1857, 1869, 1880, 1890,

[1] Thanks to Michael Pammer for help with the Austrian budgetary data.

1900, and 1910 from IHS. Data are for Transleithania. The composite population series is P1 plus P2 plus P3 plus P4 for 1818–47 and 1850–8, P1 plus P2 plus P3 for 1848–9, P1 plus P3 plus P4 for 1859–65, and P1 plus P4 for 1866–1910. All intermediate years are interpolated.

The gulden became the general monetary unit in Austria after the War of the Austrian Succession and was set at the Convention of 1753 with 1 gulden equal to 60 kreuzer. Austria decimalized in 1857, adopting a system of 1 gulden to 100 kreuzer. Revenues in gulden were converted into revenues in kreuzer by multiplying by 60. Since 1 pre-1858 gulden was equal to 1.05 gulden from 1858 onward, the pre-1858 gulden series was multiplied by 1.05. Revenues in kreuzer were then converted into revenues in silver grams for 1781–1878 by multiplying by the yearly exchange rate from Giovanni Federico and Michael Pammer. The original source is Pribram (1938, pp. 76–82). Revenues in silver grams were then converted into revenues in gold grams by dividing by the silver for gold price ratio, also from Pribram (1938, pp. 76–82). Since Pribram's data were not available for 1795–1809, the silver for gold price ratio from Officer (2010) was used for those years. These two series are nearly identical from the eighteenth century to the 1870s. The kreuzer–silver exchange rate series ended in 1878, and the krone–pound one began. This exchange rate series is also from Giovanni Federico and Michael Pammer. Revenues in gulden were converted into revenues in kronen by multiplying by 2 for 1879–1913. Revenues in kronen were then converted into revenues in pounds by multiplying by the yearly exchange rate. Revenues in pounds were then converted into revenues in gold troy ounces by dividing by the London market price of gold from Officer (2010). Revenues in gold troy ounces were then converted into revenues in gold grams by multiplying by 31.10.

E1 is central government expenditure, 1781–1913, from IHS. This series covers Austria-Hungary (i.e., Cisleithania plus Transleithania) through 1867 and Cisleithania from 1868 onward. Data do not include expenditures on tax collection through 1864. Total expenditures through 1874 are for cash payments made by the Treasury. They include obligations undertaken and the change in the Treasury's cash balance for 1875–1913. E2 is central government revenue in Transleithania, 1868–1913, from IHS. The composite series for central government expenditures is E1, 1781–1867, and E1 plus E2, 1868–1913. The same conversion process into gold grams was used for expenditures as for revenues.

England. British data on perpetual government bonds are from the GFD. For 1750–3, the 3 percent yield on annuities is used. For 1754–1913, the

British consol is used, which paid 3 percent through 1888, 2.75 percent for 1889–1906, and 2.5 percent for 1907–13. For 1750–1879, monthly data are used to compute yearly averages, for 1880–1913, weekly data. Yields are for bonds traded in London.

R1 is total revenue to the English Crown, 1650–1824, from O'Brien (2010). R2 is net receipts of the public income for Great Britain, 1692–1801, from BHS. R3 is central government revenue for Great Britain, 1750–1801, and for the United Kingdom, 1802–1913, from IHS. The composite series for central government revenues is R1, 1650–91; R2, 1692–1749; and R3, 1750–1913. The years 1654 and 1660 are interpolated.

P1 is the population of England from BHS. These figures do not include Wales (see Wrigley and Schofield, 1981, p. 10). P2 is the population of Wales for 1701, 1751, 1781, 1801, and 1831, from Deane and Cole (1967). P3 is the population of Scotland. The 1650 figure is from De Vries (1984), the 1701 figure from Brown (1991, p. 33), and the 1755 figure from BHS. All intermediate years for Wales and Scotland are interpolated. P4 is the estimated mid-year home population of the British Isles from BHS. The composite population series is P1, 1650–91; P1 plus P2 plus P3, 1692–1801; and P4, 1802–1913.

Acts of Union conjoined England and Wales in 1536, Scotland in 1707, and Ireland in 1800 (see Chapter 2). For 1650–91, revenue data for the English Crown are used. Due to a lack of data, neither Wales nor Scotland was included, though the English Crown collected revenues from those domains. To convert revenue data into per capita terms, they were divided by the English population only.[2] Revenue data are for Great Britain (England, Scotland, and Wales) for 1692–1801 and for the United Kingdom (Great Britain and Ireland) for 1802–1913. Accordingly, revenue data were divided by the populations for England, Scotland, and Wales for 1692–1801, and for England, Scotland, Wales, and Ireland for 1802–1913.

The British official price of gold in pounds per fine troy ounce, 1650–1717, and the London market price of gold in pounds per fine troy ounce, 1718–1913, are from Officer (2010). With the exception of French revolutionary and Napoleonic times (1789–1815), these two series are

---

[2] This choice biases the data against the hypothesis that the establishment of limited government in 1688 led to greater revenues. Since the pre-1692 denominator (i.e., population) was made smaller than it actually was, pre-1692 revenues per capita become higher than they actually were. Any revenue increases after parliamentary reform will thus be smaller than otherwise. Also see Chapter 3.

nearly identical. British revenues in gold troy ounces were converted into revenues in gold grams by multiplying by 31.10.

E1 is issues and assignments for the English exchequer, 1660–87, from Chandaman (1975). To calculate total expenditures, issues (listed at half-year intervals, A and B) and assignments (also listed at half-year intervals, A and B) were summed. E2 is total net expenditure including debt charges for Great Britain, 1692–1801, from BHS. E3 is central government expenditure for Great Britain, 1750–1801, and for the United Kingdom, 1802–1913, from IHS. The composite series for central government expenditures is E1, 1650–87; E2, 1692–1749; and E3, 1750–1913. The same conversion process into gold grams was used for expenditures as for revenues.

France. Since no single debt instrument analogous to the British consol existed in France before the nineteenth century, it is difficult to identify "the" interest rate paid on government loans. Bonds could be perpetual or finite, redeemable or not, and repudiated when revenues ran thin. The eighteenth-century yield data were collected by Velde and Weir (1992), who chose the October loan as the asset that best captured yields on long-term French government bonds for 1750–93. Prior to 1770, the October loan was a private debt of the Compagnie des Indes. From 1770 onward, it was a perpetual debt of the French government. For 1793–6, the Paris Stock Exchange was closed off and on. Data for 1794–1800 are not available, though a perpetual 5 percent consolidated bond was issued in 1798. This bond continued to trade until 1825, when the French government refunded it and issued a perpetual 3 percent bond, which became the primary government bond until 1949.[3] French data for the nineteenth and twentieth centuries are from Jean-Laurent Rosenthal for 1801–72 and from the GFD for 1873–1913. For 1750–1879, monthly data are used to compute yearly averages; for 1880–1913, weekly data. Yields are for bonds traded on the Paris Stock Exchange.

R1 is ordinary revenues of the French monarchy, 1650–95, from Bonney (2010b). R2 is total royal revenue in France from various sources converted into livres tournois, 1660–1775, from Bonney (2010c). R3 is French ordinary revenue, 1727–1814, from Bonney (2010d). R4 is French revenue, 1650–1870, from François Velde. R5 is ordinary central government revenue, 1815–1913, from IHS. R6 is extraordinary central government revenue, 1815–1890, from the Institut national de la statistique et des études économique (1966). The composite series

---

[3] A new 3% bond paying quarterly interest replaced the previous one in 1862.

of central government revenues is R1, 1650–6, 1662; R2, 1661–1703, 1705–15, 1727–50, 1757–8, 1761, 1763, 1773–4; R3, 1751–4, 1764–5, 1768, 1780–1, 1788–96, 1806–13; R4, 1716–26, 1759–60, 1766–7, 1769, 1772, 1775–9, 1782–7, 1791–1805, 1814; R5 plus R6, 1815–90; and R5, 1891–1913. Years 1657–60, 1755–6, 1762, and 1770–1 are interpolated.[4]

P1 is the population of France from Dupaquier (1988, vol. 2). P2 is the population of France from Mathias and O'Brien (1976). P3 is the population of France from Blayo and Henry (1975). P4 is the population of France at censuses from IHS. The composite population series is P1, 1650, 1670, 1680, 1690, 1710; P2, 1715, 1725, 1730, 1735; P3, 1740, 1745, 1750, 1755, 1760, 1765, 1770, 1775–6, 1780–1, 1785–6, 1790–1, 1795–6, 1800–1, 1805–6, 1810–11, 1815–16, 1820–1, 1825–6, 1830–1, 1835–6, 1840–1, 1845–6, 1850–1, 1855–6, 1860–1; P4, 1866, 1872, 1876, 1881, 1886, 1891, 1896, 1901, 1906, 1911, and 1921. All intermediate years are interpolated.

The Paris market price of gold in francs per gram, 1650–1913, is from Jean-Laurent Rosenthal.

E1 is royal expenditure in France, 1600–95, from Bonney (2010e). E2 is royal expenditure in France, 1670–1715, from Bonney (2010f). E3 is French ordinary expenditure, 1727–1814, from Bonney (2010d). E4 is expenditure of the French monarchy at various dates, 1773–85, from Bonney (2010g). E5 is total French expenditure, 1801–44, from Bonney (2010h). E6 is ordinary and extraordinary central government expenditure, 1815–1913, from IHS. The composite series of central government expenditures is E1, 1650–6, 1662–83; E2, 1684–1715; E3, 1727–52, 1764–5, 1767–8, 1780–1, 1788–96; E4, 1785; E5, 1801–14; and E6, 1815–1913. The same conversion process into gold grams was used for expenditures as for revenues.[5]

---

[4] Massive inflation took place after the start of the French Revolution in 1789, generating per capita revenue calculations for 1794–6 that were incredibly large. The revenue data for those years were thus interpolated using the 1793 and 1797 figures. This choice biases the data against the hypothesis that fiscal centralization (which occurred in 1790) improved public finances, since after interpolation the revenue estimates for the 1790s become much lower. Any revenue increases after tax reform will thus be smaller than otherwise. Also see Chapters 2 and 5.

[5] Massive inflation occurred in France during the 1790s, generating incredible expenditure calculations: per capita estimates were 1792, 49.24 gold grams; 1793, 95.94 gold grams; 1794, 170.87 gold grams; 1795, 204.09 gold grams; and 1796, 0.07 gold grams. By comparison, they were 7.62 gold grams in 1791 and 6.16 gold grams in 1801 (the next available observation). The expenditure data for 1792–96 were thus excluded. Also see the preceding footnote.

The Netherlands. Public bonds in the Dutch Republic (1572–1795) were issued by several authorities, including the Union, provinces, and cities. Joost Jonker, Oscar Gelderblom, and Heleen Kole collected the Dutch data used in this study for 1780–1810.[6] Prior to 1780, there were not enough data to form a complete series. For 1780–95, the source is the Dutch newspaper *Maandelijksche Hollandsche Mercurius*, which reported yields on government bonds from securities auctions in Amsterdam. Jonker et al. chose the Holland and Westfriesland perpetual 2.5 percent bond, which (like the October loan in eighteenth-century France) best captured long-term yield levels. For 1796–1813, the source is the Dutch newspaper *Prijscourant der Effecten*. Perpetual 2.5 percent national bonds are used. Data are not available for 1812. The entire national debt, with interest rates ranging from 1.25 to 7 percent, was converted into a single debt in 1814 at a rate of 2.5 percent. The data source for 1814–1913 is the GFD. For 1780–96, monthly data are used to compute yearly averages; for 1797–1812, biweekly data; for 1814–81, monthly data; for 1882, biweekly data; and for 1883–1913, weekly data. Post-1813 bonds were also traded in Amsterdam.

R1 is total tax revenues in the Dutch Republic, 1720–95, from Fritschy et al. (2007).[7] Provincial tax streams for Drenthe, Friesland, Groningen, Holland, Overijssel, and Utrecht were calculated using this source. Sums included income from direct and indirect taxes but excluded income from land sales and loans. The totals for Overijssel were used to calculate those for Brabant and Gelderland. Official quotas for Overijssel and Gelderland were 3.60 percent and 5.61 percent, respectively (see t'Hart, 1997). The totals for Gelderland were thus calculated as 1.56 times (i.e., 5.61 divided by 3.60) those for Overijssel. These totals were also used for Brabant. Data for Zeeland and its admiralty are from Veenstra (2006, 2010).[8] His data include customs (*convooien en licenten*) and tonnage (*lastgeld*) and ship (*veilgeld*) taxes. Customs tax data for the four other admiralties (Amsterdam, Friesland, Noorderkwartier, Rotterdam) are from Hovy (1966). The admiralty data also include annual payments of 364,000 guilders made by the Dutch East India Company. Total tax revenues for the Republic as a whole were calculated as sums of these diverse categories. R2 is income of the Batavian Republic and its successors, 1803–10 and 1814, and R3 is income during the reign of William I,

---

[6] Thanks to Joost Jonker for help with the Dutch yield data.
[7] Thanks to Wantje Fritschy for help with this fascinating database.
[8] Thanks to Wietse Veenstra for help with the Admiralty data.

1814, 1821, 1826, 1831, 1836, and 1840, from van Zanden and van Riel (2004). Since the totals for 1815–30 include Belgium, the average yearly net Belgian transfer according to van Zanden and van Riel (2004, p. 99) was subtracted. For example, the net transfer from Belgium for 1814–20 was 11,800,000 guilders, or 1,966,666 guilders per annum. The latter amount was thus deducted from total income for the Netherlands for each year over this six-year period. The same correction was performed for the periods 1821–5 and 1826–30.[9] The results closely matched the (interpolated) data from Fritschy and van der Voort (1997). R4 is central government revenue, 1845–1913, from IHS. The composite series of central government revenues is R1, 1720–95; R2, 1803–10; R3, 1814–40; and R4, 1845–1913. Years 1841–4 are interpolated.

P1 is the population of the Netherlands from De Vries (1984). The population data used in the time series for per capita revenues for Holland in Figure 5.5 are from Jan Luiten van Zanden. P2 is the population of the Netherlands from IHS. The composite population series is P1, 1700, 1750, 1800; and P2, 1816, 1829, 1839, 1849, 1859, 1869, 1879, 1889, 1899, 1909, and 1920. All intermediate years are interpolated. The data exclude the Southern Netherlands (see earlier discussion).

The Dutch market price of gold in guilders per gram, 1719–1913, is from W. L. Korthals Altes. The years 1749 and 1759, which were missing, are interpolated.

E1 is total expenditures in the Dutch Republic, 1720–94. The totals for Drenthe, Friesland, Groningen, Holland, Overijssel, and Utrecht were calculated from Fritschy et al. (2007). Sums include expenditures on behalf of the Generality and provincial spending. Total expenditures for Gelderland were calculated using the official quotas for Overijssel (3.60 percent) and Gelderland (5.61 percent). As for revenues, the totals for Gelderland were calculated as 1.56 times (i.e., 5.61 divided by 3.60) those for Overijssel. Data for Zeeland are from Veenstra (2010). Roughly 80 percent of defense expenditures for the Republic in 1790 were from the seven provinces and Drenthe. Fritschy et al. (2007) claim that the remaining 20 percent were from other parts: 11 percent from the Admiralties, 7 percent from Brabant, and 2 percent from additional central revenue sources. The series of expenditures by Holland on behalf of the Generality was used to calculate the remaining portion of Generality expenditures. During the 1700s, Holland paid a yearly amount of roughly 60 percent of total Generality expenditures including those of the seven provinces

---

[9] Thanks to Jan Luiten van Zanden for help with this correction.

and Drenthe, or roughly 48 percent of Generality expenditures overall. The remaining portion of yearly Generality expenditures was thus computed as 42 percent (i.e., 20 divided by 48) of Holland's expenditures on behalf of the Generality.[10] Total expenditures for the Republic as a whole were calculated as sums of these diverse categories.[11] E2 is expenditures in the Batavian Republic and its successors, 1803–10, from van Zanden and van Riel (2004). E3 is estimates of expenditures in the Netherlands, 1814–1913, from Jan Luiten van Zanden. His data exclude southern provinces like Belgium. See Fritschy and van der Voort (1997) for a comparison. The composite series of central government expenditures is E1, 1720–95; E2, 1803–10; and E3, 1814–1913. The same conversion process into gold grams was used for expenditures as for revenues.

Prussia. Prussian data on 10-year government bonds for 1815–41 are from the GFD. However, this source used Bavarian bonds for 1842–69. Prussian data on 10-year government bonds for those years were thus taken from Homer and Sylla (2005). 4s bonds are used, except for 1844–52, when 3.5s bonds are used. The Prussian data on 10-year government bonds for 1870–1913 are from the GFD. Prussian 4 percent consols are used for 1870–97, and German 3 percent Imperial loans for 1898–1913. For 1815–41, monthly data are used to compute yearly averages; for 1842–69, infrequent data; for 1870–80, monthly data; and for 1881–1913, weekly data. Yields are for bonds traded in Berlin.

R1 is net revenues of the Prussian state, 1688–1806, from Korner (2010). Revenue data are from the military treasury only for 1688–1713. R2 is total ordinary revenues, 1807–1913, from Mauersberg (1988). The composite series of central government revenues is R1, 1688–1806; and R2, 1821, 1829, 1841, 1847, 1850, 1855, 1860, 1867, 1868, 1870, 1874, 1875, 1880, 1885, 1890, 1900, 1905, and 1910. All intermediate years are interpolated.[12]

P1 is the population of Prussia from Peter Brecke. These data incorporate Prussian territorial changes over the seventeenth to the nineteenth centuries as well as possible. P2 is the population of Prussia from Mauersberg (1988). The composite population series is P1, 1688–1865; and P2, 1870, 1874, 1875, 1880, 1885, 1890, 1895, 1900, 1905, 1910, and 1914. All intermediate years are interpolated.

---

[10] The percentage of expenditures for the Admiralties was lower during the Fourth Anglo-Dutch War (1780–4), which was fought at sea.

[11] Thanks to Wantje Fritschy for help with the expenditure calculations for the Dutch Republic.

[12] Thanks to Mark Spoerer for help with the Prussian budgetary data.

One thaler equaled 60 kreuzer through 1692. The thaler became the speciesthaler in 1693 following the Conference of Leipzig, with 1 speciesthaler equal to 120 kreuzer. The speciesthaler was redefined as equal to 1.33 thalers in 1753 following the Convention of Vienna. Revenues in thalers were converted into revenues in kreuzer by multiplying by 60 for 1688–92 and by 120 for 1693–1871, and by dividing by 1.33 for 1753–1913. Revenues in kreuzer were then converted into revenues in silver grams by multiplying by the yearly exchange rate from Pribram (1938, pp. 76–82). Revenues in silver grams were then converted into revenues in gold grams by dividing by the silver for gold price ratio, also from Pribram (1938, pp. 76–82). Since Pribram's data were not available for 1795–1809, the silver for gold price ratio from Officer (2010) was used for those years. These two series are nearly identical from the seventeenth century to the 1870s. The mark–U.S. dollar exchange rate series from the GFD began in 1872. Revenues in thalers were converted into revenues in marks by multiplying by 3 for 1872–1913. Revenues in marks were then converted to revenues in U.S. dollars. Exchange rates were computed as yearly averages of closing prices taken from the last day of trading each month. Revenues in dollars were then converted into gold troy ounces by dividing by the New York market price of gold from Officer (2010). Revenues in gold troy ounces were then converted into revenues in gold grams by multiplying by 31.10.[13]

E1 is total expenditure of the Prussian state, 1688–1806, from Korner (2010). E2 is expenditures, 1821–66, from Tilly (1966, 1967). E3 is total ordinary expenditures, 1807–1913, from Mauersberg (1988). The composite series of central government expenditures is E1, 1688–1806; E2, 1838, 1849, 1853, 1856, 1866; and E3, 1821, 1829, 1841, 1847, 1850, 1855, 1860, 1867, 1868, 1870, 1874, 1875, 1880, 1885, 1890, 1900, 1905, 1910. The same conversion process into gold grams was used for expenditures as for revenues.

Spain. Like Old Regime France, Spain issued many disparate debt instruments prior to the nineteenth century (see Tortella and Comín, 2001). The Spanish yield series, however, did not begin until 1821. Data are for 10-year government bonds from the GFD. For 1823–36, 5s bonds are used. For 1836–81, 3s bonds are used. In 1881, the 3s bonds were converted into a 1 percent bond. The 1 percent bond was converted into a 1.25 percent bond in 1882, and then into a 4 percent bond. The 4 percent bond is used for 1882–1913. Monthly data are used for 1821–1913 to

---

[13] The conversion from thalers into gold grams was updated from Dincecco (2009a).

compute yearly averages. London yields are used for the entire series, except for 1913, when the Madrid yield is used.

R1 is ordinary and extraordinary revenues to the Spanish Crown, 1703 and 1713, from Lynch (1989, p. 61). R2 is ordinary and extraordinary revenues to the Spanish Crown, 1753–88, from Gelabert (2010). R3 is Ingresos Totales del Estado, 1801–42, and R4 is Derechos Reconocidos y Liquidados Totales, 1845–1913, from Carreras and Tafunell (2006). The composite series of central government revenues is R1, 1703, 1713; R2, 1753–88; R3, 1801–7, 1813–20, 1822, 1824–39, 1841–2; and R4, 1845, 1849–1913. All other years are interpolated.[14]

P1 is the population of Spain from De Vries (1984). P2 is the population of Spain from Nogal and Prados de la Escosura (2006). P3 is the population of Spain from Lynch (1989). P4 is the population of Spain from IHS. The composite population series is P1, 1700, 1850; P2, 1750, 1787; P3, 1717, 1797; and P4, 1768, 1857, 1860, 1877, 1887, 1897, 1900, 1910, and 1920. All intermediate years are interpolated.

Since buying and selling bullion outside the Spanish mint was forbidden, the Spanish market price of gold or silver is not available from the sixteenth to the nineteenth century.[15] Spanish revenues were in reales for 1703–1842 and pesetas for 1843–1913, with 1 peso equal to 20 reales or 5 pesetas. Revenues in reales were converted into revenues in pesos by dividing by 20 through 1842 and by 5 from 1843 onward. Revenues in pesos were then converted into revenues in pounds using the peso–pound exchange rate series from the GFD. Exchange rates were computed as yearly averages of closing prices taken from the last day of trading each month. Revenues in pounds were then converted into revenues in gold grams by dividing by the London market price of gold in pounds per fine troy ounce from Officer (2010). Revenues in gold troy ounces were then converted into revenues in gold grams by multiplying by 31.10.

E1 is Gastos Totales del Estado, 1801–42, and E2 is Obligaciones Totales del Estado Reconocidos y Liquidadas, 1845–1913, from Carreras and Tafunell (2006). The composite series of central government expenditures is E1, 1801–3, 1805–7, 1813–7, 1819–22, 1827–8, 1830–1, 1833–9, 1841–2; and E2, 1845, 1849–1913. The same conversion process into gold grams was used for expenditures as for revenues.

---

[14] Thanks to Carlos Álvarez Nogal for help with the Spanish revenue data.
[15] Thanks to Maria Del Pilar Nogués Marco for this information.

A.2.2. Group 2

Belgium. Belgian data on 10-year government bonds are from the GFD. For 1832–44, the 5 percent bond is used; for 1845–58, the 4.5 percent bond; and for 1859–1913, the 3 percent bond. For 1832–84, monthly data are used to compute yearly averages; for 1885–98, biweekly data; and for 1889–1913, monthly data. Yields are for bonds traded in Brussels.

R1 is central government revenue, 1831–1912, from IHS. Data are not available for 1913. The composite series of central government revenues is R1, 1831–1912.

P1 is the population of Belgium from IHS. The composite population series is P1, 1816, 1831, 1846, 1856, 1866, 1880, 1890, 1910, and 1920. All intermediate years are interpolated.

Belgium adopted the French monetary system during French revolutionary and Napoleonic times (1789–1815) with one Belgian franc equal to one French franc. The Paris market price of gold in francs per gram from Jean-Laurent Rosenthal was thus used.

E1 is central government expenditure, 1831–1912, from IHS. Data are not available for 1913. The composite series of central government expenditures is E1, 1831–1912. The same conversion process into gold grams was used for expenditures as for revenues.

Denmark. Danish data on 10-year government bonds are from the GFD. For 1821–5 and 1852–8, the 5s bond is used; for 1825–52, the 3s bond; and for 1864–94 the consolidated 4s bond. The consolidated 4s bond was converted into 3.5 percent consols in 1895, which are used through 1913. Data are not available for 1859–63. Monthly data are used to compute yearly averages for 1821–1913. Yields are for bonds traded in London.

R1 is central government revenue, 1853–1913, from IHS. These data include the Duchies of Schleswig, Holstein, and Lauenburg for 1853–64. The composite series of central government revenues is R1, 1853–1913.

P1 is the population of Denmark from IHS. These data include the Duchies of Schleswig, Holstein, and Lauenburg for 1853–64. The composite population series is P1, 1769, 1787, 1801, 1834, 1840, 1845, 1850, 1855, 1860, 1870, 1880, 1890, 1901, 1906, 1911, and 1916. All intermediate years are interpolated.

Revenues in kroner were converted into revenues in U.S. dollars by multiplying by the exchange rate from the GFD. This series began in 1864. Exchange rates were computed as yearly averages of closing prices taken from the last day of trading each month. Revenues in dollars were then converted into gold troy ounces by dividing by the New York market price of gold from Officer (2010). Revenues in gold troy ounces were then converted into revenues in gold grams by multiplying by 31.10.[16]

E1 is central government expenditure, 1854–1913, from IHS. Figures include the Duchies of Schleswig, Holstein, and Lauenburg for 1854–65. The composite series of central government expenditures is E1, 1854–1913. The same conversion process into gold grams was used for expenditures as for revenues.

Italy. Italian data on long-term government bonds are from the GFD. The average maturity was six years. For 1862–99, the consolidated 5 percent bond is used; for 1900–13, the 3.5 percent consol bond. Monthly data are used to compute yearly averages for 1862–1913. Yields are for bonds traded in London.

R1 is central government revenue, 1862–83 and 1886–1913, from IHS. The composite series of central government revenues is R1, 1862–1913. Years 1884–5 are interpolated.

P1 is the population of Italy from IHS. The composite population series is P1, 1861, 1871, 1881, 1901, 1911, and 1921. All intermediate years are interpolated.

The lira was adopted as the monetary unit of the Kingdom of Italy in 1862 with 1 lira equal to 1 French franc. The Paris market price of gold in francs per gram from Jean-Laurent Rosenthal was thus used.

E1 is central government expenditure, 1862–83 and 1886–1913, from IHS. Data are not available for 1884–5. The composite series of central government expenditures is E1, 1862–83 and 1886–1913. The same conversion process into gold grams was used for expenditures as for revenues.

Portugal. Portuguese data on 10-year government bonds are from the GFD. For 1823–95 and 1903–13, the 3 percent bond is used; for 1896–1902, the 1 percent bond. Data are not available for 1903. Monthly data are used to compute yearly averages for 1823–1913. Yields are for bonds traded in London.

R1 is government revenue, 1762–1913, from Cardoso and Lains (2010b). The composite series of government revenues is R1, 1762–76, 1797–1804, 1812, 1817, 1821, 1827–8, 1834–45, 1847, and 1852–1913.[17] All intermediate years are interpolated.

---

[16] The conversion from kroner into gold grams was updated from Dincecco (2009a).

[17] Due to new evidence published by Cardoso and Lains (2010a), the time series for Portuguese revenues and expenditures was updated from Dincecco (2009a).

P1 is the population of Portugal from IHS. The composite population series is P1, 1768, 1801, 1821, 1835, 1838, 1841, 1854, 1858, 1861, 1864, 1878, 1890, 1900, 1911, and 1920. All intermediate years are interpolated. The Azores and Maderia are included from 1841 onward.

Revenues in contos were converted into revenues in milreis by multiplying by 1,000. Revenues in milreis were then converted into revenues in pounds by dividing by the exchange rate from the GFD. Yearly averages of monthly exchange rates were used. Revenues in pounds were then converted into revenues in gold troy ounces by dividing by the London market price of gold from Officer (2010). Revenues in gold troy ounces were then converted into revenues in gold grams by multiplying by 31.10.

E1 is government expenditure, 1762–1913, from Cardoso and Lains (2010b). The composite series of government expenditures is E1, 1762–76, 1800–2, 1812, 1817, 1821, 1827–8, 1834–45, 1847, and 1852–1913. The same conversion process into gold grams was used for expenditures as for revenues.

Sweden. Swedish data on 10-year government bonds are from the GFD. For 1868–78, the 5s bond is used; for 1878–94, the 4s bond; and for 1894–1913, the 3s bond. Monthly data are used to compute yearly averages for 1868–1913. Yields are for bonds traded in London.

R1 is ordinary and extraordinary state revenue, 1722–1911, from Fregert and Gustafsson (2008). R2 is central government revenue, 1912–3, from IHS. The composite series of central government revenues is R1, 1722–1911, and R2, 1912–3.[18]

P1 is the population of Sweden from IHS. The composite population series is P1, 1750, 1760, 1770, 1775, 1780, 1785, 1790, 1795, 1800, 1805, 1810, 1815, 1820, 1825, 1830, 1835, 1840, 1845, 1850, 1855, 1860, 1870, 1880, 1890, 1900, 1910, and 1915. All intermediate years are interpolated.

Revenues in kronor were converted into revenues in guilders by multiplying by the exchange rate from the GFD. This series began in 1740. Exchange rates were computed as yearly averages of closing prices taken from the last day of trading each month. Revenues in guilders were then converted into gold grams by dividing by the Dutch market price of gold in guilders per gram from W. L. Korthals Altes. The years 1749 and 1759, which were missing, are interpolated.[19]

[18] Due to the discovery of the evidence published by Fregert and Gustafsson (2008), the time series for Swedish revenues and expenditures were updated from Dincecco (2009a).
[19] The conversion from kronor into gold grams was updated from Dincecco (2009a).

E1 is ordinary and extraordinary state expenditure, 1722–1911, from Fregert and Gustafsson (2008). E2 is central government expenditure, 1912–3, from IHS. The composite series of central government expenditures is E1, 1722–1911, and E2, 1912–3. The same conversion process into gold grams was used for expenditures as for revenues.

A.3. Descriptions of Control Variables

For further details, see Chapter 7.

War Deaths. Average military deaths per conflict year sustained by participant countries (in hundreds of thousands). All external conflicts fought in Western and Eastern Europe that involved at least one sample country according to Clodfelter (2002) were included. Clodfelter's dates for the durations of wars were used. However, formal peace treaties were not signed until years after ceasefires in some cases. The term "casualty" refers to all persons lost to active military service, including those killed in action or by disease, disabled by physical or mental injuries, captured, deserted, or missing. Due to data limitations, Clodfelter's data sometimes refer to soldiers killed or wounded in battle and deaths by disease, and not to casualties per se. Total military deaths were used in such cases. If those data were not available, then deaths from major land and sea battles and major sieges were summed. Death totals were then divided by conflict lengths to determine average military deaths per year. Non-overlapping average deaths per conflict were summed for each year that a sample country was involved in two or more wars. Sources: Clodfelter (2002) and Dincecco (2009a, app. 3).

Enemy Coalition Size. Sums of (available) total populations for coalition countries in the year that conflicts began (in tens of millions). Non-overlapping opposition coalition totals were summed for each year that a sample country was involved in two or more conflicts. Sources: Clodfelter (2002), Dincecco (2009a, app. 3), and Appendix 2.

Mercenary Dummy. Equal to 1 for each year that a country fought as part of an alliance with England, the Dutch Republic, or France. Sources: Clodfelter (2002) and Dincecco (2010a).

Default Dummy. Equal to 1 for each year that a national government partially or fully defaulted on its public debt. Sources: Reinhart et al. (2003, table 2), supplemented by Ferguson and Shularick (2006) for Belgium, Denmark, and Sweden; by Jones (1994, p. 94) for England; by Sargent and Velde (1995, p. 480) for France; by Federico (2010) for Italy; and by Fritschy and van der Voort (1997, p. 65) for the Netherlands.

Internal Conflict Dummy. Equal to 1 for each year of civil war, coup, and revolution. Insurrections, massacres, riots, and uprisings were typically excluded. Sources: Clodfelter (2002) and the *Encyclopedia Britannica* (2010).

Urbanization Rate. Annual shares of urban populations in total populations. Data are for 1650, 1700, 1750, 1850, 1890, and 1980, and are for cities with minimum populations of 10,000 through 1850, 20,000 in 1890, and 100,000 inhabitants in 1980. All intermediate years are interpolated. The data for Austria include Bohemia. Due to data limitations, figures for Germany were used for Prussia, and figures for Scandinavia were used for Denmark and Sweden. Sources: De Vries (1984, app. 3 and table 4.8) and Appendix A.2.

Country Dummy. Equal to 1 for each sample country.

Old Regime Dummy. Equal to 1 for each year before the fall of the Old Regime in 1789.

Gold Standard Dummy. Equal to 1 for each year that a country adhered to the gold standard, starting the year in which a currency became de facto and de jure convertible into gold. Sources: Meissner (2005, table 1), supplemented by Officer (2001) for England.

Average Credit Risk. Average annual yield spread using available data for all sample countries over the "safe" British consol.

Change in Gold Stock. Yearly change in the cumulative world stock of gold in millions of troy ounces. Source: Velde and Weber (2000).

Railway Nationalization Dummy. Equal to 1 for each year that a major nationalization of railways took place. Source: Bogart (2009, table 1).

Works Cited

Accominotti, O., M. Flandreau, R. Rezzik, and F. Zumer (2010). "Black Man's Burden, White Man's Welfare: Control, Devolution, and Development in the British Empire, 1880–1914." *European Review of Economic History,* 14: 47–70.

Acemoglu, D. (2005). "Politics and Economics in Weak and Strong States." *Journal of Monetary Economics,* 52: 1199–1226.

Acemoglu, D., and J. Robinson (2000). "Why Did the West Extend the Franchise? Democracy, Inequality, and Growth in Historical Perspective." *Quarterly Journal of Economics,* 115: 1167–99.

Acemoglu, D., S. Johnson, and J. Robinson (2001). "Colonial Origins of Comparative Development: An Empirical Investigation." *American Economic Review,* 91: 1369–1401.

(2002). "Reversal of Fortune: Geography and Development in the Making of the Modern World Income Distribution." *Quarterly Journal of Economics,* 117: 1231–94.

(2005). "The Rise of Europe: Atlantic Trade, Institutional Change, and Economic Growth." *American Economic Review,* 94: 546–79.

Acemoglu, D., J. Robinson, and T. Verdier (2004). "Alfred Marshall Lecture – Kleptocracy and Divide-and-Rule: A Model of Personal Rule." *Journal of the European Economic Association,* 2: 162–92.

Acemoglu, D., D. Cantoni, S. Johnson, and J. Robinson (2009a). "The Consequences of Radical Reform: The French Revolution." NBER Working Paper 14831, National Bureau of Economic Research.

Acemoglu, D., S. Johnson, J. Robinson, and P. Yared (2009b). "Reevaluating the Modernization Hypothesis." *Journal of Monetary Economics,* 56: 1043–58.

Acemoglu, D., D. Ticchi, and A. Vindigni (2011). "Emergence and Persistence of Inefficient States." *Journal of the European Economic Association,* 9: 177–208.

Adler, J., Schlesinger, and E. Olson (1952). *Public Finance and Economic Development in Guatemala.* Stanford, CA: Stanford University Press.

Aidt, T., and Jensen, P. (2009). "Tax Structure, Size of Government, and the Extension of the Voting Franchise in Western Europe, 1860–1938." *International Tax and Public Finance*, 16: 362–94.

Aidt, T., J. Dutta, and E. Loukoianova (2006). "Democracy Comes to Europe: Franchise Extension and Fiscal Outcomes, 1830–1938." *European Economic Review*, 50: 249–83.

Alesina, A., A. Devleeschauwer, W. Easterly, S. Kurlat, and R. Wacziarg (2002). "Fractionalization." *Journal of Economic Growth*, 8: 155–94.

Ashton, R. (1960). *The Crown and the Money Market, 1603–40.* Oxford: Clarendon Press.

Bai, J., and P. Perron (2003). "Computation and Analysis of Multiple Structural Change Models." *Journal of Applied Econometrics*, 18: 1–22.

Bairoch, P. (1988). *Cities and Economic Development: From the Dawn of History to the Present.* Chicago: University of Chicago Press.

Barro, R. (1979). "On the Determination of Public Debt." *Journal of Political Economy*, 87: 940–71.

   (1987). "Government Spending, Interest Rates, Prices, and Budget Deficits in the United Kingdom, 1701–1918." *Journal of Monetary Economics*, 20: 221–48.

   (1989). "The Neoclassical Approach to Fiscal Policy." In R. Barro, ed., *Modern Business Cycle Theory.* Cambridge: Cambridge University Press.

Bates, R. (2001). *Prosperity and Violence.* Cambridge, MA: Harvard University Press.

Beck, N. (2008). "Time-Series Cross-Section Methods." In J. Box-Steffensmeier, H. Brady, and D. Collier, eds., *The Oxford Handbook of Political Methodology.* Oxford: Oxford University Press.

Beck, N., and J. Katz (1995). "What to Do (and Not to Do) with Time-Series Cross-Section Data." *American Political Science Review*, 89: 634–47.

   (1996). "Nuisance vs. Substance: Specifying and Estimating Time-Series Cross-Section Models." *Political Analysis*, 6: 1–36.

Berger, H., and M. Spoerer (2001). "Economic Crises and the European Revolutions of 1848." *Journal of Economic History*, 61: 293–326.

Bernanke, B. (2006). "The Coming Demographic Transition: Will We Treat Future Generations Fairly?" Speech at the Washington Economic Club, October 4.

Besley, T., and T. Persson (2008). "Wars and State Capacity." *Journal of the European Economic Association*, 2: 522–30.

   (2009). "The Origins of State Capacity: Property Rights, Taxation, and Politics." *American Economic Review*, 99: 1218–44.

   (2010). "State Capacity, Conflict, and Development." *Econometrica*, 78: 1–34.

Blayo, Y., and L. Henry (1975). "La Population de la France de 1740 à 1860." *Population*, November: 71–122.

Bogart, D. (2005). "Did Turnpike Trusts Increase Transportation Investment in Eighteenth-Century England?" *Journal of Economic History*, 65: 439–68.

   (2009). "Nationalizations and the Development of Transport Systems: Cross-Country Evidence from Railroad Networks, 1860–1912." *Journal of Economic History*, 69: 202–37.

Bonney, R. (1995). *Economic Systems and State Finance.* Oxford: Oxford University Press.

(1999). *The Rise of the Fiscal State in Europe. 1200–1815.* Oxford: Oxford University Press.

(2010a). "The Apogee and Fall of the French Rentier Regime, 1801–1914." In J. Cardoso and P. Lains, eds., *Paying for the Liberal State: The Rise of Public Finance in Nineteenth-Century Europe,* Cambridge: Cambridge University Press.

(2010b). "Categories of Ordinary Revenues of the French Monarchy, 1600–95." European State Financial Database, administered by D. Coffman and A. Murphy, http://esfdb.websites.bta.com/Default.aspx.

(2010c). "Total Royal Revenue in France, 1660–1775, Converted into Livres Tournois." European State Financial Database, administered by D. Coffman and A. Murphy, http://esfdb.websites.bta.com/Default.aspx.

(2010d). "French Ordinary Revenue and Expenditure, 1727–1814." European State Financial Database, administered by D. Coffman and A. Murphy, http://esfdb.websites.bta.com/Default.aspx.

(2010e) "Malet's Figures for Royal Expenditure in France, 1600–95." European State Financial Database, administered by D. Coffman and A. Murphy, http://esfdb.websites.bta.com/Default.aspx.

(2010f). "Forbonnais: Royal Expenditure in France, 1670–1715." European State Financial Database, administered by D. Coffman and A. Murphy, http://esfdb.websites.bta.com/Default.aspx.

(2010g). "Revenue and Expenditure of the French Monarchy at Various Dates Between 1773 and 1785." European State Financial Database, administered by D. Coffman and A. Murphy, http://esfdb.websites.bta.com/Default.aspx.

(2010h). "Total French Expenditure, 1801–44." European State Financial Database, administered by D. Coffman and A. Murphy, http://esfdb.websites.bta.com/Default.aspx.

Bordo, M., and R. Cortés-Conde (2001). *Transferring Wealth and Power from the Old to the New World: Monetary and Fiscal Institutions in the Seventeenth through the Nineteenth Centuries.* Cambridge: Cambridge University Press.

Bordo, M., and H. Rockoff (1996). "The Gold Standard as a Good Housekeeping Seal of Approval." *Journal of Economic History,* 56: 389–428.

Bordo, M., and E. White (1991). "A Tale of Two Currencies: British and French Finance During the Napoleonic Wars." *Journal of Economic History,* 51: 303–16.

Brennan, G., and J. Buchanan (1980). *The Power to Tax: Analytical Foundations of a Fiscal Constitution.* Cambridge: Cambridge University Press.

Breuilly, J. (2003). "Napoleonic Germany and State Formation." In M. Rowe, ed., *Collaboration and Resistance in Napoleonic Europe: State Formation in an Age of Upheaval, c. 1800–15.* New York: Palgrave Macmillan.

Brewer, J. (1989). *The Sinews of Power: War, Money, and the English State, 1688–1783.* London: Unwin Hyman.

Brown, R. (1991). *Society and Economy in Modern Britain, 1700–1850.* London: Routledge.

Brown, W., and R. Burdekin (2000). "Turning Points in the U.S. Civil War: A British Perspective." *Journal of Economic History*, 60: 216–31.

Brown, W., R. Burdekin, and M. Weidenmier (2006). "Volatility in an Era of Reduced Uncertainty: Lessons from Pax Britannica." *Journal of Financial Economics*, 79: 693–707.

Burns, J. (2010). "Britain's Leader Carves Identity as Slasher of Government Bloat." *New York Times*, July 21.

Cain, P., and A. Hopkins (1994). *British Imperialism*. London: Longman.

Cameron, D. (2010). "We Must Tackle Britain's Massive Deficit and Growing Debt." Speech at Open University, June 7.

Cardoso, J., and P. Lains (2010a). *Paying for the Liberal State: The Rise of Public Finance in Nineteenth-Century Europe*. Cambridge: Cambridge University Press.

——— (2010b). "Public Finance in Portugal, 1796–1910." In J. Cardoso and P. Lains, eds., *Paying for the Liberal State: The Rise of Public Finance in Nineteenth-Century Europe*. Cambridge: Cambridge University Press.

Carstairs, A. (1980). *A Short History of Electoral Systems in Western Europe*. London: George Allen.

Carreras, A., and X. Tafunell (2006). *Estadisticas Historicas de Espana*. Madrid: Fundación BBVA.

Central Intelligence Agency (2010). "CIA World Factbook." https://www.cia.gov/library/publications/the-world-factbook.

Chandaman, C. (1975). *The English Public Revenue, 1660–88*. Oxford: Clarendon Press.

Clark, G. (1996). "The Political Foundations of Modern Economic Growth: England, 1540–1800." *Journal of Interdisciplinary History*, 26: 563–88.

Clodfelter, M. (2002). *Warfare and Armed Conflicts: A Statistical Reference to Casualty and Other Figures, 1500–2000*, 2d ed. Jefferson, NC: McFarland.

Cohen, J., and G. Federico (2001). *The Growth of the Italian Economy, 1820–1960*. Cambridge: Cambridge University Press.

Cook, B. (2002). *Belgium: A History*. New York: Peter Lang.

Comín, F. (1990). *Las cuentas de la Hacienda preliberal en España, 1801–55*. Madrid: Banco de España.

——— (2010). "Public Finance and the Rise of the Liberal State in Spain, 1808–1914." In J. Cardoso and P. Lains, eds., *Paying for the Liberal State: The Rise of Public Finance in Nineteenth-Century Europe*. Cambridge: Cambridge University Press.

Cox, G. (2011). "War, Moral Hazard, and Ministerial Responsibility: England after the Glorious Revolution." *Journal of Economic History*, 71: 133–61.

Cust, R. (1987). *The Forced Loan and English Politics, 1626–8*. Oxford: Clarendon Press.

Deane, P., and W. Cole (1967). *British Economic Growth, 1688–1959: Trends and Structure*. Cambridge: Cambridge University Press.

De Long, B., and A. Shleifer (1993). "Princes and Merchants: European City Growth Before the Industrial Revolution." *Journal of Law and Economics*, 36: 671–702.

De Vries, J. (1984). *European Urbanization, 1500–1800.* Cambridge, MA: Harvard University Press.

Dickson, P. (1967). *The Financial Revolution in England: A Study in the Development of Public Credit, 1688–1756.* New York: St. Martin's Press.

Dincecco, M. (2009a). "Fiscal Centralization, Limited Government, and Public Revenues in Europe, 1650–1913." *Journal of Economic History,* 69: 48–103.

    (2009b). "Political Regimes and Sovereign Credit Risk in Europe, 1750–1913." *European Review of Economic History,* 13: 31–63.

    (2010a). "The Political Economy of Fiscal Prudence in Historical Perspective." *Economics & Politics,* 22: 1–36.

    (2010b). "Fragmented Authority from Ancien Régime to Modernity: A Quantitative Analysis." *Journal of Institutional Economics,* 6: 305–28.

Dincecco, M., G. Federico, and A. Vindigni (2011). "Warfare, Taxation, and Political Change: Evidence from the Italian Risorgimento." Unpublished paper, IMT Lucca Institute for Advanced Studies.

Dincecco, M., and M. Prado (2011). "Warfare, Fiscal Capacity, and Performance." Unpublished paper, IMT Lucca Institute for Advanced Studies.

Doan, T. (2010). "Bai–Perron Procedure for RATS Software." Estima, http://www.estima.com.

Drelichman, M., and H. J. Voth (2008). "Debt Sustainability in Historical Perspective: The Role of Fiscal Repression." *Journal of the European Economics Association,* 6: 657–67.

    (2010). "The Sustainable Debts of Philip II: A Reconstruction of Castile's Fiscal Position, 1566–96." *Journal of Economic History,* 70: 813–42.

Dupaquier, J. (1988). *Histoire de la Population Française.* Paris: Presses Universitaires de France.

Economist, The (2006). "Impunity Rules; Guatemala." November 18.

Edling, M. (2003). *A Revolution in Favor of Government: Origins of the U.S. Constitution and the Making of the American State.* Oxford: Oxford University Press.

Elliot, J. (1986). *The Count-Duke of Olivares: The Statesman in an Age of Decline.* New Haven, CT: Yale University Press.

Epstein, S. (2000). *Freedom and Growth: Markets and States in Europe, 1300–1750.* London: Routledge.

Federico, G. (2010). "Always on the Brink: Piedmont and Italy." In J. Cardoso and P. Lains, eds., *Paying for the Liberal State: The Rise of Public Finance in Nineteenth-Century Europe.* Cambridge: Cambridge University Press.

Ferguson, N. (1998). *The House of Rothschild.* New York: Penguin.

    (2006). "Political Risk and the International Bond Market Between the 1848 Revolution and the Outbreak of the First World War." *Economic History Review,* 59: 70–112.

Ferguson, N., and M. Schularick (2006). "The Empire Effect: Determinants of Country Risk in the First Age of Globalization, 1880–1913." *Journal of Economic History,* 66: 283–312.

Flandreau, M., and F. Zumer (2004). *The Making of Global Finance, 1880–1913.* Paris: OECD.

Flora, P. (1983). *State, Economy, and Society in Western Europe, 1815–1975*, Vol. 1. Frankfurt: Campus Verlag.

Fontvieille, L. (1976). *Évolution et croissance de l'État français, 1815–1969*. Paris: Institut des Sciences Mathématiques et Economiques Appliquées.

Fregert, K., and R. Gustafsson (2008). "Fiscal Statistics for Sweden, 1719–2003." *Research in Economic History*, 25: 169–224.

Frey, B., and M. Kucher (2000). "History as Reflected in Capital Markets: The Case of World War II." *Journal of Economic History*, 60: 468–96.

Fritschy, W. (2003). "A 'Financial Revolution' Reconsidered: Public Finance in Holland During the Dutch Revolt, 1568–1648." *Economic History Review*, 56: 57–89.

(2007). "The Efficiency of Taxation in Holland." In O. Gelderblom, ed., *The Political Economy of the Dutch Republic*. London: Ashgate.

Fritschy, W., and R. van der Voort (1997). "From Fragmentation to Unification: Public Finance, 1700–1914." In M. t'Hart, J. Jonker, and J. L. van Zanden, eds., *A Financial History of the Netherlands*. Cambridge: Cambridge University Press.

Fritschy, W., M. t'Hart, and E. Horlings (2002). "Continuities and Discontinuities in Dutch Fiscal History, 1515–1913." Paper presented at the Fifteenth Economic History Congress, Buenos Aires, July 26.

Fritschy, W., L. van der Ent, V. Enthoven, R. Liesker, C. Trompetter, S. Verstegen, and W. Veenstra (2007). "Provincial Finances in the Days of the Republic of the United Netherlands." Institute for Netherlands History Project, http://www.inghist.nl.

Gelabert, J. (2010). "Revenue of the Spanish Crown, 1753–1788." European State Financial Database, administered by D. Coffman and A. Murphy, http://esfdb.websites.bta.com/Default.aspx.

Gelderblom, O., and J. Jonker (2011). "Public Finance and Economic Growth: The Case of Holland in the Seventeenth Century." *Journal of Economic History*, 71: 1–39.

Glaeser, E., R. La Porta, F. Lopez-de-Silanes, and A. Shleifer (2004). "Do Institutions Cause Growth?" *Journal of Economic Growth*, 9: 271–303.

Global Financial Data (2010). "Global Financial Database." https://www.globalfinancialdata.com.

Godechot, J., B. Hyslop, and D. Dowd (1971). *The Napoleonic Era in Europe*. New York: Holt, Rinehart, and Winston.

Grab, A. (2003). *Napoleon and the Transformation of Europe*. New York: Palgrave Macmillan.

Greene, W. (2000). *Econometric Analysis*, 4th ed. Upper Saddle River, NJ: Prentice Hall.

Griffiths, R. (1982). "The Creation of the Dutch National Economy, 1795–1909." *Tijdschrift voor Geschiedenis*, 95: 513–37.

Henderson, W. (1939). *The Zollverein*. Cambridge: Cambridge University Press.

Henshall, N. (1992). *The Myth of Absolutism: Change and Continuity in Early Modern European Monarchy*. New York: Longman.

Herbst, J. (2000). *States and Power in Africa: Comparative Lessons in Authority and Control*. Princeton, NJ: Princeton University Press.

Heston, A., R. Summers, and B. Aten (2006). "Penn World Tables, Version 6.2." Center for International Comparisons of Production, Income, and Prices, University of Pennsylvania, http://pwt.econ.upenn.edu/.

Hill, C. (1980). *The Century of Revolution, 1603–1714*. Walton-on-Thames: Nelson.

Hirst, D. (1986). *Authority and Conflict: England, 1603–58*. Cambridge, MA: Harvard University Press.

Hoffman, P. (1994). "Early Modern France, 1450–1700." In P. Hoffman and K. Norberg, eds., *Fiscal Crises, Liberty, and Representative Government, 1450–1789*. Stanford, CA: Stanford University Press.

(2009). "Why Was It that Europeans Conquered the World?" Unpublished paper, California Institute of Technology.

Hoffman, P., and K. Norberg (1994a). *Fiscal Crises, Liberty, and Representative Government, 1450–1789*. Stanford, CA: Stanford University Press.

(1994b). "Conclusion." In P. Hoffman and K. Norberg, eds., *Fiscal Crises, Liberty, and Representative Government, 1450–1789*. Stanford, CA: Stanford University Press.

Hoffman, P., and J. L. Rosenthal (1997). "The Political Economy of Warfare and Taxation in Early Modern Europe: Historical Lessons for Economic Development." In J. Drobak and J. Nye, eds., *The Frontiers of the New Institutional Economics*. St. Louis: Academic Press.

(2000). "Divided We Fall: The Political Economy of Warfare and Taxation." Unpublished paper, California Institute of Technology.

Hohenberg, P., and L. Lees (1985). *The Making of Urban Europe, 1000–1950*. Cambridge, MA: Harvard University Press.

Hollinger, P. (2010). "France: Pension Tensions." *Financial Times*, May 26.

Holmes, G. (1993). *The Making of a Great Power: Late Stuart and Early Georgian Britain, 1660–1722*. London: Longman.

Holtman, R. (1967). *The Napoleonic Revolution*. Baton Rouge: Louisiana State University Press.

Homer, S., and R. Sylla (2005). *A History of Interest Rates*, 4th ed. Hoboken, NJ: Wiley.

Hovy, J. (1966). *Het voorstel von 1751 tot instelling van een beperkt vrijhavenstelsel in de Republiek (propositie tot een gelimiteerd porto-franco)*. Groningen: J. B. Wolters.

Husted, T., and L. Kenny (1997). "The Effect of the Expansion of the Voting Franchise on the Size of Government." *Journal of Political Economy*, 105: 54–82.

Institut national de la statistique et des études économiques (1966). *Annuaire statistique*. Paris.

International Monetary Fund (2005). "Staff Report for the 2005 Article IV Consultation: Guatemala." Country Report No. 05/362.

International Monetary Fund (2010). "Government Financial Statistics." http://www.imfstatistics.org/imf.

Jacks, D. (2005). "Intra- and International Commodity Market Integration in the Atlantic Economy, 1800–1913." *Explorations in Economic History*, 42: 381–413.

Jackson, H. (1974). *A Short History of France from Early Times to 1972*. Cambridge: Cambridge University Press.

Jin, H. Y. (2005). "Were Kim Jong-Il Sleeps and Works." *Daily NK*, March 15.
Johnson, N. (2006). "Banking on the King: The Evolution of the Royal Revenue Farms in Old Regime France." *Journal of Economic History*, 66: 963–91.
Jones, J. (1972). *The Revolution of 1688 in England*. London: Weidenfeld and Nicolson.
(1994). "Fiscal Polities, Liberties, and Representative Government during the Reigns of the Last Stuarts." In P. Hoffman and K. Norberg, eds., *Fiscal Crises, Liberty, and Representative Government, 1450–1789*. Stanford, CA: Stanford University Press.
Kang, D. (2002). *Crony Capitalism: Corruption and Development in South Korea and the Phillipines*. Cambridge: Cambridge University Press.
Karaman, K. and Ş. Pamuk (2010). "Ottoman State Finances in European Perspective, 1500–1914." *Journal of Economic History*, 70: 593–629.
Keller, W., and C. Shiue (2007). "Markets in China and Europe on the Eve of the Industrial Revolution." *American Economic Review*, 97: 1189–1216.
Kenny, L., and J. Lott (1997). "Did Women's Suffrage Change the Size and Scope of Government?" *Journal of Political Economy*, 107: 1163–98.
Kiser, E., and J. Schneider (1994). "Bureaucracy and Efficiency: An Analysis of Taxation in Early Modern Prussia." *American Sociological Review*, 59: 187–204.
Knack, S., and P. Keefer (1995). "Institutions and Economic Performance: Cross-Country Tests Using Alternative Measures." *Economics & Politics*, 7: 207–27.
Korner, M. (2010). "Total Revenue and Expenditure of the Prussian State, 1688–1806." European State Financial Database, administered by D. Coffman and A. Murphy, http://esfdb.websites.bta.com/Default.aspx.
La Porta, R., F. Lopez-de-Silanes, and A. Shleifer (2008). "The Economic Consequences of Legal Origins." *Journal of Economic Literature*, 46: 285–332.
La Porta, R., F. Lopez-de-Silanes, A. Shleifer, and R. Vishny (1997). "Legal Determinants of External Finance." *Journal of Finance*, 52: 1131–50.
(1998). "Law and Finance." *Journal of Political Economy*, 106: 1113–55.
(1999). "The Quality of Government." *Journal of Law, Economics, and Organization*, 15: 222–79.
Levi, M. (1988). *Of Rule and Revenue*. Berkeley: University of California Press.
Lindert, P. (1994). "The Rise of Social Spending, 1880–1930." *Explorations in Economic History*, 31: 1–37.
(2004). *Growing Public: Social Spending and Economic Growth Since the Eighteenth Century*. Cambridge: Cambridge University Press.
(2009). "Revealing Failures in the History of School Finance." NBER Working Paper 15491, National Bureau of Economic Research.
Lynch, J. (1989). *Bourbon Spain, 1700–1808*. Oxford: Basil Blackwell.
Maandelijksche Hollandsche Mercurius. Amsterdam, 1780–95.
Magnusson, L. (2000). *An Economic History of Sweden*. London: Routledge.
(2009). *Nation, State, and the Industrial Revolution: The Visible Hand*. London: Routledge.
Major, R. (1994). *From Renaissance Monarchy to Absolute Monarchy: French Kings, Nobles, and Estates*. Baltimore: Johns Hopkins University Press.

Marshall, M., and Jaggers, K. (2008). "Polity IV Project: Political Regime Characteristics and Transitions, 1800–2007." Center for Systemic Peace, George Mason University, http://www.systemicpeace.org/polity/polity4.htm.

Mathias, P., and P. O'Brien (1976). "Taxation in Britain and France, 1715–1810: A Comparison of the Social and Economic Incidence of Taxes Collected for the Central Governments." *Journal of European Economic History*, 5: 601–50.

Mauersberg, H. (1988). *Finanzstrukturen deutscher Bundesstaaten zwischen 1820 und 1944*. St. Katharinen: Scripta Mercaturae Verlag.

Mauro, P., N. Sussman, and Y. Yafeh (2002). "Emerging Market Spreads: Then versus Now." *Quarterly Journal of Economics*, 117: 695–733.

McGuire, M., and M. Olson (1996). "The Economics of Autocracy and Majority Rule: The Invisible Hand and the Use of Force." *Journal of Economic Literature*, 34: 72–96.

Meissner, C. (2005). "A New World Order: Explaining the Emergence of the Classic Gold Standard." *Journal of International Economics*, 6: 385–406.

Migdal, J. (1988). *Strong Societies and Weak States: State–Society Relations and State Capabilities in the Third World*. Princeton, NJ: Princeton University Press.

Mitchell, B. (1988). *British Historical Statistics*. Cambridge: Cambridge University Press.

(2003). *International Historical Statistics: Europe, 1750–2000*. New York: Palgrave Macmillan.

Mitchener, K., and M. Weidenmier (2005). "Empire, Public Goods, and the Roosevelt Corollary." *Journal of Economic History*, 65: 658–92.

Mokyr, J. (1998). "The Second Industrial Revolution, 1870–1914." In Valerio Castronono, ed., *Storia dell'economia Mondiale*. Rome: Laterza.

(1999). *The British Industrial Revolution: An Economic Perspective*. Boulder, CO: Westview.

(2010). Review of *1688: The First Modern Revolution*, by Steven Pincus. *Journal of Economic History*, 70: 510–14.

Moore, B. (1966). *Social Origins of Dictatorship and Democracy*. Boston: Beacon Press.

Myers, B. (2010). *The Cleanest Race: How North Koreans See Themselves – And Why It Matters*. Brooklyn: Melville House.

Neal, L. (1990). *The Rise of Financial Capitalism: International Capital Markets in the Age of Reason*. Cambridge: Cambridge University Press.

(2010). "Conclusion: The Monetary, Fiscal, and Political Architecture of Europe, 1815–1914." In J. Cardoso and P. Lains, eds., *Paying for the Liberal State: The Rise of Public Finance in Nineteenth-Century Europe*. Cambridge: Cambridge University Press.

Nogal, C., and L. Prados de la Escosura (2006). "La decadenza spagnola nell'età moderna: Una revisione quantitativa." *Rivista di Storia Economica*, 21: 59–90.

Nordstrom, B. (2002). *The History of Sweden*. Westport, CT: Greenwood Press.

North, D. (1981). *Structure and Change in Economic History*. New York: Norton.

North, D., and R. Thomas (1973). *The Rise of the Western World: A New Economic History*. Cambridge: Cambridge University Press.

North, D., J. Wallis, and B. Weingast (2009). *Violence and Social Orders: A Conceptual Framework for Interpreting Recorded Human History*. Cambridge: Cambridge University Press.

North, D., and B. Weingast (1989). "Constitutions and Commitment: The Evolution of Institutions Governing Public Choice in Seventeenth-Century England." *Journal of Economic History*, 49: 803–32.

Nunn, N. (2009). "The Importance of History for Economic Development." *Annual Review of Economics*, 1: 65–92.

Nye, J. (2007). *War, Wine, and Taxes: The Political Economy of Anglo-French Trade, 1689–1900*. Princeton, NJ: Princeton University Press.

O'Brien, P. (1983). *Railways and the Economic Development of Western Europe, 1830–1914*. New York: St. Martin's Press.

(2001). "Fiscal Exceptionalism: Great Britain and its European Rivals, from Civil War to Triumph at Trafalgar and Waterloo." Working Paper 65/01, London School of Economics.

(2005). "Fiscal and Financial Pre-Conditions for the Rise of British Naval Hegemony, 1485–1815." Working Paper 91/05, London School of Economics.

(2010). "Total Revenue to the English Crown, 1485–1815." European State Financial Database, administered by D. Coffman and A. Murphy, http:// esfdb.websites.bta.com/Default.aspx.

Obstfeld, M., and A. Taylor (2003). "Sovereign Risk, Credibility, and the Gold Standard: 1870–1913 versus 1925–31." *Economic Journal*, 113: 241–75.

Officer, L. (2001). "Gold Standard." EH.net, http://eh.net.

(2010). "The Price of Gold, 1257–2009." MeasuringWorth, http://www. measuringworth.com.

Pammer, M. (2010). "Public Finance in Austria-Hungary, 1820–1913." In J. Cardoso and P. Lains, eds., *Paying for the Liberal State: The Rise of Public Finance in Nineteenth-Century Europe*. Cambridge: Cambridge University Press.

Persson, K. (1999). *Grain Markets in Europe, 1500–1900*. Cambridge: Cambridge University Press.

Persson, T., and G. Tabellini (2003). *The Economic Effects of Constitutions*. Cambridge, MA: MIT Press.

Pincus, S. (2009). *1688: The First Modern Revolution*. New Haven, CT: Yale University Press.

Pribram, A. (1938). *Materialien zur Geschichte der Preise und Löhne in Österreich, Band I*. Vienna: Carl Ueberreuters Verlag.

Price, R. (1993). *A Concise History of France*. Cambridge: Cambridge University Press.

Prijscourant der Effecten. Amsterdam, 1796–1813.

Queisser, M. (1999). "Pension Reform: Lessons from Latin America." Organisation for Economic Co-operation and Development Policy Brief No. 15.

Quinn, S. (2001). "The Glorious Revolution's Effect on English Private Finance: A Microhistory, 1680–1705. "*Journal of Economic History*, 61: 593–615.

Reinhart, C., and K. Rogoff (2009). *This Time Is Different: Eight Centuries of Financial Folly*. Princeton, NJ: Princeton University Press.

Reinhart, C., K. Rogoff, and M. Savastano (2003). "Debt Intolerance." *Brookings Papers on Economic Activity*, 1: 1–74.

Ringrose, D. (1968). "Transportation and Economic Stagnation in Eighteenth-Century Castile." *Journal of Economic History*, 28: 51–79.

(1970). *Transportation and Economic Stagnation in Spain*. Durham, NC: Duke University Press.

Rosenthal, J. L. (1992). *The Fruits of Revolution: Property Rights, Litigation, and French Agriculture, 1700–1860*. Cambridge: Cambridge University Press.

(1998). "The Political Economy of Absolutism Reconsidered." In R. Bates, A. Greif, M. Levi, J. L. Rosenthal, and B. Weingast, eds., *Analytic Narratives*. Princeton, NJ: Princeton University Press.

(2010). Review of *The British Industrial Revolution in Global Perspective*, by Robert Allen. *Journal of Economic History*, 70: 242–5.

Rosenthal, J. L., and R. B. Wong (2011). *Before and Beyond Divergence: The Politics of Economic Change in China and Europe*. Cambridge, MA: Harvard University Press.

Sacks, D. (1994). "The Paradox of Taxation: Fiscal Crises, Parliament, and Liberty in England, 1450–1640." In P. Hoffman and K. Norberg, eds., *Fiscal Crises, Liberty, and Representative Government, 1450–1789*. Stanford, CA: Stanford University Press.

Sargent, T., and F. Velde (1995). "Macroeconomic Features of the French Revolution." *Journal of Political Economy*, 103: 474–518.

Schön, L. (2010). "The Rise of the Fiscal State in Sweden, 1800–1914." In J. Cardoso and P. Lains, eds., *Paying for the Liberal State: The Rise of Public Finance in Nineteenth-Century Europe*. Cambridge: Cambridge University Press.

Schultz, K., and B. Weingast (1998). "Limited Governments, Powerful States." In R. Siverson, ed., *Strategic Politicians, Institutions, and Foreign Policy*. Ann Arbor: University of Michigan Press.

Shapiro, G., and J. Markoff (1998). *Revolutionary Demands: A Content Analysis of the Cahiers de Doléances of 1789*. Stanford, CA: Stanford University Press.

Smith, Adam. (2003). *The Wealth of Nations*. First published in 1776. New York: Bantam Dell.

Smith, Alan. (1997). *The Emergence of a Nation State: The Commonwealth of England, 1529–1660*. London: Longman.

Spoerer, M. (2010). "The Evolution of Public Finances in Nineteenth-Century Germany." In J. Cardoso and P. Lains, eds., *Paying for the Liberal State: The Rise of Public Finance in Nineteenth-Century Europe*. Cambridge: Cambridge University Press.

Stasavage, D. (2003). *Public Debt and the Birth of the Democratic State: France and Great Britain, 1688–1789*. Cambridge: Cambridge University Press.

(2005). "Cities, Constitutions, and Sovereign Borrowing in Europe, 1274–1785." *International Organization*, 61: 489–526.

(2011). *States of Credit: Size, Power, and the Development of European Polities*. Princeton, NJ: Princeton University Press.

Stockholm International Peace Research Institute (2010). "SIPRI Military Expenditure Database, 2009." http://www.sipri.org.

Stone, L. (1979). *The Crisis of the Aristocracy, 1558–1641.* Oxford: Clarendon Press.

Summerhill, W. (2011). *Inglorious Revolution: Political Institutions, Sovereign Debt, and Financial Underdevelopment in Imperial Brazil.* New Haven, CT: Yale University Press, forthcoming.

Sussman, N., and Y. Yafeh (2000). "Institutions, Reforms, and Country Risk: Lessons from Japanese Government Debt in the Meiji Era." *Journal of Economic History,* 60: 442–67.

(2006). "Institutional Reforms, Financial Development, and Sovereign Debt: Britain, 1690–1790." *Journal of Economic History,* 66: 906–35.

Sutherland, D. (1986). *France 1789–1815: Revolution and Counterrevolution.* Oxford: Oxford University Press.

t'Hart, M. (1997). "The Merits of a Financial Revolution: Public Finance, 1550–1700." In M. t'Hart, J. Jonker, and J. L. van Zanden, eds., *A Financial History of the Netherlands.* Cambridge: Cambridge University Press.

Ticchi, D., and A. Vindigni (2009). "War and Endogenous Democracy." Unpublished paper, Princeton University.

Tilly, C. (1990). *Coercion, Capital, and European States, 990–1990.* London: Blackwell.

Tilly, R. (1966). "The Political Economy of Public Finance and the Industrialization of Prussia, 1815–66." *Journal of Economic History,* 26: 484–97.

(1967). "Public Finance and the Industrialization of Prussia, 1815–66: A Correction." *Journal of Economic History,* 27: 391.

Tomz, M. (2007). *Reputation and International Cooperation: Sovereign Debt across Three Centuries.* Princeton, NJ: Princeton University Press.

Tortella, G. (2000). *The Development of Modern Spain: An Economic History of the Nineteenth and Twentieth Centuries.* Cambridge, MA: Harvard University Press.

Tortella, G., and F. Comín (2001). "The Merits of a Financial Revolution: Public Finance, 1550–1700." In M. Bordo and R. Cortés-Conde, eds., *Transferring Wealth and Power from the Old to the New World: Monetary and Fiscal Institutions in the Seventeenth through the Nineteenth Centuries.* Cambridge: Cambridge University Press.

Tracy, J. (1986). *A Financial Revolution in the Habsburg Netherlands: "Renten" and "Renteniers" in the County of Holland, 1515–65.* Berkeley: University of California Press.

United Nations (2010). "Human Development Indicators." http://hdr.undp.org/en/.

U.S. Department of State (2010). "Country Profile: North Korea." http://www.state.gov.

Van Zanden, J. L. (1996). "The Development of Government Finances in a Chaotic Period, 1807–50." *Economic and Social History of the Netherlands,* 7: 53–71.

Van Zanden, J. L., E. Buringh, and M. Bosker (2011). "The Rise and Decline of European Parliaments, 1188–1789." *Economic History Review,* forthcoming.

Van Zanden, J. L., and M. Prak (2006). "Towards an Economic Interpretation of Citizenship: The Dutch Republic between Medieval Communes and Modern Nation-States." *European Review of Economic History,* 10: 111–45.

Van Zanden, J. L., and A. van Riel (2004). *The Strictures of Inheritance: The Dutch Economy in the Nineteenth Century.* Princeton, NJ: Princeton University Press.

(2010). "The Development of Public Finance in the Netherlands, 1815–1914." In J. Cardoso and P. Lains, eds., *Paying for the Liberal State: The Rise of Public Finance in Nineteenth-Century Europe.* Cambridge: Cambridge University Press.

Veenstra, W. (2006). *"Geld is de zenuw van de oorlog." De financiën van de Zeeuwse Admiraliteit in de achttiende eeuwe (1698–1795).* M.A. thesis, University of Leiden.

(2010). *Gewestelijke financiën ten tijde van de Republiek der Verenigde Nederlanden. Deel 7. Zeeland (1573–1795).* Institute for Netherlands History Project, http://www.inghist.nl.

Velde, F., and D. Weir (1992). "The Financial Market and Government Debt Policy in France, 1746–93." *Journal of Economic History,* 52: 1–39.

Velde, F., and W. Weber (2000). "A Model of Bimetallism." *Journal of Political Economy,* 108: 1210–34.

Vicens Vive, J. (1969). *An Economic History of Spain.* Princeton, NJ: Princeton University Press.

Wade, R. (1990). *Governing the Market: Economic Theory and the Role of Government in East Asian Industrialization.* Princeton, NJ: Princeton University Press.

White, E. (1995). "The French Revolution and the Politics of Government Finance, 1770–1815." *Journal of Economic History,* 55: 227–55.

(2001). "France and the Failure to Modernize Macroeconomic Institutions." In M. Bordo and R. Cortés-Conde, eds., *Transferring Wealth and Power from the Old to the New World: Monetary and Fiscal Institutions in the Seventeenth through the Nineteenth Centuries.* Cambridge: Cambridge University Press.

Willard, K., T. Guinnane, and H. Rosen (1996). "Turning Points in the Civil War: Views from the Greenback Market." *American Economic Review,* 86: 1001–18.

Wooldridge, J. (2003). *Introductory Econometrics: A Modern Approach,*2d ed. Mason, OH: Thomson South-Western.

Woolf, S. (1991). *Napoleon's Integration of Europe.* London: Routledge.

World Bank (2009). "World Development Indicators." http://data.worldbank.org/indicator.

Wrigley, E., and R Schofield (1981). *The Population History of England, 1541–1871: A Reconstruction.* Cambridge, MA: Harvard University Press.

Ziblatt, D. (2006). *Structuring the State: The Formation of Italy and Germany and the Puzzle of Federalism.* Princeton, NJ: Princeton University Press.

Index

Index